FARTHEST NORTH

FARTHEST NORTH

*Endurance and Adventure in
the Quest for the North Pole*

Edited by
CLIVE HOLLAND

CARROLL & GRAF PUBLISHERS, INC.
New York

Carroll & Graf Publishers, Inc.
19 West 21st Street
New York
NY 10010-6805

First published in the UK
by Robinson Publishing Ltd 1994

First Carroll & Graf edition 1999

ISBN 0-7867-0680-5

Printed and bound in the EC

Contents

Illustration on front of jacket shows the Fram, *Fridtjof Nansen's ship.*

Preface

This book tells the story of the quest for the North Pole from earliest times to the recent past. It is an enthralling story spanning four centuries and embracing many different motives, many different modes of travel, and many remarkable men.

As far as possible, the story is told in the explorers' own words. As compiler, my own role is mainly to provide continuity and context: to blend together extracts from the explorers' narratives into one unfolding historical drama.

The book is also a celebration of courageous men and heroic deeds. All manner of dangers, hardships and suffering are portrayed in these narratives; death was never far away on pioneering journeys to seek the Pole.

For the most part the explorers tell their stories wonderfully well. It is strange how men of no literary pretensions, but facing extremes of physical hardship and a range and intensity of emotions that few of us will ever meet – deepest despair, misery, agony, the ever-present prospect of imminent death, or the exhilaration of a hard-earned success – can achieve a height of eloquence worthy of any poet. In the world of exploration, the most famous example of this ability is Captain Robert Falcon Scott of the Antarctic. As he lay dying in his tent after losing the race for the South Pole, Scott wrote: 'Had we lived, I should have had a tale to tell of the hardihood, endurance, and courage of my companions which would have stirred the heart of every Englishman.' Yet Scott did not need to live in order to stir hearts; his posthumously published journal, letters and notes contain some of the most moving prose in the English language; they have stirred hearts throughout the world ever since.

Readers of this book will find that Scott was not the only explorer with the ability to give full and vivid expression to his thoughts and emotions. Many of those who sought the North Pole also experienced the full spectrum of emotional experiences, and somehow found the resources to express them in their journals with a lucidity that is sometimes chilling, but never dull.

CLIVE HOLLAND
CAMBRIDGE
March 1994

A Note on Distances

Polar explorers usually recorded distances either in nautical miles, or in degrees (°), minutes (') and, more rarely, seconds (") of latitude. A minute is approximately one nautical mile, which was deemed by the British Admiralty to be 6,080 feet (about 2,026½ yards, or 1.85 kilometres). It is therefore longer than the well-known English statute mile (1,760 yards, or 1,609 km). Other definitions of the nautical mile differ from the Admiralty version, but only by a few feet. One degree of latitude equals 60 minutes, so a degree equals about 60 nautical miles. So the distance from 80° North to the North Pole at 90° North is about 600 nautical miles. A second is one-sixtieth of a minute, and was normally used for the most important observations, when precision was required.

It is useful to bear these figures in mind when visualizing how far explorers had to travel to reach the Pole.

– 1 –

The Impossible Dream

1527–1773

The quest for the North Pole has for long been one of the great adventure stories in the history of exploration. It has all the best ingredients: ever-present danger; heroic courage; tragedy and triumph; sensationalism; the quest for glory, fame and wealth; unsolved mystery; astounding incompetence; deep hatreds; and a feud so bitter that it still simmers 80 years after the event.

The North Pole is a strange target for an explorer to aim at, for there is nothing there. It is an imaginary point in the middle of an ice-covered ocean. Its significance, of course, is that it is the northern end of the axis on which the Earth rotates, but ancient Greek astronomers worked that out long ago, without ever leaving home. The Pole has never needed to be 'discovered'; its location has never been in doubt. What the traveller finds there is just a layer of ice ten feet thick covering 14,000 feet of empty ocean, and the strange phenomenon of the sun circling continuously above the horizon for six months of the year, then disappearing completely for the other six. This annual sunrise and sunset apart, even time ceases to exist at the North Pole, for here all the world's time zones converge and the hour becomes both everything and nothing. The place is inhospitable and remote: the nearest land is some 400 miles away at the equally remote northern tip of Greenland. There is virtually no wildlife except the occasional migrating bird. Not even polar bears bother to wander so far from land, and there is no obvious reason for humans to make the effort either.

And yet there is. There is a mysterious magic in standing at that particular place that has long beguiled mankind. A century ago brave men died trying to get there. And nowadays tourists pay tens of thousands of dollars to be taken there by icebreaker, stick a wooden pole in the snow and be photographed standing next to it. They are happy to delight in the immense beauty of the rest of the Arctic Ocean, with the delicate blue-green tinges of the upturned hummocks of ice floes driven together by immense forces of wind and current. But the Pole is where they want to stand. It is irrational and few can adequately explain it. For travellers now, getting to the North Pole is just an irresistibly enticing, romantic but ultimately pointless thing to do. For some of those explorers who vied with one another to get there first, whose stories form the subject of this book, it was the most important thing in life.

But it was not always so. During the sixteenth, seventeenth and eighteenth centuries, those few who thought about the North Pole at all thought of it in extremely practical economic terms: they were looking for a new shipping route to the Orient. In the sixteenth century, Spain and Portugal took a stranglehold on the southern routes, by way of the Atlantic, Indian and Pacific oceans, so threatening the valuable Oriental trade of two other powerful maritime nations, Britain and the Netherlands. The problem, and the ingenious solution of exploring for a new northern route, was first expressed in print in 1527, in a proposal to King Henry VIII from the merchant Robert Thorne of London. It was first published in 1589 by the eminent sixteenth-century geographer Richard Hakluyt in his influential book *Principall Navigations*.

> I know it is my bounden duetie to manifest this secret unto your Grace, which hitherto, as I suppose, hath beene hid: which is, that with a small number of ships there may be discovered divers New lands and kingdomes, in the which without doubt your Grace shall winne perpetuall glory, and your subiectes infinite profite. To which places there is left one way to discover, which is into the North: for that of the foure parts of the world, it seemeth three parts are discovered by other Princes. For out of Spaine they have discovered all the Indies and Seas Occidentall, and out of Portingall all the Indies and Seas Orientall: so that by this part of the Orient and Occident, they have compassed the world . . . So that now rest to be discovered the said North partes, the which it seemeth to me, is onely your charge and

dutie. Because the situation of this your Realme is thereunto nearest and aptest of all other: and also for that you have alreadie taken it in hande. And in mine opinion it will not seeme well to leave so great and profitable an enterprise, seeing it may so easily, and with so litle cost, labour, and danger, be followed and obteined: . . . and considering well the courses, truely the danger and way is shorter to us, than to Spaine or Portingall, as by evident reasons appeareth.

And now to declare something of the commoditie and utilitie of this Navigation and discoverie, it is very cleere and certaine, that the Seas that commonly men say, without great danger, difficulties and perill . . . it is impossible to passe, that those same seas be navigable and without any such danger, but that shippes may passe and have in them perpetuall cleereness of the day without any darkeness of the night: which thing is a great commoditie for the navigants, to see at all times round about them . . . They being past this little way which they named so dangerous, (which may be two or three leagues before they come to the Pole, and as much more after they passe the Pole) it is cleere that from thence foorth the seas and landes are as temperate as in these partes, and that then it may be at the will and pleasure of the mariners, to choose whether they will saile by the coastes that be colde, temperate or hot. For they being past the Pole, it is plaine, they may decline to what part they list.

If they will goe toward the Orient, they shall injoy the regions of all the Tartarians that extend toward the midday, and from thence they may goe and proceed to the land of the Chinas, and from thence to the land of Cathaia Orientall, which is of all the maine land most Orientall that can be reckoned from our habitation. And if from thence they doe continue their navigation, following the coasts that returne toward the Occident, they shall fall in with Malaca, and so with all the Indies which we call Orientall, and following that way, may returne hither by the Cape of Buona Speransa [Cape of Good Hope] and thus they shall compasse the whole worlde. And if they will take their course after they be past the Pole, toward the Occident, they shall goe in the backe side of the new found land [North

America], which of late was discovered by your Graces subiectes, untill they come to the back side and South Seas of the Indies Occidental. And so continuing their voyage they may returne thorow the Streight of Magellan to this countrey, and so they compasse also the world by that way: and if they goe this third way, and after they be past the Pole, goe right toward the Pole Antarctike, and then decline toward the lands and Islands situated betweene the Tropikes, and under the Equinoctiall, without doubt they shall finde there the richest landes and Islands of the world of golde, precious stones, balmes, spices, and other thinges that we heere esteeme most: which is come out of strange countreyes, and may returne the same way.

By this it appeareth, your Grace hath not onely a great advantage of the riches, but also your subiectes shall not travell halfe of the way that the other doe, which goe round about as aforesaide.

And so, man's quest for the North Pole began on a note of unlimited optimism. To Thorne, the Pole was the key that opened access to almost the entire world and its riches, east, west and south. It was a much shorter route to the Orient than the southern routes (which is true). Beside the Orient, it also offered access to the west coast of America and the southern Pacific (also true). More fancifully, he believed that the Arctic presented few navigational dangers, except, perhaps, within a few leagues of the Pole itself; that it had a generally temperate climate; and that its perpetual summer daylight offered explorers and navigators a clear advantage over other routes. Britain's very own northern route would be shorter, safer, and in every way better than the routes held by rivals. The early optimism began to fade rapidly when expeditions began actually to explore towards the Pole. But elements of that optimism persisted for over 300 years before the impossible dream of a practical sea route over the Pole faded slowly to nothing, to be replaced gradually by a desire among explorers to attain the Pole for its own sake; a heroic but purely symbolic conquest.

As it happened Thorne's proposal had no immediate effect, but it is clear that other merchants were beginning to think along very similar lines. Finally, some 25 years after Thorne's letter, they began to take positive action, and in 1553 the first of a long series of British expeditions set out to search for a new Arctic route to the Orient. That first expedition headed for the seas north of Russia, which was only one of three separate Arctic routes examined by British and Dutch explorers during the next 75 years. One, known as the Northwest Passage, would have taken them through the waters of the present-day Canadian Arctic. Another, the Northeast Passage, is a sea route along the north coast of Russia and Siberia, and was already partially known to Russian navigators. The third, the polar passage, would have been the shortest, as it would have passed directly north from Europe, then straight across the Arctic Ocean by way of the Pole. The notion of sixteenth-century, 70-ton sailing vessels crossing an ice-filled ocean may seem like folly now, but at that time the Arctic was almost completely unexplored. Nothing was known of the pack ice, or the many other perils that unsuspecting explorers were about to encounter. The existence of the Arctic Ocean was unknown to them; it could, for all they knew, have been a shallow, island-studded and navigable sea. So, understandably, merchants and explorers were absurdly over-optimistic; their expeditions dangerously, hopelessly under-equipped. But it does not take long to recognize the defiant impenetrability of a vast sheet of ice stretching almost unbroken to the horizon, and the earliest flushes of enthusiasm for a polar route to the Pacific, in both Britain and the Netherlands, were very short lived. In the first period of search for a northern passage, both countries sent out only one expedition to explore that route.

After the first Northeast Passage expeditions in the 1550s, several expeditions sought passages through the Barents Sea (north of European Russia), and Davis Strait (between Greenland and Baffin Island). They gave explorers a clearer understanding of general Arctic conditions, but their progress toward finding a passage was minimal. For that reason, the Dutchman Willem Barentsz, and the Englishman Henry Hudson attempted more northerly routes at the turn of the sixteenth and seventeenth centuries.

Barentsz went first. He had made two previous Northeast Passage expeditions in 1594 and 1595, and had made some valuable discoveries in northwest Novaya Zemlya. But the Barents Sea is one of the Arctic's milder seas: nothing had prepared him for the ordeal he was about to undergo. In 1596, merchants of Amsterdam fitted out two ships to continue the search for a passage to China through the waters of the Russian Arctic. The ships were commanded by Jacob van Heemskerck and Jan Corneliszoon Rijp (Barentsz was their chief pilot), and the two ships left Amsterdam on 10 May. Three weeks later, at 71°N, the officers began to learn to their great surprise that this was not to be the Northeast Passage expedition they had expected, but more nearly an expedition towards the Pole. At this point they should have begun to head east around the northern tip of Scandinavia into the Barents Sea and towards the Vaigats – one of the main straits leading eastwards from the Barents Sea into the Kara Sea (the strait is now named Yugorskiy Shar) – but Jan Corneliszoon insisted on a much more northerly course. At the same time, some of the crew were startled by their first sight of ice. The story is told by Gerrit De Veer, an officer on one of the ships, in a contemporary translation.

John Cornelis ship held aloofe from us, and would not keepe with us, and would hold no course but North North-east, for they alleged, that if we went any more Easterly, that then we should enter into the Wey-gates, but wee being not able to perswade them, altered our course one point of the Compasse, to meet them, and sayled North-east and by North, and should otherwise have sayled North-east, and somewhat more east.

The fifth [June], wee saw the first Ice, which we wondered at, at the first, thinking that it had beene white Swannes, for one of our men walking in the Fore-decke, on a sudden began to cry out with a loud voyce, and said; that hee saw white Swannes: which wee that were under Hatches hearing, presently came up, and perceiving that it was Ice that came driving from the great heape, showing like Swannes, it being then about Eevening, at midnight we sayled through it, and the Sunne was about a degree elevated above the Horizon in the North.

The sixth, about foure of the clock in the after-noone, wee entred againe into the Ice, which was so strong that we could not passe through it, and sayled South-west and by West, till eight Glasses were runne out, after that we kept on our course North, North-east, and sayled along by the Ice . . .

The ninth of June we found the Iland that lay under 74 degrees and 30 minutes, and as we ghest, it was about five miles [20 nautical miles] long. The tenth, we put out our Boate, and therewith eight of our men went on Land, and as we past by John Cornelisons ship, eight of his men also came into our Boate, whereof one was the Pilot. Then William Barents asked him, whether we were not too much Westward, but hee would not acknowledge it: whereupon there passed many words betweene them, for William Barents sayd, he would prove it to be so, as in truth it was.

The island where they landed was Bear Island (now Bjørnøya), a new discovery. And Corneliszoon's stubborn defiance of his fellow officers, and insistence on heading north, was putting them on course for another, more dramatic discovery, that was to assume great importance in the quest for the North Pole. The expedition continued on its northward course, and De Veer takes up the story again a week later.

The sixteenth, with the like speed we sayled North and by East, with mistie weather; and as we sayled, we heard the Ice before we saw it; but after, when it cleared up, we saw it, and then woond off from it, when as we ghest had sayled thirtie [*ie* 120] miles. The seventeenth and eighteenth we saw great store of Ice, and sayled along by it, untill we came to the point, which we could not reach, for that the wind was South-east, which was right against us; yet we lavered a great while to get beyond it, but we could not doe it. The nineteenth, we saw Land againe, then we tooke the height of the Sun, and found that . . . we were under 80 degrees and 11 minutes, which was the height of the Pole there. This Land was very great, and we sayled Westward along by it,

till we were under 79 degrees and a halfe, where we found a
good road, and could not get neare to the Land, because the
wind blew North-east, which was right off from the Land:
the Bay reacheth right North and South into the Sea.

De Veer's casual references to land belie the importance of the
expedition's achievement, for what he records here is the discovery of Svalbard (formerly Spitsbergen; the name Spitsbergen,
once applied to the whole archipelago, is now applied only to
the main island). Their latitude at the time was not 81°11' N but
79°49' N (De Veer missed a step in the calculation), which means
that they must have sighted land in the extreme northwest of
the archipelago, near Amsterdam Island and the northwestern
tip of the island of Spitsbergen. Svalbard, and this part of it in
particular, was later to figure very prominently in the quest for
the North Pole. It was the most convenient part of the Arctic
for European explorers to launch their attempts on the Pole,
and the warm waters of the Gulf Stream, which flow along the
western coasts of Svalbard, helped to keep the sea in this region
relatively ice-free up to an exceptionally high latitude. But just
to the north of Svalbard, at about 80°N in unfavourable seasons,
or up to about 82°N in favourable ones, explorers inevitably
came up against the southern edge of the permanent pack ice,
which sometimes stretched like a forbidding wall, unbroken,
between Svalbard and Greenland (at the Greenland end the ice
extends much farther south, usually to about 75°N). Although
De Veer's account is vague, it was probably this pack edge that
the expedition encountered and sailed along on 17 and 18 June.
On subsequent North Pole expeditions, explorers time and again
headed north hoping that an exceptionally favourable season
might allow them access to the Pole and beyond, only to find
all their hopes denied them, sooner or later, by this unyielding
barrier. And it took a remarkably long time, over three and a half
centuries, for the world of exploration to learn that wherever
ships sought to approach the Pole, be it from Svalbard waters,
or the Barents Sea, Baffin Bay or Bering Strait, the wall of ice
unfailingly awaited them.

De Veer does not say so, but it was presumably the encounter
with the edge of the pack on 17–18 June which forced the
Dutch expedition to turn back. In any event, after lingering

for a week to explore the northwestern coasts of Svalbard, they began coasting south, making further discoveries, then on 1 July arrived back at Bear Island. There, the expedition divided. Jan Corneliszoon expressed a wish to return to northern Spitsbergen to explore the land at about 80°N. Unfortunately, his subsequent activities are not recorded, but it is known that he achieved nothing new. Heemskerck and Barentsz returned to the original plan of searching for a Northeast Passage. They spent a winter in northern Novaya Zemlya (by far the most northerly wintering of any expedition to that date), lost their ship, then during their voyage south in boats in summer 1597, Barentsz, who had long been ill, died. These events, however, are not a part of this story.

Ten years later, Henry Hudson made the first British attempt to reach the Orient by way of the North Pole, under instructions from one of the great international trading companies of the day, the Muscovy Company. This company owed its existence to the very first Northeast Passage expedition, which took place in 1553–4. It had failed utterly to make progress toward the Orient, but part of it had reached the White Sea, and eventually Moscow. There, its leader Richard Chancellor negotiated Britain's first trading relations with Russia, and in 1555 the Muscovy Company was founded to carry out the trade. It sent ships annually to the White Sea and north Russia, but its activities also included occasional exploring voyages in the Arctic. It began to diversify its interests into hunting when one of its ships discovered walruses on Bear Island. Later, it became Britain's first and largest Arctic whaling company. Having originated as a Northeast Passage expedition, the company never quite abandoned its interest in a short northern route to the Orient, and Hudson's North Pole expedition of 1607 was one of several sent out by the company to search for such a route.

Virtually nothing at all is known about Henry Hudson beyond his four voyages in search of an Arctic passage to the Orient in the last five years of his life, 1607–11. It can only be said that by 1607 he was already a distinguished sea captain in the service of the Muscovy Company. After his North Pole voyage, he undertook a Northeast Passage expedition in 1608, a combined Northeast/Northwest Passage expedition in 1609 (during which he discovered the Hudson River, New York), and in 1610–11 a

Northwest Passage expedition to Hudson Bay, during which he
and several others were set adrift in a boat by mutineers. He was
never seen again.

On 1 May 1607, Hudson and his 11-man crew put to sea from
Gravesend in the 40-ton bark *Hopewell*. Hudson was aware of the
discoveries of the Dutch in 1596, and after a little exploration
on the east coast of Greenland, he headed for the west coast of
Spitsbergen where he knew he could reach a high latitude. He
carried out some more exploration on that coast, then he made
his run for the north. In the following extract from his notes,
'Newland' is Svalbard, and he was heading into the waters to
the north of northwest Spitsbergen.

The eleventh [July], very cleere weather, with the winde at
south-east-south; we were come out of the blue sea into
our greene sea againe, where we saw whales. Now, having
a fresh gale of wind at south south-east, it behooved mee
to change my course, and to sayle to the north-east, by
the souther end of Newland. But being come into a greene
sea, praying God to direct mee, I steered away north
ten leagues. After that we saw ice on our larboord, we
steered away east and by north three leagues, and left the
ice behind us. Then wee steered away north till noone.
This day wee had the sunne on the meridian south and
by west, westerly, his greatest height was 37 degrees, 20
minutes. By this observation we were in 79 degrees, 17
minutes; we had a fresh gale of wind and a smooth sea,
by meanes whereof our ship had out-runne us. At ten this
eevening cleere weather, and then we had the company of
our troublesome neighbours, ice with fogge. The wind was
at south south-west. Heere we saw plentie of seales, and
we supposed beares had beene heere, by their footing and
dung upon the ice. This day, many of my companie were
sicke with eating of beares flesh the day before unsalted.

The twelfth, for the most part, was thicke fogge; wee steered
betweene south and by east, and south south-east 2½
leagues, to cleere us of the ice. Then we had the wind at
south; wee steered till noone north-east five leagues. This
morning we had our shroudes frozen. At noone, by our

accompt, we were in 80 degrees, being little wind at west south-west, almost calme with thicke fogge. This afternoone we steered away north and sometimes north-east. Then we saw ice ahead off us; we cast about and stood south-east, with little wind and fogge. Before we cast about by meanes of the thicke fogge, we were very neere ice, being calme, and the sea setting on to the ice, which was very dangerous. It pleased God at the very instant to give us a small gale, which was the meanes of our deliverance; to Him be praise therefore. At twelve this night it cleared up, and out of the top William Collins, our boatswaine, saw the land, called Newland by the Hollanders, bearing south south-west twelve leagues from us.

The thirteenth, in the morning, the wind at south and by east, a good gale, we cast about and stood north-east and by east, and by observation we were in 80 degrees, 23 minutes. This day we saw many whales. This fore-noone proved cleere weather, and we could not see any signe of ice out of the top. Betweene noone and three of the clocke, we steered away north-east and by east five leagues; then we saw ice on head off us; we steered east two glasses, one league, and could not be cleare of the ice with that course. Then we steered away south-east two leagues ½, after we sayled east and by north, and east foure leagues, till eight the next morning.

The fourteenth, in the morning, was calme with fogge. At nine, the wind at east, a small gale with thicke fogge; wee steered south-east and by east, and running this course we found our greene sea againe, which by proofe we found to be freest from ice, and our azure blue sea to be our icie sea.

The expedition spent the remainder of that day in a bay some-where in northeast Svalbard, then, that same night, headed north again. In the following extract, the location of 'Collins Cape' is unknown, but he was still off northwest Spitsbergen.

The fifteenth, in the morning, was very cleere weather, the

sunne shining warme, but little wind at east southerly. By
a south-east sunne we had brought Collins Cape to beare off
us south-east, and we saw the high land of Newland, that
part by us discovered on our starboord, eight or ten leagues
from us, trending north-east and by east, and south-west
and by west, eighteene or twentie leagues from us to the
north-east, being a very high mountaynous land, like ragged
rockes with snow betweene them. By mine account, the
norther part of this land which now we saw, stretched into
81 degrees. All this day proved cleere weather, little wind,
and reasonable warme.

The sixteenth, in the morning warme and cleere weather;
the wind at north. This morning we saw that we were
compassed in with ice in abundance, lying to the north, to
the north-west, the east and south-east; and being runne
toward the farthest part of the land by us discovered,
which for the most part trendeth nearest hand north-east
and south-west, wee saw more land joyning to the same,
trending north in our sight, by meanes of the cleernesse of
the weather, stretching farre into 82 degrees, and by the
bowing or shewing of the skie much farther. Which when
I first saw, I hoped to have had a free sea between the
land and the ice, and meant to have compassed this land
by the north. But now, finding by proofe it was unpossible,
by means of the abundance of ice compassing us about by
the north and joyning to the land, and seeing God did
blesse us with a faire wind to sayle by the south of this
land to the north-east, we returned, bearing up the helme,
minding to hold that part of the land which the Hollanders
had discovered in our sight; and if contrary winds should
take us, to harbour there, and to trie what we could finde to
the charge of our voyage, and to proceed on our discoverie
as soone as God should blesse us with winde. And this I can
assure at this present, that betweene 78 degrees and ½ and
82 degrees, by this way there is no passage: but I think this
land may bee profitable to those that will adventure it.

Soon after, Hudson left the ice, and he spent the next week
cruising in open water to the west of Svalbard, apparently

uncertain what to do next. At this point, many an explorer would have used that emphatic journal entry 'there is no passage' as the perfect guarantee of a sympathetic reception back home if he abandoned the search there and then. But Hudson was no quitter, as his entire record as an explorer shows; if he failed in one direction, he would try again in another, and he never returned home without satisfying himself that he had tried everything. That very quality played a large part in provoking the mutiny against him in 1611. On 24 July he made his final run to the north, but this time farther west, with a secondary aim of perhaps passing around the north coast of Greenland.

The seven and twentieth, extreme thicke fog, and little wind at east and by south. Then it proved calme, and the sea very loftie. Wee heard a great rutte or noise with the ice and sea, which was the first ice we heard or saw since we were at Collins Cape: the sea heaving us westward toward the ice. Wee heaved out our boat, and rowed to towe out our ship farther from the danger; which would have beene to small purpose, by meanes the sea went so high: but in this extremitie it pleased God to give us a small gale at north-west and by west, we steered away south-east, 4 leagues, till noone. Here wee had finished our discoverie, if the wind had continued that brought us hither, or if it had continued calme; but it pleased God to make this north-west and by west wind the meane of our deliverance: which wind wee had not found common in this voyage. God give us thankfull hearts for so great deliverance. Here we found the want of a good ship-boat, as once we had done before at Whales Bay: we wanted also halfe a dozen long oares to rowe in our ship. At noone the day cleered up, and we saw by the skie ice bearing off us, from west south-west to the north and north north-east. Then we had a good gale at west; we steered away south till foure, 7 leagues. From foure to six, south 4 leagues, and found by the icy skie and our neereness to Groneland that there is no passage that way: which, if there had beene, I meant to have made my returne by the north of Groneland to Davis his Streights, and so for England. Here finding we had the benefit of a westerly wind, which all this voyage we had found scant,

we altered our course and steered to the eastward, and
ran south-east foure leagues. From eight this eevening till
noone the next day, east south-east, 30 leagues. All this day
and night proved very cold, by meanes, as I suppose, of the
winds comming off so much ice.

Here, Hudson gives a fine description of how the edge of the
pack sweeps down from 80° and above off Svalbard to much
lower latitudes off northeast Greenland, making that part of
the Greenland coast unapproachable. Having now tried every
possible direction between Greenland and Svalbard, Hudson
abandoned the search and returned to the Thames, arriving on
15 September.

The negative results of the expeditions of Barentsz and Hudson
virtually put an end to exploration towards the North Pole for
over a century and a half. The Muscovy Company included an
order to explore towards the Pole in its instructions to two or
three other expeditions, including one by its senior officer Jonas
Poole in 1611, but there is no evidence that they made any
serious effort to progress beyond Svalbard. Seventeenth-century
ships were simply not equal to the awesome power of the drifting
pack, and these two expeditions had proved that a ship that
cannot safely enter the pack cannot approach the Pole.

However, Hudson's expedition had one consequence of enormous importance. On his return home he reported to the
Muscovy Company on the large numbers of whales to be found
in the bays of the west coast of Spitsbergen. The company sent
a ship to confirm the report, and in 1611 it sent two ships to
Svalbard to initiate the Arctic whaling industry. Soon, other
companies and other nations began to compete for the whales,
and from the modest beginnings of two ships, the whaling fleet
grew greatly in size, until at times in the eighteenth century over
300 ships per year roamed the Greenland Sea. The industry also
had some influence over the quest for the North Pole, for whaling
captains were, of necessity, expert observers of the edge of the
pack ice extending from Greenland to Svalbard. The vicinity of
the pack edge was one of the whalers' main hunting areas,
because it was the whales' main feeding ground. There, the
meeting of cold waters from the north with warm waters from
the south generated masses of plankton, which provided food

for the shrimp-like krill, which in turn was the basic diet of the whalers' target, the Greenland Right Whale. So, season after season, whalers in their dozens roamed the boundary of the pack between Greenland and Svalbard, and repeatedly confirmed that there was no passage to the Pole by that way. Yet, as will shortly be seen, it was the reports of whalers that, paradoxically, provided the very basis on which further expeditions were sent to search for a polar passage by that route.

The eighteenth century saw very little more progress in the quest for the North Pole than the seventeenth. It was marked only by two serious Russian attempts to cross the Arctic Ocean, and, in Britain, by an entertaining series of events involving one of Arctic history's most enjoyable eccentrics, and leading to one British attempt.

The two Russian expeditions were intended to find the shortest sea route from European Russia to its far eastern Siberian dominions. It was mere coincidence that the shortest route passed almost directly over the North Pole. Both expeditions were financed by the Russian government and commanded by the naval officer Vasiliy Yakovlevich Chichagov. The plan was proposed by the distinguished scientist M.V. Lomonosov (whose name was later given to a major underwater ridge on the sea-bed of the Arctic Ocean), and, like the expeditions of Barentsz and Hudson, consisted of an attempt to reach the North Pole and beyond from Svalbard waters.

Only limited information is available on Chichagov's two attempts, but neither achieved much more than Barentsz and Hudson had managed. In July 1765, with three ships, Chichagov headed north into the ice off northwest Spitsbergen, but reached only 80°26'N. Given a second chance in 1766, he sailed to the same area, but scarcely exceeded his previous achievement, reaching 80°28'N. It was a new record, just passing Hudson's farthest north, but it offered no encouragement for the Russian government to continue seeking a sea route to eastern Siberia. Russia pulled out of exploration in the Arctic Ocean until icebreakers became available in the twentieth century.

The only other serious attempt on the North Pole in the eighteenth century was a British Royal Naval expedition in

1773, led by Captain the Honourable Constantine John Phipps, with two ships, HMS *Racehorse* and HMS *Carcass*. Among the most fascinating aspects of this expedition are the strange circumstances under which it was organized, for it was the result of campaigning by just one man, whose prolonged research into the possibility of attaining the North Pole had convinced him that 'the Polar Seas are, at least sometimes, navigable.' This man was the Honourable Daines Barrington (1727–1800), and the fascination in his campaigns rises from the man himself, who was the very model of an amiable eccentric, the unusual nature of his evidence of a polar passage, and the fact that he was able to persuade anyone at all that the polar seas might be navigable.

Daines Barrington was the son of the first Viscount Barrington. His family's influence, rather than any conspicuous talent, brought him a series of elevated occupations in the course of his life. In the 1750s he attained high office as a judge. In private life he was an incorrigible ferret, and he tirelessly gathered information on any subject that captured his interest, from the history of playing cards to the writings of King Alfred, and from the Cornish language to natural history. His prolific output of published works included essays on these and many other subjects, but most of his publications were almost entirely without merit, and his only work described as having lasting value was a history of statute law. He achieved a certain amount of fame in his day, both as judge and author, and perhaps especially as one of the correspondents to whom Gilbert White's *Natural History of Selborne* is addressed. But among his peers, it seems, he was equally renowned for being remarkably dim-witted. A contemporary and more enduringly famous student of the law, Jeremy Bentham (1748–1832), recorded of his judicial career that 'He was not intentionally a bad judge, though he was often a bad one.' The satirical poet Peter Pindar wrote of Barrington, in an imaginary conversation between himself and Sir Joseph Banks (1743–1820) about the Royal Society:

> *Sir Joseph*   Pray then, what think ye of our famous Daines?
> *Peter*   *Think*, of a man denied by Nature *brains*!

Altogether it appears that respect for his intellectual accomplishments failed to match the genuine affection that he apparently inspired.

One of Barrington's obsessions, in the 1770s, was the navigability of the Arctic Ocean, and the possibility of attaining the North Pole by ship. He was an early champion of a theory that later came to be known as the 'Open Polar Sea', which proclaimed that, although there was often a band, or wall of ice surrounding the Arctic Ocean at about 80°N, the ocean itself was free of ice. So, if an expedition could find a break in the wall, navigation to the Pole presented no problem. In supporting his case, he referred back to a statement in the Royal Society of London's prestigious *Philosophical Transactions* for 1675:

> It is well known to all that sail Northward, that most of the Northern Coasts are frozen up many leagues, though in the open sea it is not so, *No, nor under the Pole itself,* unless by accident.

It appears that Barrington also believed that, in some years, the encircling wall of ice did not appear at all, so that ships could sail to the Pole and beyond unhindered. In the light of the contrary observations of many thousands of whalers over about 150 years, it was an implausible theory. In addition, his case should have been irreparably damaged by the quality of his evidence for an 'Open Polar Sea'. Typically, it consisted of second- or third-hand alehouse yarns that circulated among the crews of whaling ships, often about events so vaguely remembered and so distant in time that they were hopelessly unreliable. The following extracts are typical of his evidence as a whole.

In 1662–3, a Mr Oldenburg of the Royal Society interviewed a whaler named Mr Grey, who reported:

> I once met, upon the Coast of Greenland, a Hollander, that swore he had been but half a degree from the Pole, showing me his Journal, which was also attested by his mate; where they had seen no ice or land, but all water.

In about 1675, Captain John Wood (who later led an unsuccessful Northeast Passage expedition) reported a conversation between a whaler, Captain Goulden, and King Charles II:

> Captain Goulden, who had made above thirty voyages to

Greenland, did relate to his majesty that, being at Greenland some twenty years before, he was in company with two Hollanders to the eastward of Edge's Island; and that the whales not appearing on the shore, the two Hollanders were determined to go farther Northward, and in a fortnight's time returned and gave it out, that they had sailed into the Latitude 89°, and that they did not meet with any ice, but free and open sea; and that there run a very hollow grown sea, like that of the Bay of Biscay.

One of the most implausible of all the stories is third-hand, far distant in time, and even armed with excuses for its own unreliability, but Barrington admits no doubts about its validity and defends it vigorously as one of his favourite 'proofs'. It was related by a Dutchman named Dallie to a man named Campbell 30 years previously, and concerns a voyage on which Dallie served in an unknown capacity some 60 years previously. Campbell had told the story to Barrington at some unrecorded date, but had subsequently died.

Between fifty and sixty years ago it was usual to send a Dutch ship of war to superintend the Greenland Fishery, though it is not known whether this continues to be a regulation at present.

Dr Dallie (then young) was on board the Dutch vessel employed on this service; and, during the interval between the two fisheries, the captain determined . . . to try whether he could not reach the Pole; and accordingly penetrated (to the best of Dr Campbell's recollection) as far as North Latitude 88°, when the weather was warm, the sea perfectly free from ice, and rolling like the Bay of Biscay. Dallie now pressed the Captain to proceed; but he answered, that he had already gone too far by having neglected his station, for which he should be blamed in Holland: on which account, also, he would suffer no Journal to be made, but returned as speedily as he could to Spitzbergen.

In 1773, Barrington equipped himself with a sheaf of similar implausible yarns, and persuaded the Council of the Royal

Society to approach the Board of Admiralty with a request to send out an expedition to investigate the navigability of the route from Svalbard to the North Pole. And the Admiralty complied. The chain of events and the ready compliance of both those institutions is bizarre. It is difficult to understand how the highest officials of the world's most powerful navy and one of the world's most distinguished scientific societies could reject the observations of thousands of whalers in favour of Barrington's little collection of half-baked seamen's tales, but his campaign did result in the despatch of a major exploring expedition.

It was commanded by Captain Constantine John Phipps, with the ships HMS *Racehorse* and HMS *Carcass* (the latter commanded by Skeffington Lutwidge). Its instructions were to follow the familiar northward course towards northwest Spitsbergen, then to determine how far navigation was possible from there to the North Pole.

The two ships left the Thames on 26 May 1773, and by early July the expedition was ready for its first serious engagement with the ice.

9th [July]. Having a fair opportunity, and SW wind, stood to the Westward; intending, when the weather was clear, to make the ice to the Northward, and run along it. About twelve, clearer; saw the fast ice to the Northward, and the appearance of loose ice to the NW: stood directly for it, and got amongst it between two and three; steering as much to the Northward as the situation of the ice would permit. At six observed the dip 81°52'. At half past seven, found the ice quite fast to the West, being in longitude 2°2'E, by our reckoning, which was the farthest to the Westward of Spitsbergen that we got this voyage. At eight the fog was so very thick, that we could neither see which way to push for an opening, nor where the *Carcass* was, though very near us. That we might not risk parting company with her, I was obliged to ply to windward under the topsails, tacking every quarter of an hour to keep in the opening in which we were, and clear of the ice which surrounded us. At four in the afternoon we were in 80°36'.

10th. We lost the *Carcass* twice in the night, from the very thick fog, and were working all night amongst the ice, making very short tacks; the opening being small, and the floating ice very thick about the ship. The situation of the people from the very fatiguing work and wet weather, made the most minute precautions necessary for the preservation of their health: we now found the advantage of the spirits which had been allowed for extraordinary occasions; as well as the additional cloathing furnished by the Admiralty. Notwithstanding every attention, several of the men were confined with colds, which affected them with pains in their bones; but, from the careful attendance given them, few continued in the sick list above two days at a time. At nine in the morning, when it cleared a little, we saw the *Carcass* much to the Southward of us. I took the opportunity of the clear weather to run to the Westward, and found the ice quite solid there; I then stood through every opening to the Northward, but there also soon got to the edge of the solid ice. I was forced to haul up to weather a point which ran out from it. After I had weathered that, the ice closing fast upon me, obliged me to set the foresail, which, with the fresh wind and smooth water, gave the ship such way as to force through it with a violent stroke. At one in the afternoon, immediately on getting out into the open sea, we found a heavy swell setting to the Northward; though amongst the ice, the minute before, the water had been as smooth as a mill pond. The wind blew strong at SSW. The ice, as far as we could see from the mast head, lay ENE: we steered that course close to it, to look for an opening to the Northward. I now began to conceive that the ice was one compact impenetrable body, having run along it from East to West above ten degrees. I purposed however to stand over to the Eastward, in order to ascertain whether the body of ice joined to Spitsbergen. This the quantity of loose ice had before rendered impracticable; but thinking the Westerly winds might probably by this time have packed it all that way, I flattered myself with the hopes of meeting with no obstruction till I should come to where it joined the land; and in case of an opening, however small, I was determined at all events to push through it.

Another northward thrust, later in July, brought them to the highest latitude attained on the voyage.

27th [July]. Working still to the NE, we met with some loose ice; however from the openness of the sea hitherto, since we had passed Deer Field, I had great hopes of getting far to the Northward; but about noon, being in the latitude of eighty and forty-eight, by our reckoning, we were stopped by the main body of the ice, which we found lying in a line, nearly East and West, quite solid. Having tacked, I brought to, and founded close to the edge of the ice, in 79 fathom, muddy bottom.

The wind being still Easterly, I worked up close to the edge of the ice, coasting it all the way. At six in the evening we were in longitude 14°59'30"E, by observation.

28th. At midnight the latitude observed was 80°37'. The main body of the ice still lying in the same direction, we continued working to the Eastward, and found several openings to the Northward, of two or three miles deep; into every one of which we ran, forcing the ship, wherever we could, by a press of sail, amongst the loose ice which we found here in much larger pieces than to the Westward. At six in the morning the variation, by the mean of six azimuths, was 11°56'W; the horizon remarkably clear. At noon, being close to the main body of the ice, the latitude by observation was 80°36': we sounded in 101 fathom, muddy ground. In the afternoon the wind blew fresh at NE, with a thick fog; the ice hung much about the rigging. The loose ice being thick and close, we found ourselves so much engaged in it, as to be obliged to run back a considerable distance to the Westward and Southward, before we could extricate ourselves: we afterwards had both the sea and the weather clear, and worked up to the North Eastward. At half past five the longitude of the ship was 15°16'45"E. At seven the Easternmost land bore E ½ N distant about seven or eight leagues, appearing like deep bays and islands, probably those called in the Dutch charts the *Seven Islands*; they seemed to be surrounded with ice. I stood to the Southward, in hopes of getting to the

Southeastward round the ice, and between it and the land, where the water appeared more open.

Phipps's hopes were soon thwarted, though, and within a few days they were hopelessly trapped in the ice.

August 1st. The ice pressed in fast; there was not now the smallest opening; the two ships were within less than two lengths of each other, separated by ice, and neither having room to turn. The ice, which had been all flat the day before, and almost level with the water's edge, was now in many places forced higher than the main yard, by the pieces squeezing together. Our latitude this day at noon, by the double altitude, was 80°37'.

2nd. Thick foggy wet weather, blowing fresh to the Westward; the ice immediately about the ships rather looser than the day before, but yet hourly setting in so fast upon us, that there seemed to be no probability of getting the ships out again, without a strong East, or North East wind. There was not the smallest appearance of open water, except a little towards the West point of the North East land. The Seven islands and North East land, with the frozen sea, formed almost a bason [basin], leaving but about four points opening for the ice to drift out, in case of a change of wind.

3rd. The weather very fine, clear, and calm; we perceived that the ships had been driven far to the Eastward; the ice was much closer than before, and the passage by which we had come in from the Westward closed up, no open water being in sight, either in that or any other quarter. The pilots having expressed a wish to get if possible farther out, the ships companies were set to work at five in the morning, to cut a passage through the ice, and warp through the small openings to the Westward. We found the ice very deep, having sawed sometimes through pieces twelve feet thick. This labour was continued the whole day, but without any success; our utmost efforts not having moved the ships above three hundred yards to the Westward through the ice, at the same time that they had been driven (together with the ice itself, to which they were fast) far to the NE and Eastward, by the current; which had also forced the loose ice from the Westward, between the islands, where it became packed, and as firm as the main body.

They were now farther to the northeast of Svalbard than any exploring expedition before them, though it is possible that whalers may have been there previously. The 'Seven Islands' and 'North East Land' mentioned by Phipps (shown on modern maps with their Norwegian names, Sjuøyane and Nordaustlandet) are about as far to the north and east as sailing ships could go in most seasons. The main problem facing Phipps now was that the strong east, or northeast wind that he needed to free the ships failed to come as soon as he wished. For a while he was driven to contemplate abandoning the ships, even though on 7 August a gentle but more encouraging easterly wind finally arose, and the ice loosened a little.

> Finding the ice rather more open near the ships, I was encouraged to attempt moving them. The wind being Easterly, though but little of it, we set the sails, and got the ships about a mile to the Westward. They moved indeed, but very slowly, and were not now by a great deal so far to the Westward as where they were beset. However, I kept all the sail upon them, to force through whenever the ice slacked the least. The people behaved very well in hauling the boat; they seemed reconciled to the idea of quitting the ships, and to have the fullest confidence in their officers. The boats could not with the greatest diligence be got to the water side before the fourteenth; if the situation of the ships did not alter by that time, I should not be justified in staying longer by them. In the mean time I resolved to carry on both attempts together, moving the boats constantly, but without omitting any opportunity of getting the ships through.

On 10 August, the desired wind finally blew for him: 'The wind springing up to the NNE in the morning, we set all the sail we could upon the ship, and forced her through a great deal of very heavy ice: she struck often very hard, and with one stroke broke the shank of the best bower anchor. About noon we had got her through all the ice, and out to sea.'

A few days later, Phipps headed for home, and he reached the Thames on 24 September.

A final fascinating aspect of the Phipps expedition was that its most junior member later rose to be one of the greatest and most famous naval officers of all time. The 14-year-old Horatio Nelson served as a midshipman on the *Carcass*, and during the course of the expedition he fought his first and least glorious battle. One of his early biographers, Robert Southey (1774–1843), tells the story.

> One night, during the mid-watch, he stole from the ship with one of his comrades, taking advantage of a rising fog, and set off over the ice in pursuit of a bear. It was not long before they were missed. The fog thickened, and Captain Lutwidge and his officers became exceedingly alarmed for their safety. Between three and four in the morning the weather cleared, and the two adventurers were seen, at a considerable distance from the ship, attacking a huge bear. The signal for them to return was immediately made: Nelson's comrade called upon him to obey it, but in vain; his musket had flashed in the pan; their ammunition was expended; and a chasm in the ice, which divided him from the bear, probably preserved his life. 'Never mind,' he cried; 'do but let me get a blow at this devil with the butt-end of my musket, and we shall have him.' Captain Lutwidge, however, seeing his danger, fired a gun, which had the desired effect of frightening the beast; and the boy then returned, somewhat afraid of the consequences of his trespass. The captain reprimanded him sternly for conduct so unworthy of the office which he filled, and desired to know what motive he could have for hunting a bear. 'Sir,' said he, pouting his lip, as he was wont to do when agitated, 'I wished to kill the bear, that I might carry the skin to my father.'

The Phipps expedition gave an effective demonstration that there was no access to the Arctic Ocean between Greenland and Svalbard. His report on his experiences were hardly encouraging. He reported a 'wall of ice' extending between Svalbard and Greenland, 'without the smallest appearance of any opening'.

Even so, the failure of Phipps to make substantial progress beyond Barentsz, Hudson and Chichagov did not at first bring a halt to Barrington's campaign. In 1774 he presented two lectures to the Royal Society on the subject of the Pole, and in 1775 and 1776 he published his 'proofs' in further attempts to gain support. But by now events were moving rapidly away from him. The Admiralty's interest in polar routes had shifted to the Northwest Passage, and in 1776 it despatched Captain James Cook (1728–79) on the last of his three great voyages of exploration, to search for the Passage from its Pacific end back to the Atlantic. In 1780 the expedition returned without success and without Cook; he had died in a scuffle on a beach with a group of Hawaiian Islanders. A decade later, France erupted into revolution, then Europe erupted into war, and suddenly the Royal Navy had more pressing matters on its mind.

– 2 –

The Dream Fades

1818–27

The French Revolution of 1789 and the subsequent Napoleonic wars in Europe, which brought Arctic exploration almost to a standstill for nearly 30 years, were also the agents of its regeneration in 1818. When the Treaty of Paris restored peace in 1815, the Royal Navy was left with a major problem. It had huge resources of ships and manpower, and very little employment for either. The easiest and first solution adopted by the Admiralty was simply to discharge in excess of 100,000 seamen and throw them off the ships and onto the streets. The concept of unfair dismissal had yet to be invented. But there was still a huge surplus of officers who were not so easily disposed of. Many simply drew their half-pay and never worked again. But to keep the navy alive at all, useful employment had to be found for at least some of the officers, men and ships. A partial solution to this problem was eventually discovered by one of the greatest promoters of polar exploration, John Barrow (1764–1848), Second Secretary of the Admiralty. Barrow, who in earlier life had travelled widely, and had taken a voyage on a Spitsbergen whaler, had a passion for geography and exploration, and proposed exploration as a suitable occupation for the Royal Navy in peacetime. In particular, he proposed the revival of the search for Arctic passages to the Pacific. Barrow, like his predecessors, believed that practical benefits might come from such voyages. He expressed his argument very clearly.

It may . . . be asked, as it has been asked by some of that class known as Utilitarians, *cui bono* are these northern voyages undertaken? If they were merely to be prosecuted for the sake of making a passage from England to China, and for no other purpose, their utility might fairly be questioned. But when the acquisition of knowledge is the groundwork of all the instructions, under which they are sent forth, when the commanding officer is directed to cause constant observations to be made for the advancement of every branch of science – astronomy, navigation, hydrography, meteorology, including electricity and magnetism, and to make collections of subjects in natural history, – in short, to lose no opportunity of acquiring new and important information and discovery; and when it is considered that these voyages give employment to officers and men, in time of peace, and produce officers and men not to be surpassed, perhaps not equalled, in any other branch of the service, the question *cui bono* is easily answered in the words of the minister of Queen Elizabeth – 'Knowledge is Power'.

Barrow went on to enumerate the benefits that northern exploration had already brought to Great Britain: the cod fisheries of Newfoundland; the Arctic whaling industry; an enormous fur trading industry that stretched all the way across northern Canada. He was, of course, correct in every particular. The desire to explore is an emotion essential to mankind. Survival, progress and prosperity stem from it. Successful societies explore first, and determine later what good may have come from it. But just as today there are persons churlish enough to doubt the value of the exploration of space, so then there were persons who doubted the value of exploring the Earth. On this occasion, however, Barrow was fortunate.

The Admiralty accepted his argument, and authorized the planning of a Northwest Passage expedition in 1818. This expedition, led by Commander John Ross, was deemed a poor effort, having failed to sail beyond Baffin Bay, but it set in train a series of some 30 naval expeditions which, during the next 40 years, explored and charted large coastal areas of east and west Greenland and a huge area of the Canadian Arctic archipelago, plotted nearly the whole Arctic coastline of the North American continent, and discovered a Northwest Passage.

Barrow was also an adherent of Daines Barrington's belief in an ice-free Arctic Ocean, and his interest in re-examining the subject prompted a publisher to issue a new edition of

Barrington's North Pole publications in 1818. It is extraordinary how, in the face of all the evidence, the subject of the 'Open Polar Sea' recurs in the history of the North Pole. We may forgive Barrington, who was more of an armchair enthusiast than professional geographer, and, to be fair, he had little reliable evidence to work with. But it is more difficult to understand why, with the evidence against it still accumulating, the theme was taken up again and again by eminent geographers and explorers in the nineteenth century. Yet different versions of the theory persisted until about 1880. According to Barrow's version, the 'wall of ice' that Phipps and many whaling masters encountered between Greenland and Svalbard could easily and frequently be breached, permitting passage into an ice-free sea beyond.

> Captain Phipps seems to think that 'the summer was uncommonly favourable for his purpose,' because it 'afforded him the fullest opportunity of ascertaining repeatedly the situation of that wall of ice, extending for more than twenty degrees between the latitudes of eighty and eighty-one, without the smallest appearance of any opening'. There is reason to believe, however, that few years occur in which there are not many openings in the wall of ice which usually stretches between the eastern coast of Greenland and the northern-most parts of Spitzbergen, and consequently the summer in which Captain Phipps made the attempt to get to the northward was particularly unfavourable.

The only other eye-witness evidence available to Barrow was from whalers, who visited the region every year. One of the most respected of them all, William Scoresby Sr, is known to have reached 81°30'N on the ship *Resolution* in 1806, and that was generally regarded as being a new record. Between Phipps's voyage in 1773 and that organized by Barrow in 1818, over 3,300 other whaling ships visited the Arctic, and only one claimed to have sailed beyond that: in 1786 James Wyatt, of the ship *Whale*, reported that he sailed to 89°N, but ruined his story by claiming that the Pole was marked by a volcano. The evidence was overwhelmingly against Barrow's belief in a narrow and broken wall of ice between Svalbard and Greenland, with an open sea beyond. But in matters concerning the North

Pole, and especially the 'Open Polar Sea' beyond it, the ability of otherwise rational men to delude themselves was remarkable.

On the other hand, whalers did often report 'open' seasons when it might have been possible to penetrate farther north than usual, and three such seasons in succession occurred in the years before 1818. That was encouragement enough for the Admiralty to mount a second expedition to the Arctic in 1818 to test Barrow's theory. The leader was Captain David Buchan (1780–1838) on HMS *Trent*, and he was accompanied by Lieutenant John Franklin commanding HMS *Dorothea*. The ships had a complement of 56 and 40 respectively. Buchan's instructions were to sail directly north between Greenland and Spitsbergen, and in the event of finding an open sea, to continue directly to Bering Strait. The expedition left London on 25 April, and on 4 June reached Magdalena Bay (now Magdalenefjorden) near the northwest corner of Spitsbergen. From there, they made their first attempt to progress northward three days later, but the result was predictable. In his narrative of the voyage Lieutenant Frederick William Beechey of the *Trent* relates their many problems.

June 1818. – The expedition quitted Magdalena Bay on the 7th June, to renew the examination of the ice; and, after steering a few leagues to the northward, found it precisely in the same situation and state as we had left it on the 2nd instant.

We were no sooner clear of the land, than we concluded, by a heavy swell rolling up from the south-west, that it had been blowing hard at sea during the time we were snugly at anchor, and that we had thus escaped at least one gale of wind. The breeze was now moderating, and we stood along the margin of the ice, searching for an opening, and remarking as we went what very little effect had been produced upon it by the gale.

While thus occupied the breeze suddenly deserted us, and the vessels being rendered unmanageable by the heavy swell which continued to roll towards the ice, they were, in spite of all our efforts, driven into the pack. With a view of averting this occurrence, the boats had been employed in towing the vessels until the latest moment, but unfortunately those of the *Trent* were cut off from communication with her by the breaking of the line.

By the aid of a light breeze of wind off the ice, both vessels succeeded in gaining the open sea, but they had scarcely proceeded an hour before they were again becalmed, and, in spite of every exertion, they were a second time driven into the packed ice.

The turbulent scene from which we had but recently escaped was but a faint prelude to that which now presented itself. During the interval the swell had materially increased, and now rolled furiously in upon the ice. The pieces at the edge of the pack were at one time wholly immersed in the sea, and at the next raised far above their natural line of flotation, while those further in, being more extensive, were alternately depressed or elevated at either extremity as the advancing wave forced its way along. The see-saw motion which was thus produced was alarming, not merely in appearance, but, in fact; and must have proved fatal to any vessel that had encountered it, as floes of ice, several yards in thickness, were continually crashing and breaking in pieces, and the sea for miles was covered with fragments ground so small that they actually formed a thick, pasty substance – in nautical language termed 'brash ice' – which extended to the depth of five feet.

Amidst this giddy element, our whole attention was occupied in endeavouring to place the bow of the vessel, the strongest part of her frame, in the direction of the most formidable pieces of ice – a manoeuvre which, though likely to be attended with the loss of the bowsprit, was yet preferable to encountering the still greater risk of having the broadside of the vessel in contact with it. For this would have subjected her to the chance of dipping her gunwale under the floes as she rolled; an accident which, had it occurred, would either have laid open her side or have overset the vessel at once. In either case the event would probably have proved fatal to all on board, as it would have been next to impossible to rescue any person from the confused moving mass of brash ice, which covered the sea in every direction.

With much difficulty we effected our laborious task; until

we were fortunately spared the anticipated collision by the brash ice becoming thicker as we proceeded, and at length quite impenetrable, so that the brig by this means was kept at a distance of about a hundred yards from the heaviest pieces. Thus situated, we passed the night in the greatest anxiety, at one time fancying the distance between the ice and the vessel was diminishing, and at another that it was somewhat increased, and only earnestly hoping throughout, that a breeze would spring up from the northward, and release us from our perilous position.

The attention of the seamen was in some degree diverted from the contemplation of this scene of difficulty by the necessity of employing them all at the pump; for the leak was by no means diminished, and the duties of the day having called them from this occupation, a considerable quantity of water had by this time found its way to the well.

Towards morning, our hopes of a breeze off the ice were realized, and by seven o'clock we had the satisfaction to get quite clear of the ice. We shortly rejoined our commodore, who had escaped the danger to which we had been exposed by being at a greater distance from the pack when the wind failed.

The ships now steered to the westward to reconnoitre the state of the ice in that direction, and, in longitude 4°30′E, fell in with several whale-ships, by which we were informed that the ice was quite compact to the westward, and that fifteen vessels were beset in it. This unpromising intelligence, coupled with the apparent tending of the ice to the southward, satisfied Captain Buchan that our best chance of success was by keeping near the land of Spitzbergen, and he in consequence once more directed the course of the vessels to the eastward.

Following this sound advice, the expedition returned to the coast of Spitsbergen, and made its way back north to Cloven Cliff (now Klovningen), a tiny island that marks the northwestern extremity of Svalbard. Then, with dwindling spirits and faltering hopes, the explorers attempted for a second time to make progress northward into the Arctic Ocean, only to become stuck fast in the ice.

Our position was off a part of the northern coast of Spitzbergen, where Baffin, Hudson, Poole, and indeed almost all the early voyagers to this country had been stopped; for it appears that, with scarcely any exception, they succeeded in navigating the western coast of this island, and in doubling Cloven Cliff; but in no well-authenticated voyage is there any record of their having passed much beyond our present situation. We were also not far from the spot where Captain Phipps so nearly abandoned his vessels, as to have actually commenced drawing his boats over the ice towards the open water, in the expectation of being able to proceed in them to a port in Spitzbergen, where he knew he should find some Dutch whalers at anchor. Our hopes of being able to effect anything of consequence in a north-eastern direction were, therefore, considerably diminished, and setting aside the appearances from our mast-head, we were aware, from reading the narratives of the old voyagers, that there never had been so material an alteration in the position of the ice in this part as to promise any great advance toward the attainment of the object we had in view. It was, however, our duty to make the attempt, and ever sanguine of success whilst the ice admitted of the smallest progress, we thought we might be more fortunate than those who had preceded us.

As the tide changed, the pieces of ice immediately around us began to separate, and some of them to twist round with a loud grinding noise, urging the vessels, which were less than a mile from the land, still nearer and nearer to the beach. Captain Buchan, seeing the imminent risk to which this movement exposed the expedition, left nothing untried that seemed likely to increase our distance from the shore; and succeeded in fastening his lines to a large piece of ice that was twisting round, and which, as it turned, brought his ship gradually on the outside of it. The *Trent* endeavoured to follow her example; but so rapid was the motion of the ice that although only a few yards from the *Dorothea*, she found it wholly impracticable, and it was not until after twenty hours' hard labour that we succeeded in again placing the vessels together.

Both vessels were now hauled into small bays in the floe, and secured there by ropes fixed to the ice by means of large iron hooks, called ice-anchors.

The advantages of such a situation must be evident to every seaman, the vessel being by this means protected from the passing ice by the projecting points ahead and astern of her; and the floes being sometimes deeper in the water than the ships, there is in such a case no danger of their touching the ground.

We continued fast to this floe of ice for thirteen days, shifting the ships from one part of it to another, as the motion brought them between it and the shore. As this could be effected only by main force, the crew were so constantly engaged in this harassing duty, that their time was divided almost entirely between the windlass and the pump; until the men at length became so fatigued that our sick-list was seriously augmented. The subject of the leak was never for any length of time absent from our thoughts; but we now began to reflect seriously on the propriety of hoisting out part of the provisions upon the ice, in the hope of making some discovery that might lead to the remedy of so serious an evil. While this was in contemplation, it fortunately happened that, on one very still night, as we lay quietly by the side of the floe, the surgeon's assistant thought he heard the water rushing into the vessel beneath where he slept.

Elated at the idea of at least discovering the defect, the spirit-room was immediately cleared, and it was not long before our suspicions were confirmed. On cutting through the lining opposite the spot whence the noise proceeded, the water rushed into the hold in a stream full four feet in height. We now found that a bolt-hole had been left open in the bottom of the vessel, and that the water had found its way down between the timbers into the well. Fortunately, its dimensions did not admit of a greater quantity of water passing through than could be kept under by the pumps, otherwise the vessel must have foundered at sea. We could easily account for the leak having scarcely shown itself before the brig quitted the river, by supposing the hole to have been partly pitched over, a covering which, of course, very soon washed away at sea. By this fortunate discovery we were able in a few minutes to apply an effectual remedy, and to partake of the satisfaction arising from finding ourselves in as tight and safe a vessel as we could wish – a satisfaction which, I am sure, the reader will fully appreciate.

After 13 days of perilous besetment in the ice, the two ships finally regained the open sea, and again found sanctuary in a harbour in northwest Spitsbergen. From there they made yet another attempt to get through the ice to the north, starting on 6 July. This time, they found that the wind had created many new channels of open water in the ice, and had also changed direction to favour a northward thrust. On the next day, prospects still looked good.

The ships continued to advance rapidly along the narrow channels between the floes, trimming their sails at each turn of the canal, and receiving occasional assistance from a light line cast to a few active men upon the ice, whose exertions were at one time necessary in order to check the bow or quarter of the vessel, and otherwise assist the helm when the turnings of the channel were abrupt; at others, to prevent the vessel falling to leeward when her way had been deadened by the resistance of some heavy piece of ice which she had encountered in her path. A proficient in the art of marine drawing might here have found a beautiful subject for his pencil. The endless and ever-varying forms of the ice; the glassy smooth canals winding among the floes, and reflecting the bright blue colour of their banks; the vessels in various positions, trimming their sails to maintain their course; groups of figures, busily occupied upon the ice; and many other objects which would have presented themselves to a practised eye, would have supplied materials for a picture which I shall not spoil by attempting to describe.

Noon came, and still the prospect was favourable even from the most elevated point of our mast-head. As the day advanced, however, we had our misgivings: some occasional closing of the canals, and other obstructions, foreboded disappointment; and, toward evening, it became too evident that we had overrated the advantages of the morning. The scene was indeed changed, the channels by degrees disappeared, and the ice, with its accustomed rapidity, soon became packed, encircled the vessels, and pressed so closely upon them, that one boundless plain of rugged snow extended in every direction. Even the sea, in which we had sailed but a few hours before, was now far beyond our horizon, and its position could be determined only by a dark lowering sky that overhung the southern quarter.

After a few hours the ice opened, but the channels were narrow and very partial. We waited some little time in the hope that they would increase, and that the ships might again use their sails, but were soon convinced of the hope-lessness of getting to the northward by such means alone.

As we were now fairly entered into the pack, and the summer was already well advanced, Captain Buchan deter-mined to prove, by a desperate effort, what advance it was possible to make by dragging the vessels through the ice whenever the smallest opening occurred. We accordingly took the earliest opportunity of commencing this laborious experiment, which was performed by fixing large ropes to iron hooks driven into the ice, and by heaving upon them with the windlass, a party removing obstructions in the channels with saws. After working several hours in this manner, we reached a tolerably clear channel, and with the aid of our sails ran a few miles to the northward, encountering in the way heavy pieces of ice, which we could not avoid running against. Our progress, however, was arrested before noon by the closing of the channels; and a very heavy pressure of the pieces about us rendered it necessary to put the vessels into a small bay, formed in a field of ice that was at hand.

This was the most northerly position reached by the expedition during the voyage, and it would have been a great gratification could we have obtained an observation of the sun to determine the exact latitude; a measure which was rendered still more desirable by a difference of several miles which occurred in the reckoning of the two ships. By that kept on board the *Dorothea* the latitude was 80°31'N; while that of the *Trent* was 80°37'N, the mean of which is 80°34'N.

We had not been long secured to the field of ice before we had the mortification of finding ourselves drifting fast to the southward, both by the lead-line and by the bearings of the land; and the next day, though by warping we thought we had gained several miles, our latitude was less by nearly four leagues than it was when we first made fast, viz. 80°23'N.

Having failed once again, but at least having achieved his highest latitude at 80°34'N (still short of the latitudes attained by Phipps in 1773 and Scoresby in 1806), Buchan, like Hudson before him, decided on one last push to the north from Greenland rather than Svalbard waters, and accordingly headed west. In common with Hudson he was not readily willing to quit, but in heading for Greenland he succeeded only in becoming trapped in the ice in the midst of a gale, and putting the expedition in an even more perilous position.

No language, I am convinced, can convey an adequate idea of the terrific grandeur of the effect now produced by the collision of the ice and the tempestuous ocean. The sea, violently agitated and rolling its mountainous waves against an opposing body is at all times a sublime and awful sight; but when, in addition, it encounters immense masses, which it has set in motion with a violence equal to its own, its effect is prodigiously increased. At one moment it bursts upon these icy fragments, and buries them many feet beneath its wave, and the next, as the buoyancy of the depressed body struggles for reascendancy, the water rushes in foaming cataracts over its edges; whilst every individual mass, rocking and labouring in its bed, grinds against and contends with its opponent until one is either split with the shock or upheaved upon the surface of the other. Nor is this collision confined to any particular spot; it is going on as far as the sight can reach; and when from this convulsive scene

below, the eye is turned to the extraordinary appearance of
the blink in the sky above, where the unnatural clearness
of a calm and silvery atmosphere presents itself, bounded by
a dark hard line of stormy clouds, such as at this moment
lowered over our masts, as if to mark the confines within
which the efforts of man would be of no avail, the reader
may imagine the sensation of awe which must accompany
that of grandeur in the mind of the beholder.

At this instant, when we were about to put the strength
of our little vessel in competition with that of the great
icy continent, and when it seemed almost présumption
to reckon on the possibility of her surviving the unequal
conflict, it was gratifying in the extreme to observe in all
our crew the greatest calmness and resolution. If ever the
fortitude of seamen was fairly tried, it was assuredly not
less so on this occasion; and I will not conceal the pride I
felt in witnessing the bold and decisive tone in which the
orders were issued by the commander of our little vessel,
and the promptitude and steadiness with which they were
executed by the crew.

We were now so near the scene of danger as to render
necessary the immediate execution of our plan, and in
an instant the labouring vessel flew before the gale. Each
person instinctively secured his own hold, and with his
eyes fixed upon the masts, awaited in breathless anxiety the
moment of concussion. It soon arrived, – the brig, cutting
her way through the light ice, came in violent contact with
the main body. In an instant we all lost our footing, the
masts bent with the impetus, and the cracking timbers from
below bespoke a pressure which was calculated to awaken
our serious apprehensions. The vessel staggered under the
shock, and for a moment seemed to recoil; but the next
wave, curling up under her counter, drove her about her
own length within the margin of the ice, where she gave
one roll, and was immediately thrown broadside to the wind
by the succeeding wave, which beat furiously against her
stern, and brought her lee-side in contact with the main
body, leaving her weather-side exposed at the same time
to a piece of ice about twice her own dimensions. This
unfortunate occurrence prevented the vessel penetrating

sufficiently far into the ice to escape the effect of the gale, and placed her in a situation where she was assailed on all sides by battering-rams, if I may use the expression, every one of which contested the small space which she occupied, and dealt such unrelenting blows that there appeared to be scarcely any possibility of saving her from foundering. Literally tossed from piece to piece, we had nothing left but patiently to abide the issue, for we could scarcely keep our feet, much less render any assistance to the vessel.

Both ships were severely damaged in this incident, but after several hours the gale subsided, and the expedition was able to reach a safe harbour in northwest Spitsbergen. After repairs to some of the damage, the two ships began their long limp home on 30 August, and arrived safely on 22 October.

That heroic failure, four near-disastrous forays into the ice, persuaded even John Barrow that ships could not penetrate towards the North Pole beyond about 80–81°N. He and the Admiralty began at last to concede that there was no navigable polar passage to the Pacific, and probably no practical or economic value in attaining the Pole at all. A major shift was at last beginning to take place. The Pole was no longer to be viewed as the halfway point in a sea route: it was becoming an object of curiosity in its own right. What was there? What might be found on the way to it? Was it sea or land? The shift now was towards geographical exploration for its own sake.

Those questions still enthralled Barrow, and Buchan's failure did not quell his interest. He had accepted that, in order to reach the North Pole, explorers would probably have to walk for most of the way. In the mid-1820s, he began preparing another proposal to the Admiralty, for an expedition to attempt to attain the Pole both on foot over ice, and by boat in open water. Remarkably, in this reversal of attitude, Barrow once again took his cue from Phipps, whose observation of a solid wall of ice he had once derided. He made note of two passages in Phipps's narrative, describing 'the main body of the ice to be lying in a line, nearly east and west, quite unbroken' and 'one continued plain of smooth unbroken ice, bounded only by the horizon'. He also referred to the whaling master William Scoresby Jr (whose observations on the Arctic were no less respected than those of his father, who still held the record northern latitude of 81°30'N). Scoresby testified that 'I once saw a field [of ice] that was so free from either fissure or hummock, that I imagine, had it been free from snow, a coach might have been driven many leagues over it in a direct line, without obstruction or danger.'

On this basis, Barrow collaborated with two naval explorers who had already distinguished themselves in the Arctic, John Franklin (1786–1847) and William Edward Parry (1790–1855), to prepare detailed plans for the expedition to be laid before the Admiralty. The method they proposed for travelling over the ice, though, was not a coach but an ingenious new invention suggested by Franklin and developed by Parry, and which they named a 'sledge-boat'. The name describes it well: it was a flat-bottomed boat, 20 feet long and seven feet wide, with two sledge runners mounted underneath. The plan was that two of these 'sledge-boats', each manned by two officers and 12 seamen, would set out over the ice from the north coast of Spitsbergen. They were also to use four lightweight sledges. The plan received strong endorsement from the Royal Society, and Parry was selected to command it. It was the first realistic attempt to reach the Pole, and the first scientific expedition to the Arctic Ocean: under guidance from the Royal Society, the officers were to make a wide range of physical and natural history observations.

The expedition left London on HMS *Hecla* on 25 March 1827 and headed first for Hammerfest in Norway, where they picked up eight reindeer which were intended to haul the sledges. This was never a practical idea for travel on open water alternating with hummocky sea ice, and they were not used. Instead, they returned to the original plan of using men.

The use of British seamen as sledge teams, as a cheap and plentiful alternative to animals, soon became an entrenched tradition in the Royal Navy, even though man-hauling has been described as one of the most arduous labours known to man. Unlike the light and flexible Eskimo sledge, which lent itself readily to haulage by dogs, the naval sledge was a heavy, rigid affair built by dockyard carpenters using sturdy hardwoods. Parry's versions also had steel-shod runners, which served only to increase friction by sticking to the ice. Nor were there any other concessions to the compelling need to travel light; the sledges were heavily laden with iron cooking utensils, tents, carpenter's tools, masts and paddles, spare clothing, food to last them for several weeks, rum, even books. The total weight of each of Parry's sledges amounted to 3,753 pounds, or an incredible 268 pounds (19.1 stones) per man.

On reaching northwest Spitsbergen, Parry found that he could sail along the island's north coast, and eventually reached the Seven Islands (Sjuøyane), where he laid depots of provisions for the sledge parties. He then returned to the north coast of Spitsbergen, where he found a suitable harbour for his ship in Sorgfjorden.

On 21 June, Parry set out for the Pole with his two sledge-boats, named *Enterprise* and *Endeavour*. The second sledge was commanded by Lieutenant James Clark Ross (1800–62), who later, like Parry, rose to fame as one of the Royal Navy's most experienced and successful polar explorers. On 24 June, the boats reached the ice and turned into sledges, and the four smaller sledges were brought into use.

We set off on our first journey over the ice at ten p.m. on the 24th, Table Island bearing SSW, and a fresh breeze blowing from WSW, with thick fog, which afterwards changed to rain. The bags of pemmican were placed upon the sledges, and the bread in the boats, with the intention of securing the latter from wet; but this plan we were very soon obliged to relinquish. We now commenced upon very slow and laborious travelling, the pieces of ice being of small extent and very rugged, obliging us to make three journies, and sometimes four, with the boats and baggage, and to launch several times across narrow pools of water. This, however, was nothing more than we had expected to encounter at the margin of the ice, and for some distance within it; and every individual exerted himself to the very utmost, with the hope of the sooner reaching the main or field ice. We stopped to dine at five a.m. on the 25th, having made, by our log (which we kept very carefully, marking the courses by compass, and estimating the distances), about two miles and a half of northing; and

again setting forward, proceeded till eleven a.m. when we
halted to rest, our latitude by observation at noon being 81°
15'13".

Setting out again at half past nine in the evening, we
found our way to lie over nothing but small loose rugged
masses of ice, separated by little pools of water, obliging us
constantly to launch and haul up the boats, each of which
operations required them to be unloaded, and occupied
nearly a quarter of an hour. It came on to rain very hard
on the morning of the 26th; and finding we were making
very little progress (having advanced not more than half a
mile in four hours), and that our clothes would be soon
wet through, we halted at half past one, and took shelter
under the awnings. The weather improving at six o'clock,
we again moved forward, and travelled till a quarter past
eleven, when we hauled the boats upon the only tolerably
large floe-piece in sight. The rain had very much increased
the quantity of water lying upon the ice, of which nearly
half the surface was now covered with numberless little
ponds of various shapes and extent. It is a remarkable
fact that we had already experienced, in the course of
this summer, more rain than during the whole of seven
previous summers *taken together*, though passed in latitudes
from 7° to 15° lower than this. A great deal of the ice
over which we passed today presented a very curious
appearance and structure, being composed, on its upper
surface, of numberless irregular needle-like crystals, placed
vertically, and nearly close together; their length varying,
in different pieces of ice, from five to ten inches, and their
breadth in the middle about half an inch, but pointed at
both ends. The upper surface of ice having this structure
sometimes looks like greenish velvet; a vertical section of
it, which frequently occurs at the margin of floes, resembles,
while it remains compact, the most beautiful satin-spar, and
asbestos, when falling to pieces. At this early part of the
season this kind of ice afforded pretty firm footing; but
as the summer advanced, the needles became more loose
and movable, rendering it extremely fatiguing to walk over
them, besides cutting our boots and feet, on which account
the men called them 'penknives'. It appeared probable to

us that this peculiarity might be produced by the heavy drops of rain piercing their way downwards through the ice, and thus separating the latter into needles of the form above described, rather than to any regular crystallization when in the act of freezing; which supposition seemed the more reasonable, as the needles are always placed in a vertical position, and never occur except from the upper surface downwards.

We pursued our journey at half past nine p.m., with the wind at NE, and thick weather, the ice being so much in motion as to make it very dangerous to cross with loaded boats, the masses being all very small. Indeed, when we came to the margin of the floe-piece on which we had slept, we saw no road by which we could safely proceed, and therefore preferred remaining where we were, to the risk of driving back to the southward on one of the smaller masses. On this account we halted at midnight, having waded three-quarters of a mile through water from two to five inches deep upon the ice. The thermometer was at 33°. In the course of this short journey we saw several rotges [little auks] and dovekies [black guillemots], and a few kittiwakes, ivory gulls, and mallemuckes [fulmars].

The weather continued so thick that we could only see a few yards around us; but the wind backing to the southward, and beginning to open out the loose ice at the edge of the floe, we proceeded at half past ten p.m., and after crossing several small pieces, came to the first tolerably heavy ice we had yet seen, but all broken up into masses of small extent. At seven a.m. on the 28th, we came to a floe covered with high and rugged hummocks, which opposed a formidable obstacle to our progress, occurring in two or three successive tiers, so that we had no sooner crossed one than another presented itself. Over one of these we hauled the boats with extreme difficulty by a 'standing pull', and the weather being then so thick that we could see no pass across the next tier, we were obliged to stop at nine a.m. While performing this laborious work, which required the boats to be got up and down places almost perpendicular, James Parker, my coxswain, received a severe contusion in his back by the boat falling upon him from a hummock, and the boats were constantly subject to very heavy blows, but sustained no damage.

In this laborious, painful manner they inched their way forward, sometimes making little more than a mile after six hours' toil; sometimes less than 150 yards after two hours. Nevertheless, it was progress, however slow, and on 10 July Parry might have drawn some satisfaction from being the first explorer in the world to achieve a latitude of 82°N, though there is no indication that he derived any pleasure from it.

At half-past two we reached a floe, which appeared at first a level and large one; but on landing we were much mortified to find it so covered with immense ponds, or rather small lakes of fresh water, that to accomplish two miles in a north direction, we were under the necessity of walking from three to four, the water being too deep for wading, and from two hundred yards to one-third of a mile in length. Towards the northern margin we came among large hummocks, having very deep snow about them, so that this floe, which had appeared so promising, proved very laborious travelling, obliging us, in some parts, to make three journeys with our loads; that is, to traverse the same road five times over. We halted at six a.m., having made only one mile and three quarters in a NNW direction, the wind still blowing fresh from the eastward, with a thick fog. We were in latitude 82°3'19", and longitude by chronometers 23°17'E, and we found the variation of the magnetic needle to be 13°41', westerly. We moved again at seven p.m., with the weather nearly as foggy as before, our road lying across a very hummocky floe, on which we had considerable difficulty in getting the boats, the ice being extremely unfavourable both for launching and hauling them up. We afterwards passed over two or three other small floes, and crossed a lane of water a mile long in an east and west direction, but not more than two hundred yards wide from north to south. After stopping an hour at midnight to dine, we were again annoyed by a heavy fall of rain, a phenomenon almost as new to us in these regions, until this summer, as it was harassing and

unhealthy. Being anxious, however, to take advantage of
a lane of water that seemed to lead northerly, we launched
the boats, and by the time that we had crossed it, which gave
us only half a mile of northing, the rain had become much
harder, and our outer clothes, bread-bags, and boats were
thoroughly wet. To keep our shirts dry (which was the more
necessary as we had only one spare one between every two
individuals) we got under the shelter of our awnings, and
the rain abating in half an hour, again proceeded, giving
the men a small quantity of rum and a mouthful of biscuit,
by way of refreshing them a little in this uncomfortable
condition.

After that small gesture of kindness, the dreadful toil resumed.
On the same day, the parties endured 12 hours' hard labour in
return for an advance of seven and a half miles. But, as if all the
many varieties of hardship they had endured so far were not
enough, Parry was already beginning to hint in his journal that
there was one more hidden, silent obstacle to their progress. By
19 July, the hints were getting stronger.

It is remarkable that we had hitherto been so much
favoured by the wind, that only a single northerly one,
and that very moderate, and of short duration, appears
upon our journals up to this day, when a breeze sprung
up from that quarter, accompanied by a thick fog. Though
this wind appeared to be the means of opening several lanes
of water, of which we gladly took advantage when we set
out at eight p.m., yet we were aware that any such effect
could only be produced by the ice drifting to the southward,
and would, therefore, have willingly dispensed with this
apparent facility in proceeding. We found the temperature
of the sea-water, in a large lane, to be 34°, and once as
high as 34½°, which, as before remarked, is very unusual
in the middle of a large body of ice. We hauled over one
very heavy floe, about half a mile in length, of which
the thickness was from fifteen to twenty feet, with huge
hummocks at the margin, indicating a tremendous pressure
at some time or other. On the morning of the 20th we came
to a good deal of ice, which formed a striking contrast with

the other, being composed of flat bay-floes, not three feet thick, which would have afforded us good travelling, had they not recently been broken into small pieces, obliging us to launch frequently from one to another. These floes had been the product of the last winter only, having probably been formed in some of the interstices left between the larger bodies; and, from what we saw of them, there could be little doubt of their being all dissolved before the next autumnal frost. We halted at seven a.m., having, by our reckoning, accomplished six miles and a half in a NNW direction, the distance traversed being ten miles and a half. It may, therefore, be imagined how great was our mortification in finding that our latitude, by observation at noon, was only 82°36'52", being less than *five* miles to the northward of our place at noon on the 17th, since which time we had certainly travelled *twelve* in that direction.

Under these discouraging circumstances, which we carefully avoided making known to the men, we pursued our journey at eight p.m., the wind blowing from the NWbN with overcast but clear weather. A little small snow fell during the night, composed of very minute irregular needles. We were, as usual, much annoyed by the numerous loose pieces over which we had to pass, but a large proportion of these being composed of flat bay-ice, we made tolerable progress. At eleven p.m. we could see nothing before us but this thin ice, much of which was not fit to bear the weight of our boats and provisions, and more caution than ever was requisite in selecting the route by which we were to pass. At five a.m., on the 21st, having gone ahead, as usual, upon a bay-floe, to search for the best road, I heard a more than ordinary noise and bustle among the people who were bringing up the boats behind. On returning to them, I found that we had narrowly, and most providentially, escaped a serious calamity; the floe having broken under the weight of the boats and sledges, and the latter having nearly been lost through the ice. Some of the men went completely through, and one of them was only held up by his drag-belt being attached to a sledge which happened to be on firmer ice. Fortunately the bread had, by way of security, been kept in the boats, or this additional weight would undoubtedly have sunk the sledges, and probably some of the men with them. As it was, we happily escaped, though we hardly knew how, with a good deal of wetting; and, cautiously approaching the boats, drew them to a stronger part of the ice, after which we continued our journey till half past six a.m., when we halted to rest, having travelled about seven miles NNW. We here found the dip of the magnetic needle to be 82°21'.8, and the variation 19°5' westerly, our longitude by chronometers being 19°52' east, and the latitude 82°39'10", being only two miles and a quarter to the northward of the preceding day's observation, or four miles and a half to the southward of our reckoning.

The drift of the ice was beginning to carry them south almost as fast as they could walk north. The tone of Parry's journal from here on becomes increasingly dispirited, but to maintain the spirits of the men he and his fellow officers were having to keep up a deception that they were still making good progress. Even so, the men were beginning openly to express doubt. On one occasion Parry recorded that the day had been 'a disheartening one to those who knew to how little effect we were struggling; which, however, the men did not, though they often laughingly remarked that "we were a long time getting to this 83°!"' On 26 July, he faced an inevitable decision when the speed of the drift overtook them.

The weather improving towards noon on the 26th, we obtained the meridian altitude of the sun, by which we found ourselves in latitude 82°40'23"; so that, since our last observation (at midnight on the 22nd), we had lost by drift no less than thirteen miles and a half; for we were now more than three miles to the *southward* of that observation, though we had certainly travelled between ten and eleven due north in this interval! Again, we were but one mile to the north of our place at noon on the 21st, though we had estimated our distance made good at twenty-three miles. Thus it appeared that, for the last five days, we had been struggling against a southerly drift exceeding four miles per day.

It had, for some time past, been too evident that the nature of the ice with which we had to contend was such, and its drift to the southward, especially with a northerly wind, so great, as to put beyond our reach any thing but a very moderate share of success in travelling to the northward. Still, however, we had been anxious to reach the highest latitude which our means would allow, and, with this view, although our whole object had long become unattainable, had pushed on to the northward for thirty-five days, or until half our resources were expended, and the middle of our season arrived. For the last few days the eighty-third parallel was the limit to which we had ventured to extend our hopes; but even this expectation had become considerably weakened since the setting in of the last northerly wind, which continued to drive us to the southward, during the necessary hours of rest, nearly as much as we could gain by eleven or twelve hours of daily labour. Had our success been at all proportionate to our exertions, it was my full intention to have proceeded a few days beyond the middle of the period for which we were provided, trusting to the resources we expected to find at Table Island. But this was so far from being the case, that I could not but consider it as incurring useless fatigue to the officers and men, and unnecessary wear and tear for the boats, to persevere any longer in the attempt. I determined, therefore, on giving the people one entire day's rest, which they very much needed, and time to wash and mend their clothes, while the officers were occupied in making all the observations which might be interesting in this latitude; and then to set out on our return on the following day. Having communicated my intentions to the people, who were all much disappointed in finding how little their labours had effected, we set about our respective occupations, and were much favoured by a remarkably fine day.

The dip of the magnetic needle was here 82°21′6, and the variation 18°10′ westerly, our latitude being 82°40′23″, and our longitude 19°25′ east of Greenwich. The highest latitude we reached was probably at seven a.m., on the

23rd, when, after the midnight observation, we travelled, by our account, something more than a mile and a half, which would carry us a little beyond 82°45'.

On the journey back, travelling conditions were rather better. Because of the lateness of the season there was more open water in which to launch their boats, so, despite some of the men having chilblains, sores on their feet, and swollen legs, they made the journey ten days faster. On their last day of travelling, Parry recorded:

Having now, by means of the drift-wood, converted our paddles into oars, and being occasionally favoured by a light breeze, with a perfectly open sea, we made tolerable progress, and at half-past four p.m., on the 21st of August, when within three or four miles of Hecla Cove, had the gratification of seeing a boat under sail coming out to meet us. Mr Weir soon joined us in one of the cutters; and, after hearing good accounts of the safety of the ship, and of the welfare of all on board, together with a variety of details, to us of no small interest, we arrived on board at seven p.m., after an absence of sixty-one days, being received with that warm and cordial welcome, which can alone be felt, and not described.

They left for home the day after, and reached London on 6 October.

By any standards, this was a most remarkable journey. Despite the appalling conditions they encountered, the inadequacy and great weight of their equipment, and their poor physical condition on the return journey, they had covered a very creditable distance. By Parry's reckoning, they had covered a straight-line distance of 569 nautical miles; taking into account the southerly drift and the number of times they had to walk backwards and forwards to advance their baggage, the full distance was nearer 978 geographical miles (1,127 land or statute miles). Few sledge travellers after them could claim such distances. Also, they had learned more about the nature of sea ice on the Arctic Ocean than any expedition before them, or any after them for nearly 50 years.

Their misfortune was their choice of starting place. Parry could not have known it, but the trans-polar current from Bering Strait ensures that most of the ice that empties out of the Arctic Ocean does so through the strait between Spitsbergen and Greenland; their southward drift was inevitable from the outset. Parry's misfortune was also regrettable in terms of advances in exploration of the Arctic Ocean. A latitude of 82°45'N is most impressive in the circumstances, but is less impressive on paper: it is still well over 400 nautical miles from the Pole. His terrible ordeal in getting only that far gave the impression that the North Pole was unattainable. And as his observations on the extent of the ice also knocked on the head any lingering ideas of an ocean navigable by ship or an 'Open Polar Sea', there seemed nothing further to be done. The Royal Navy abandoned the Arctic Ocean for nearly 50 years, and no other nation or institution appeared willing to take up the challenge. Not, that is, until a German geographer emerged with a new set of theories in the 1850s.

– 3 –

Revival of the 'Open Polar Sea'

1852–73

August Petermann was a geographer of great eminence. He was born in 1822 in Bleichroede am Elberfelde, Germany. He became a student of geography at the age of 17, and by 1843 he was already producing published work. A few years later his interest in the Arctic was aroused by the Northwest Passage expedition of Sir John Franklin, which disappeared into the Canadian Arctic in 1845, never to be seen again. In the early 1850s he became a tireless campaigner in favour of sending out more and more expeditions to search for Franklin. Franklin's disappearance gave rise to a huge search operation, consisting of over 20 expeditions, lasting from 1847 to 1859, and covering a vast, previously unexplored area of the Canadian Arctic archipelago. Petermann was only one of many geographers who contributed theories regarding the Franklin expedition's whereabouts – but they were nearly all wrong, and it was not until 1859 that the explorer Francis Leopold McClintock (1819–1907) found indisputable proof that all the expedition's 129 men had perished by about 1848, on or near King William Island in the central Canadian Arctic. However, the foundation of Petermann's later Arctic career was not his contribution to the Franklin search, but an article he published in 1852, setting out his own novel theories about an ice-free polar sea. Petermann's belief in the 'Open Polar Sea' had rather more merit than some earlier theories, for at least they were based on scientific observations, and, although as wrong-headed as all the other theories, they did at least open up new areas of the Arctic for exploration. At the heart of his ideas was the conviction that the warm waters of the Gulf Stream opened up the seas between Greenland and Svalbard, and to the north of Russia and Siberia, to a far greater extent than anywhere else in the Arctic Ocean. 'The Gulf Stream discharges its warm waters into the eastern parts of the Polar Sea as if it wanted to break a path for a ship going in that direction . . . Therefore I have no doubt that a sturdy steamship could, in the appropriate season, complete the trip from the Thames to the North Pole and back – or to some land around the Bering Strait – in two or three months.' This was actually a very astute observation considering that in the early 1850s Petermann had hardly a shred of serious scientific evidence to support it. The Gulf Stream does indeed carve a path through the Arctic waters to the north of Russia. Parts of the Barents Sea are often ice-free to 80°N and beyond in the summer months, though not as reliably as the waters between Greenland and Svalbard. The seas of the Russian and Siberian Arctic are generally more accessible in summer than other parts of the Arctic Ocean. Also, things had changed since Parry's day. Parry had only sail; 'sturdy steamships' for use in the Arctic were becoming increasingly available from the 1850s onwards. The trouble with Petermann's theory is that the warming effect fades progressively as the explorer continues sailing northwards, so that when about 80° is reached in the Barents Sea, exactly the same problems arise as between Greenland and Spitsbergen. Likewise, beyond the Barents Sea, the Kara Sea to the east of it becomes progressively more difficult to navigate until, in many seasons, it is completely blocked by ice at its eastern end. These facts, however, were not yet known to science. Petermann's continuing belief in an open passage to the Pole between Greenland and Svalbard is surprising in view of the historical evidence available to him, but his enduring interest in the marine currents of the Russian Arctic, as a key to the navigability of the Arctic Ocean, stimulated numerous North Polar and scientific expeditions to that little-known area.

In 1855, Petermann started his own journal, *Petermanns Geographische Mitteilungen*, and he repeatedly used its great influence in the geographical world to spread his views on the Arctic in general and the 'Open Polar Sea' in particular. In the same manner as Barrington before him, he gathered and published reports of whalers, walrus hunters and others to demonstrate the easy navigability of many areas of the Arctic. Unlike Barrington, he published only reliable, verifiable reports, and his work carried authority. Later, he used that authority to promote the organization of exploring and scientific expeditions to test his theories. For much of his life, he campaigned tirelessly for expeditions to probe towards the North Pole from the Russian Arctic and Bering Strait. By the time of his death in 1878, his conviction of the existence of an 'Open Polar Sea' had faded. But for over 20 years from 1852, he considered himself the world's greatest authority on the subject.

Ironically, then, at the very beginning of his campaign, the first expeditions of his era to test the possibility of sailing on an 'Open Polar Sea' did so in a region where Petermann firmly believed the feat to be impossible. In 1853, the American explorer Elisha Kent Kane (1820–57) set out from New York on the ship *Advance* heading for northern Baffin Bay. Ostensibly, his aim was to search for Sir John Franklin's expedition of 1845, but there is a suspicion that he had a far greater interest in exploring a route to the Pole by way of the narrow channel separating Greenland and Ellesmere Island, Canada. Introducing his book, he writes, 'We were to pass up Baffin's Bay . . . to its most northern attainable point; and thence, pressing on toward the Pole as far as boats and sledges could carry us, examine the coast-lines for vestiges of the lost party.' The reference to the 'lost party' here is a thin veil covering his real intentions; Franklin's instructions had sent him nowhere near that area. However, the expedition did serve a serious geographical purpose, for this was only the second expedition ever to attempt the exploration of the channel between Greenland and Ellesmere Island, and the first, under Edward Inglefield in 1852, had reached only 78°28′N.

Kane's ship *Advance* was able to penetrate a little way beyond Inglefield's farthest, and in autumn 1853 Kane put the ship into winter quarters in a bay that he named Rensselaer Harbor, at 78°37′N on the Greenland side. Soon after, travelling parties using boats and sledges explored northwards through the channel, laying depots of provisions in preparation for sledge journeys in the following spring. They reached almost 80°N, and in doing so discovered a broad area of the channel that was later named Kane Basin.

The first of the travelling parties in 1854 was led by Kane, using dog-sledges, from 27 April to 14 May. His hope was to explore the coast of Greenland to its most northerly point, but the journey was cut short by poor health and the destruction of food depots by bears and he reached only 79°05'N. A second party, led by the ship's surgeon, Isaac Israel Hayes, was more successful and explored the coast of Ellesmere Island to 79°45'N. During June and early July, the last of the season's travelling parties, led by the steward William Morton, reached the expedition's northernmost point at about 80°30'N. Morton's party discovered a strait leading north beyond Kane Basin, which Kane named Kennedy Channel.

After those important achievements, the fortunes of the Kane expedition changed abruptly. It proved impossible to free the *Advance* from the ice in her harbour, and the expedition was forced to winter again. In autumn, attempts by some of the party to sail to safety in the ship's boats were unsuccessful. In winter, sickness broke out and provisions became perilously short. In spring 1855, aided by Eskimos, they were finally able to travel by boat and on foot to the safety of the Danish colony of Upernavik in west Greenland.

Despite its misfortunes, the Kane expedition gave great encouragement to others. He had found that the channel between Greenland and Ellesmere Island extended far to the north, and this gave rise to renewed hope that it might lead on into the Arctic Ocean. Kane returned home fully convinced that it did; he was sure that at the end of the channel would be found 'a wide open and ice-free Arctic Sea', but his enthusiasm deeply annoyed Petermann, who thought Kane was drawing attention away from the real routes to the Pole. He wrote in his *Mitteilungen*, 'Being, perhaps, the most determined defender of the theory of a relatively open and ice-free Polar Sea, I feel duty bound to state that Kane's report is apt to cause endless confusion, and to open the door to erroneous ideas if the public really believed him.' He was convinced that only the Russian side of the ocean could be ice-free, and ships heading for the Pole by Kane's route were doomed to fail. Once again, Petermann was right for the wrong reasons. That same trans-polar drift that had thwarted Parry in 1827 also had the effect of accumulating ice in great thicknesses to the north of Greenland and Ellesmere Island; some of the thickest ice in the whole ocean is to be found there.

In addition, unlike the ice encountered by Parry, it could not drift south: the presence of land to the south kept it relatively motionless. So he was correct in claiming that ships could not go there; until as recently as 1993, no ship ever has. But when, later in the nineteenth century, explorers realized that to get to the Pole they would need to walk, this became one of the main highways.

Petermann's annoyance had no effect on the American explorers, who were developing their own independent theories of an 'Open Polar Sea' in parallel with his. The friction between the two groups later became acute. Immediately after Kane's expedition, his ship's surgeon, Isaac Israel Hayes (1832–81), began planning his own expedition by the same route. In setting out his plans, Hayes chose, amazingly, to revive John Barrow's supposedly discredited notion of a belt of ice encircling an ice-free ocean at about 80°N.

Accepting the deductions of many learned physicists that the sea about the North Pole cannot be frozen, that an open area of varying extent may be found within the Ice-belt which is known to invest it, I desired to add to the proofs which had already been accumulated by the early Dutch and English voyagers, and, more recently, by the researches of Scoresby . . . and Parry, and still later by Dr Kane's expedition.

It is well known that the great difficulty which has been encountered, in the various attempts that have been made to solve this important physical problem, has been the inability of the explorer to penetrate the Ice-belt with his ship, or to travel over it with sledges sufficiently far to obtain indisputable proof. My former experience led me to the conclusion that the chances of success were greater by Smith Sound than by any other route, and my hopes of success were based upon the expectation which I entertained of being able to push a vessel into the Ice-belt to about the 80th parallel of latitude, and thence to transport a boat over the ice to the open sea which I hoped to find beyond. Reaching this open sea, if such fortune awaited me, I proposed to launch my boat and to push off northward. For the ice transportation, I expected to rely, mainly, upon the dog of the Esquimaux.

After a campaign lasting several years, Hayes succeeded in raising sponsorship from several American societies and the general public, and on 7 July 1860 he sailed from Boston on the ship *United States*. In his first season he was less successful than Kane had been, and by the onset of winter he had barely entered the channel leading north from Baffin Bay. He wintered at 78°20′N near the Eskimo settlement of Etah in northwest Greenland.

His spring travelling in 1861 was also only moderately successful, and he added little to what Kane's men had already discovered. Although he claimed to reach 81°35′N, to the north of Kennedy Channel, subsequent explorers cast doubt on that, and suggested he had reached only about 80°14′N. He remained convinced that the 'Open Polar Sea' was accessible by that route, but when he returned home in October 1861 the Civil War, which had broken out earlier in the year, frustrated his hopes of returning for a second attempt.

A decade later, one of America's most experienced polar explorers, Charles Francis Hall (1821–71), took up the challenge of the Kane Basin/Kennedy Channel route to the Pole. During the 1860s, Hall had spent some seven years in the Canadian Arctic, learning Eskimo techniques of travel and survival. By the end of those experiences, he had sufficient authority as an explorer to persuade the United States government to sponsor an attempt on the Pole, and the National Academy of Sciences to prepare a scientific programme for him.

On 3 July 1871 Hall's ship left New London for the Arctic. In contrast with the experiences of Kane and Hayes, Hall's initial success was spectacular. He sailed rapidly through Smith Sound, Kane Basin and Kennedy Channel, and at the end of August he entered a new broad part of the channel, later named Hall Basin. Continuing north even beyond that, he reached a latitude of 82°11′N, on the very edge of the Arctic Ocean. This was a new record for a ship, surpassing the 81°42′N   ʾned by Nordenskiöld's *Sofia* in 1868. At that point, Hall tu.   oack to seek a safe winter harbour. He found one at about 81°30′N on the coast of Greenland; he named it 'Thank God Harbor', and it was situated in a bay that he named after his ship, *Polaris*.

At this stage, Hall seemed well set to make one of the most impressive challenges on the North Pole to that date. He was in a snug harbour at a very high latitude, and – though he did not know it – in the right place to start a sledge journey to the Pole. But then something mysterious and tragic happened; and the mystery is so deep that it is still today not fully explained. Hall fell suddenly and inexplicably ill. The events that followed are recorded by Hall's assistant navigator, George Emory Tyson. His first mention of the mystery is made in his diary entry for 24 October.

Captain Hall is sick; it seems strange, he looked so well. I have been in the cabin to see him. He is lying in his berth, and says he feels sick in the stomach. This sickness came on immediately after drinking a cup of coffee. I think it must be a bilious attack, but it is very sudden. I asked him if he thought he is bilious, and told him I thought an emetic would do him good. He said if it was biliousness it would. Hope he will be better tomorrow.

Oct. 25. Captain Hall is no better. Mr Morton and Mr Chester watched with him last night; they thought part of the time he was delirious.

Evening. Captain Hall is certainly delirious; I don't know what to make of what he says. He sent for me as if he had something particular to say, but – I will not repeat what he said; I don't think it means any thing. No talk of any thing in the ship but Captain Hall's illness; if it had only been the 'heat of the cabin', which some of them say overcame him, he could have got out into the air, and he would have felt better. I cannot hear that he ate any thing to make him sick; all he had was that cup of coffee . . .

Nov. 1. Captain Hall is a little better, and has been up, attempting to write; but he don't act like himself – he begins a thing and don't finish it. He begins to talk about one thing, and then goes off onto something else: his disease has been pronounced paralysis, and also apoplexy. I can't remember of any one dying of apoplexy in the north except Captain M'Clintock's engineer, and he died very suddenly; went to bed at 9 p.m., and was found dead in his state-room in the morning. I always thought that might have been heart disease. Hope the captain will rally.

Nov. 3. Captain Hall very bad again. He talks wildly – seems to think someone means to poison him; calls for first one and then another, as if he did not know who to trust. When I was in, he accused —— and —— of wanting to poison him. When he is more rational he will say, 'If I die, you must still go on to the Pole'; and such like remarks. It's a sad affair; what will become of this expedition if Captain Hall dies, I dread to think.

Nov. 5. No change for the better – worse, I think. He appears to be partially paralysed. This is dreadful. Even should he recover his senses, what can he do with a paralysed body?

Nov. 8. Poor Captain Hall is dead; he died early this morning. Last evening Chester said the captain thought himself that he was better, and would soon be around again. But it seems he took worse in the night. Captain Buddington came and told me he 'thought Captain Hall was dying'. I got up immediately, and went to the cabin and looked at him. He was quite unconscious – knew nothing. He lay on his face, and was breathing very heavily; his face was hid in the pillow. It was about half-past three o'clock in the morning that he died. Assisted in preparing the grave, which is nearly half a mile from the ship, inland; but the ground was so frozen that it was necessarily very shallow; even with picks it was scarcely possible to break it up.

Nov. 11. At half-past eleven this morning we placed all that was mortal of our late commander in the frozen ground. Even at that hour of the day it was almost dark, so that I had to hold a lantern for Mr Bryan to read the prayers. I believe all the ship's company was present . . . It was a gloomy day, and well befitting the event. The place also is rugged and desolate in the extreme. Away off, as far as the dim light enables us to see, we are bound in by huge masses of slate rock, which stands like a barricade, guarding the barren land of the interior; between these rugged hills lies the snow-covered plain; behind us the frozen waters of Polaris Bay, the shore strewn with great ice-blocks. The little hut which they call an observatory bears aloft, upon a tall flag-staff, the only cheering object in sight; and that is sad enough today, for the Stars and Stripes droop at half-mast . . .

Thus ends poor Hall's ambitious projects; thus is stilled the effervescing enthusiasm of as ardent a nature as I ever knew. Wise he might not always have been, but his soul was in this work, and had he lived till spring, I think he would have gone as far as mortal man could go to accomplish his mission. But with his death I fear that all hopes of further progress will have to be abandoned.

The circumstances of Hall's death have been examined many times, but still the true cause of his death remains a mystery. After the expedition, a naval inquiry concluded that he had died of apoplexy, but that opinion has never been viewed as fully satisfactory. Hall's accusation that certain of his officers were trying to poison him cannot be ignored. It is known that the ship's captain, Sidney Budington; and the surgeon, Emil Bessels, quarrelled with him before he was taken ill. Either, or both, could certainly have poisoned him; there was plenty of arsenic on the ship (in the nineteenth century it was a medicine as well as a poison). There would also certainly have been men on board who, having been frozen in so far north, feared for their lives, and would have wanted to prevent Hall's ambition from detaining them for a day longer than necessary in the following year. But did they do so by killing him?

The weather conditions of the Arctic offer a strange opportunity to seek an answer to the questions hanging over Hall's death. He was buried in frozen rock, and so preserved in ice. Nearly 100 years later, in 1968, on an expedition led by Hall's biographer, Chauncey Loomis, his well-preserved body was exhumed and examined. An autopsy conducted by the grave, and later forensic examination of his hair and fingernails, showed that he had taken large quantities of arsenic. But whether or not the poison killed him will never be known; nor will it ever be known who administered it. Bessels could have done so, but

Hall also had his own supply; he could have simply overdosed. We cannot know.

One thing only is certain: Tyson's fears for the future of the expedition were fully justified. After Hall's death it virtually disintegrated; all enthusiasm for the Pole journey disappeared. As soon as the ship was released from the ice in August 1872, the expedition headed for home. For those on board, though, the adventure had scarcely even begun. Before they reached Baffin Bay and relative safety, the ship again became beset in the ice. As it drifted south, the crew began preparations to abandon ship. In mid-October, as they approached Baffin Bay, 19 of them were out on the ice when the floe on which they stood broke away and drifted out of reach of the *Polaris*. There then began a saga as thrilling as any other in polar history. Throughout the winter of 1872–3, their floe drifted south through Baffin Bay and Davis Strait. They survived only because they had the good fortune to have the expedition's two Eskimo assistants with them: the Greenlander Hans Hendrik, and the Canadian Ebierbing (nicknamed Joe). Between them, these two men kept the party alive by imposing their native survival techniques, and hunting continuously through the winter. Nevertheless, by April 1873, they were heading out into the Atlantic Ocean and their floe was getting smaller. They were saved only by the sheer luck of encountering the Newfoundland sealer *Tigress* off the coast of Labrador.

By contrast, the experiences of the 14 men left on the ship appear mundane. After a winter in the ice, they abandoned ship on 3 June 1873, and headed south in boats. Three weeks later, they were rescued by the Scottish whaling ship *Ravenscraig*.

Hall's tragic death, and the extraordinary events surrounding the ending of his expedition, served one useful purpose: the survivors brought back the news that they had penetrated to 82°N by the Kane Basin route. This therefore became one of the most popular routes for later attempts on the North Pole. First, however, came the climax of Petermann's campaign for a sea route to the Pole through European Arctic waters, followed by an interval of British interest in the Americans' route.

– 4 –

The German and Austrian Expeditions

1868–74

In the years following his disputative stance against the Kane expedition, August Petermann's interest in Arctic affairs appears to have dimmed for a full decade and his attention turned mainly to Africa – apart, that is, from a short period in the early 1860s when he took time off to express similar opposition to the Hayes expedition. However, he returned to the subject with a vengeance in 1865 when he chose to enter into a spectacular dispute with a veteran British polar explorer, Sherard Osborn. Captain Osborn, as a young lieutenant, had commanded ships on two naval Franklin search expeditions, in 1850–1 and 1852–4. The Royal Navy had sent out nearly twenty such expeditions between 1848 and 1854. In starting a campaign for the renewal of British naval exploration in the Arctic, Osborn noted that ten years had elapsed since the return of the last naval expedition. (He also noted wryly that sending naval personnel on expeditions to the Arctic had proved to be far safer, and far more popular among the men, than the navy's prevailing practice of sending them to die of tropical diseases during patrols off the coasts of Africa and China.) His fear was that, if the navy did not soon return to the Arctic, then the hard-earned polar experience of a whole generation of naval officers and men would be lost – future generations would need to re-learn those skills unaided. In a lecture to the Royal Geographical Society in January 1865, Osborn argued forcefully for the renewal of Arctic exploration, and he proposed that an expedition be sent out in an attempt to attain the Pole. However – and this is what rekindled Petermann's fire – he rejected Petermann's Gulf-Stream routes,

and proposed instead the American route. He argued that the
mixture of drifting ice and open water on Petermann's routes
would always prevent both ships and sledges from reaching the
Pole that way; whereas the Americans' experience indicated a
probability of continuous ice all the way to the Pole. He also
pointed out that ice travel was a particular British skill: during
the Franklin search, many sledging parties had accomplished
journeys of several hundred miles in the ice-filled channels
of the Canadian Arctic, and some of those had covered well
over 1,100 nautical miles – more than enough for an estimated
round trip to the Pole of 1,000 from the limit of the Americans'
exploration. Petermann responded furiously with a long letter to
the President of the Royal Geographical Society, listing a string of
reasons why the Pole could be reached by ship from Spitsbergen,
and could never be reached by the American route. Passages in
his letter seem to suggest that he was now convinced that he
somehow 'owned' the subject of the North Pole and was not
to be disregarded; this was frustration, perhaps, that in 13 years
nobody had yet bothered to act on his own version of the 'Open
Polar Sea' theory, but it was decidedly tetchy.

> If I may be permitted to submit to you, and the geographers
> of England, some remarks about Captain Osborn's lecture,
> and the discussion relating to it . . . then I have a duty to
> recommend the choice of the Spitsbergen route instead of
> Smith Sound. As I have been recommending this route as
> the proper direction for Arctic research for 13 years, I would
> like to refer to some of my earlier publications on Arctic
> geography in general, and limit myself for now to a short
> summary of some of the main facts which in my opinion
> must come into consideration.

From there he went on to list 16 of his publications from the
period 1852–3; and he followed up his letter with four more
long articles in the 1865 volume of his *Mitteilungen*, hammering
home all his points. An increasingly bitter and extremely public
dispute between Petermann and Osborn ensued, observed in
stunned amazement by geographers all over Europe. Not only
geographers were involved. *The Times* of London hinted overtly
that Petermann was driven chiefly by German nationalism and

a desire to hinder British attempts on the Pole in pursuit of 'cheap honours for his politically disrupted country'. Petermann responded with a reference to 'greedy British money bags' attempting to make the scientific world 'dance to the pipe of John Bull'. It really was an extraordinarily unseemly dispute, but at least it brought Petermann back on the scene.

It took ten years for Osborn's plan to come to fruition, but by the end of 1865 Petermann's period of dormancy was over. He desperately wanted a ship at the Pole, and if Britain would not do it, and America would not do it, then Germany must. He began to campaign for a German North Polar expedition. By 1868 he had raised enough funding from the German scientific community to send out the ship *Grönland* to explore towards the North Pole from about 75°N on the east coast of Greenland. The expedition's leader was Karl Koldewey (1837–1908). Ice stopped them from getting even a sighting of the Greenland coast, and the expedition's most northerly advance, to 80°30'N, was made by the traditional route along the west coast of Spitsbergen. It was a disappointment, but this expedition was seen primarily as a preliminary survey in preparation for a more ambitious one in 1869.

In 1869 Petermann's second expedition used the ships *Germania* and *Hansa*, and was again commanded by Karl Koldewey. In spite of the problems with ice encountered by the *Grönland*, this expedition, too, was instructed to attempt to reach the North Pole from northeast Greenland and, from the point of view of approaching the Pole, was an even greater disappointment. The two ships became accidentally separated at about 74°N off east Greenland. *Hansa* drifted south, stuck fast in the ice, and in October, sank after being crushed at about 71°N. The crew spent a miserable winter in a hut on the ice. In May 1870 they set off in boats for west Greenland, where there were Danish settlements. They were rescued at Julianehåb in southwest Greenland in June. The *Germania* party fared better. They were able to reach the Greenland coast at about 74°N and did some exploration there, but their attempt to sail to the Pole failed dismally: *Germania* reached only 75°30'N before meeting a solid barrier of ice. They returned south to a harbour in the area of their exploration, then in 1870 carried out some further exploration on foot. This was the most successful part of the voyage. Sledging parties explored the coast in an area north of all previous explorations in east Greenland, reaching 77°01′N, in an area they named after their emperor, Wilhelm. After some more exploration farther south, they returned home in September.

The exploration achieved by this expedition was valuable, but in terms of fulfilling Petermann's dream of a ship at the Pole, it was sheer disaster. He never looked at the Greenland/Svalbard passage to the Pole again.

In 1869 Petermann equipped two much smaller expeditions to lay some scientific foundations for future exploration towards the Pole. He persuaded a sealing company to put scientists on two of its ships, *Albert* and *Bienenkorb*. On *Albert* Emil Bessels (1847–88) sailed to 80°14′N off northwest Spitsbergen, then cruised in the northern Barents Sea making observations on the Gulf Stream. Meanwhile, F.J. Dorst on the *Bienenkorb* attempted to make oceanographical and meteorological observations off northeast Greenland, but met the same exceptionally bad ice and weather conditions as Koldewey's expedition, and his work was cut short.

Petermann remained determined to continue his quest. After these failures he switched his attention to his other favoured Gulf-Stream route, in the Barents Sea between Svalbard and Novaya Zemlya. Initially his chief problem was that by the end of Koldewey's second expedition, Germany was at war with France. To escape that difficulty, while ensuring that his next expedition would still be primarily Germanic in flavour, he looked south to the Austro-Hungarian Empire. There he found a financial supporter in the person of Count Johann von Wilczek (1837–1922), who was to remain a generous sponsor of Austrian polar expeditions for over a decade. Together, they organized a preliminary expedition in 1871 to cruise in the northern Barents Sea in search of a possible starting point for an expedition towards the Pole. The leaders were Karl Weyprecht (1838–81) and Julius von Payer (1842–1915), and their ship was a chartered Norwegian sailing ship, the *Isbjørn* of Tromsø. This expedition traced the southern edge of the drifting ice zone from Svalbard eastwards, and reached its farthest north at 78°05′N, 56°E, to the northwest of Novaya Zemlya. They persuaded themselves that the ice in the northern Barents Sea was not impenetrable, and on their return home reported in favour of mounting a major expedition to head for the Pole in that region.

The culmination of Petermann's quest to prove the possibility of taking a ship to the North Pole came with the Austro-Hungarian exploring expedition of 1872–4. The report of Weyprecht and Payer on the good prospects of sailing far to the north through the Barents Sea found favour in high places, and after their return the Austrian government undertook to join Wilczek in sponsoring an attempt on the Pole by that route. Weyprecht and Payer were invited to lead it, on the ship *Tegetthoff*. Their instructions were unusually vague, and they were not ordered specifically to seek the Pole; their actions were to be determined by circumstance.

As it happened, circumstances led them towards the Pole, but their greatest achievement had little to do with the Pole itself. They sailed from Bremerhaven in north Germany on 13 June 1872, and within a month were heading northeast across the Barents Sea. They met ice unexpectedly far south, at about 74°N, but they found open water along the coast of Novaya Zemlya, and they used that to progress towards the north. As they entered the ice, they continued to force a northward passage, and at the end of August *Tegetthoff* became firmly beset among the floes. The ship drifted north with the ice throughout September, and by the beginning of October was at 77°N. The northerly drift continued throughout the winter, and the following spring and summer. Then, on 30 August 1873, when they had reached 79°43′N, they sighted land. This was a discovery of great importance in the history of exploration towards the Pole. They named it Franz Josef Land (now, in Russian, Zemlya Frantsa-Iosifa) in honour of their emperor, and later it became not only a starting-place for expeditions seeking the Pole, but also the focus of some famously memorable, magical events. Later, they were to find that their discovery was not just one island, but a large archipelago of many islands, but first they had to endure yet another winter of drifting helplessly in the ice, tantalizingly close to this new land.

Between March and May 1874, Payer led three sledge journeys to explore the eastern part of the archipelago. On the second, from 26 March to 22 April, he explored almost directly northwards through a strait that he named 'Austria Sound' (now Austriyskiy Proliv), and it was this journey that guided later explorers to a new starting point for the Pole. Payer describes the most northerly part of his exploration. As he started on the last few marches, he and his men were still recovering from a terrifying incident in which one of them, Antonio Zaninovich, had fallen into a deep crevasse in a glacier, together with a laden sledge. Both he and the sledge were eventually hauled out, but the rescue left the whole party exhausted. After a night's rest, however, Payer and two others felt able to press on north, while the others returned south to their previous camp to await Payer's return.

We now left the glacier and the icebergs, and by midnight had reached Cape Habermann. Here we slept, and the dogs with us, as uncomfortably as possible. On the morning of the 11th of April (the thermometer marking $-13°\cdot3$ R [Réaumur]), we started at an hour when we would much rather have continued to sleep. Our thirst was so great that we felt ourselves equal to drinking up a stream. Haller, Sussich, Lukinovich had during the night returned to Cape Schrötter. Before they started Haller earnestly besought me to come back as soon as possible; for the recent event, he said, had not been without its disquieting effects on the men. On the whole, we might congratulate ourselves on being able to continue our journey, without having received any serious damage, though no longer over the treacherous glacier.

A sharp turn to the left brought us to the west coast of Crown-Prince Rudolf's Land, along which we pursued our route northwards. When we reached Cape Brorok, where by an observation we found our latitude at noon to be 81°45', the weather became wonderfully bright, and the warm sunlight lay on the broken summits of the Dolerite mountains, which, though covered with gleaming ice, were free from snow. To the north-west we saw at first nothing but ice up to the horizon; even with the telescope of the theodolite I could not decide for the existence of land, which Orel's sharp eye discovered in the far distance. In the Arctic regions, it often happens that banks of fog on the horizon assume the character of distant ranges, for the small height to which these banks rise in the cold air causes them to be very sharply defined. It is very common also to make the same mistake in the case of mists arising from the waste water of enormous glaciers. We marched on northward close under the land, and for the first time over smooth undulating ice, in high spirits at the increasing grandeur of the scenery and at the happy issue of our adventure of yesterday. Thirst compelled us frequently to halt in order to liquefy snow; sometimes we melted it as we marched along, and our sledge with smoke curling up from the cooking-machine then resembled a small steamer.

By and by we came to more snow, and the ice, through which many fissures ran, became gradually thinner; but when we reached the imposing headland, which we called Cape Auk, the ice lay in forced-up barriers. A strange change had come over the aspect of nature. A dark water-sky appeared in the north, and heavy mists rolled down to the steep promontories of Karl Alexander Land; the temperature rose to $-10.1°$ R, our track became moist, the snow-drifts collapsed under us with a loud noise, and if we had previously been surprised with the flight of birds from the north, we now found all the rocky precipices of Rudolf's Land covered with thousands of auks and divers. Enormous flocks of birds flew up and filled the air, and the whole region seemed alive with their incessant whirring. We met everywhere with traces of bears and foxes. Seals lay on the ice, but sprang into the water before we got within shot of them. But notwithstanding these signs of a richer animal life, we should not be justified in inferring, from what we saw in a single locality, that life increases as we move northwards. It was a venial exaggeration, if amid such impressions we pronounced for the nearness of an open Polar sea, and without doubt all adherents of this opinion, had they come with us to this point and no further, would have found in these signs fresh grounds to support their belief. In enumerating these observations, I am conscious what attractions they must have for every one who still leans to the opinion that an open ocean will be found at the Pole; subsequent experience, however, will show how little is their value in support of this antiquated hypothesis.

Our track was now very unsafe; it was only the icebergs which seemed to keep the ice in the bays. A strong east wind would certainly have broken it up and cut off our return, at least with the sledge. There were no longer the connected floes of winter, but young ice only, covered with saline efflorescence, dangerously pliable, and strewn over with the remains of recent pressures. The ice was broken through in many places by the holes of seals. It was expedient therefore to tie ourselves together with a long rope, and each of us, as he took his turn in leading, constantly sounded the ice. Passing by Cape Auk, which resembled a gigantic aviary, we followed the line of Teplitz Bay, into which a stream of glaciers, descending from high mountains in the interior, discharged itself. Icebergs lay along the terminal glacier wall which formed its shore. Ascending one of these masses, we found granite erratics on its surface and saw the open sea stretching far to the west. There seemed to be ice only on the extreme horizon. As the ice sheet over which our track lay became thinner and more pliable, and constantly threatened to give way under us, the height and length of its piled-up barriers increased also, and because the high glacier walls made it impossible to travel over the land, we had no other resource than to open up a track through the hummocky ice by pick and shovel. At last even this expedient failed to help us; our sledge, constantly damaged, and as constantly repaired, had to be unloaded, the dogs unharnessed, and everything transported separately. Evening had now arrived; ahead of us lay the two rock towers, which we called Cape Säulen, and open coast water here began.

Beautiful and sublime was this far-off world. From a height we looked over a dark 'ice-hole', studded with icebergs like pearls, and over these lay heavy clouds through which the sunbeams fell on the gleaming water. Right over the true sun shone a second, though somewhat duller sun; the icebergs of Crown-Prince Rudolf's Land, appearing enormously high, sailed through the still region amid rolling mist and surrounded by vast flocks of birds. Close under Cape Säulen (the Cape of Columns) we came upon the steep edge of the glaciers and dragged up our baggage with a long rope. While Orel got ready our encampment for the night in the fissure of a glacier, and completed as usual his meteorological observations and soundings, I ascended a height to reconnoitre our track for the next day. The sun was setting amid a scene of majestic wildness; its golden rays shot through dark banks of mist, and a gentle wind, playing over the 'ice-hole', formed ever-widening circles on its mirror-like surface. Land was no longer visible towards the north, it was covered with a dense 'water-sky'. A bird flew close past me; at first I took it for a ptarmigan, but it was probably a snipe. It ought to be remarked that during the two days which we spent near this 'ice-hole' we never once saw a whale. As soon as with half-closed eyes we had eaten our supper, we fell fast asleep, for our longing to sleep was yet greater than our exhaustion and our thirst. The dogs availed themselves of this opportunity to devour several pounds of bear's flesh and empty a tin of condensed milk, which, however, did not prevent them from barking impudently the next morning for more.

The 12th of April was the last day of advance in a northerly direction. Though the weather was not clear, yet it was clearer than it had been for some time. When we started we buried our baggage in the fissure of the glacier where we had slept, in order to protect it from bears, which roamed about on all sides. Our march lay over snowy slopes to the summits of the coast range – from 1,000 to 3,000 feet high. The masses of mist lying on the horizon had retreated before the rays of the morning sun, and all the region with its lines of ice-forms was bathed in light; and southward, open water stretched to the shores of Cape Felder. As we followed this lofty coast range, mountains with glaciers sloping down their sides towards the sea seemed to rise before us. An hour before noon we reached a rocky promontory 1,200 feet high, afterwards called Cape Germania. Here we rested, and from a meridian observation we found our latitude to be 81°57'. Following the coast as it trended towards the north-east, we came on a glacier, with a steep inclination and frequent crevasses, which compelled us to leave the sledge behind before we attempted to cross it. But the increasing insecurity of our track over fissures, our want of provisions, and the certainty that since noon we had reached 82°5′NL by a march of five hours, at last brought our advance northward to a close. With a boat we might certainly have gone some miles farther.

We now stood on a promontory about a thousand feet high, which I named Cape Fligely, as a small mark of respect and gratitude towards a man of great distinction in geographical science. Rudolf's Land still stretched in a northeasterly direction towards a cape – Cape Sherard Osborn – though it was impossible to determine its farther course and connection. The view we had from this height was of great importance in relation to the question of an open Polar sea. Open water there was of considerable extent and in very high latitudes; of this there could be no question. But what was its character? From the height on which we stood we could survey its extent. Our expectations had not been sanguine, but moderate though they were, they proved to be exaggerated. No open sea was there, but a 'Polynia' surrounded by old ice, within which lay masses of younger ice. This open space of water had arisen from the action of the long prevalent ENE winds. But of more immediate interest than the question of an open Polar sea was the aspect of blue mountain-ranges lying in the distant north, indicating masses of land, which Orel had partially seen the day before, and which now lay before us with their outlines more defined. These we called King Oscar Land and Petermann Land; the mountainous extremity on the west of the latter lay beyond the 83rd degree of north latitude. This promontory I have called Cape Vienna, in testimony of the interest which Austria's capital has ever shown in geographical science, and in gratitude for the sympathy with which she followed our wanderings, and finally rewarded our humble merits.

Proudly we planted the Austro-Hungarian flag for the first time in the high north, our conscience telling us that we had carried it as far as our resources permitted. It was no act asserting a right of possession in the name of a nation, as when Albuquerque or Van Diemen unfurled the standards of their country on foreign soil, yet we had won this cold, stiff, frozen land with not less difficulty than these discoverers had gained those paradises. It was a sore trial to feel our inability to visit the lands lying before us, but withal we were impressed with the conviction that this day was the most important of our lives, and ever since the memory of it has recurred unbidden to my recollection . . .

The following document we inclosed in a bottle and deposited in a cleft of rock:

> Some members of the Austro-Hungarian North Pole Expedition have here reached their highest point in 82.5° NL, after a march of seventeen days from the ship, lying inclosed in ice in 79°51′NL. They observed open water of no great extent along the coast, bordered by ice, reaching in a north and northwesterly direction to masses of land, whose mean distance from this highest point might be from sixty to seventy miles, but whose connection it was impossible to determine. After their return to the ship, it is the intention of the whole crew to leave this land and return home. The hopeless condition of the ship and the numerous cases of sickness constrain them to this step.

> Cape Fligely, *April 12th 1874.*
> (Signed)   ANTONIO ZANINOVICH, *Seaman,*
>   EDWARD OREL, *Midshipman,*
>   JULIUS PAYER, *Commander.*

This 'Rudolf's Land' (Ostrov Rudol'fa), the most northerly island in the group, was later to be the starting point, or intended starting point, for several expeditions attempting to reach the Pole. 'King Oscar Land' and 'Petermann Land' which Payer thought he saw to the north, were mere illusions, mirages – a common phenomenon in the Arctic that also deceived several other explorers.

After Payer had completed his explorations, the need to return home after two years in the Arctic compelled the explorers to abandon *Tegetthoff* in mid-May and take to their boats. On 24 August, they were rescued by Russian vessels off the coast of Novaya Zemlya.

By any normal standards this expedition was a triumph. It had made a major advance in Arctic exploration and discovery and important contributions to Arctic science, and from the

point of view of national pride, it had given the name of the
Austro-Hungarian emperor a prominent position on the map.
But, of course, it had penetrated no farther north than many
other North Pole expeditions, and had given new strength to the
belief, shared by most polar geographers other than Petermann,
that any successful expedition to the North Pole would have to
walk for most of the way. Petermann became despondent,
resigned to the weakness of a theory that he had defended
passionately for over 20 years, but also, towards those whom
he had once opposed with equal passion, conciliatory. In 1874,
he wrote to the Royal Society: 'It is fortunate for science that
the North Pole has not yet been reached. So, why insist on one
way if there are so many ways? They all lead in the end to
the one goal that really matters: better knowledge of the Arctic
regions.' Finally, therefore, Petermann was able to withdraw
from his rigid stance. For the remaining few years of his life,
he turned his attention away from the Pole, and towards more
intensive studies of the Gulf Stream and other Arctic marine
currents. Sadly, though, the despondency he had felt on the
return of *Tegetthoff* turned increasingly to clinical depression
and on 25 September 1878 he committed suicide. Yet, even
in death, he continued to influence the course of exploration
in the Arctic Ocean. His ideas about polar currents were of
enduring influence, and his ideas about passages to the Pole
influenced one more major expedition: that of the American
George Washington De Long (1844–81), who had Petermann
in mind when he organized his Polar expedition of 1879–81.

In the years when Petermann was advocating the Svalbard
route to the Pole, and sending out preliminary expeditions to
investigate it, a prominent Swedish explorer was also seeking
to investigate that route: this was Adolf Erik Nordenskiöld, who
later rose to fame as leader of the first expedition to navigate
the Northeast Passage. Nordenskiöld's great distinction as an
explorer rests chiefly on his pioneering achievements in the
fields of Arctic science and commercial shipping, but he had
a streak of adventure in him, and on two occasions, in 1868
and 1872–3, he attempted to approach the Pole. His first
expedition was of some minor significance in the history of

the North Pole, because he managed to take his ship *Sofia* to a new record northern latitude for any ship, 81°42′N, to the north of Svalbard, finally beating the record established by Scoresby in 1806.

Nordenskiöld's second attempt to approach the Pole was less successful. In 1872, he embarked on a wintering expedition with the intention of attaining the Pole by the novel means of reindeer-hauled sledges. Everything went wrong. As he entered winter quarters on the north coast of Spitsbergen, two support ships that were intended to return home before winter became trapped in the ice. So, during the winter, he found himself catering for 67 men on provisions intended for only 22. Then all but one of his reindeer escaped, rendering the Pole journey impossible. He made a short journey north with his single reindeer in spring 1873, but he turned back on meeting difficult ice conditions before he reached 81°N, and while he was still among the northernmost islands of the archipelago. The expedition did not fail: it completed a scientific programme, and Nordenskiöld contented himself with making the first crossing of North East Land (Nordaustlandet) instead of trying to claim the Pole.

– 5 –

The British Arctic Expedition

1875–6

While Petermann was stimulating interest in Arctic exploration in Germany and Austro-Hungary, his bitter rival Sherard Osborn was trying doggedly and with infinite patience to do the same thing in Britain. After the loss of the Franklin expedition in 1845, and over ten years of intensive search for it by nearly 30 expeditions in the 1840s and 1850s, the British public's appetite for polar exploration had been sated, and the government's willingness to bear the great expense of it had been exhausted. The search expeditions had discovered many thousands of miles of coastline among the Canadian Arctic islands, but it appeared too remote and too inaccessible to be of any conceivable benefit to the nation. In response to Osborn's appeal, the suspicion must have been that an expedition to the North Pole would yield the same valueless result. Having first stated his case for a British naval attempt to reach the North Pole in 1865, he was required to repeat the argument very many times during the next decade to win support; but slowly, very slowly, the resistance of government and public was eroded. Finally, in August 1874, the government yielded and agreed to organize the venture. In the words of one veteran of the Franklin search, 'the public mind was now ripe, and the time had come at last when this country was to resume her foremost place, and put forth her whole strength in the renewal of Arctic discovery.' The expedition was lavishly fitted out at the then considerable expense of £150,000. Two naval ships, HMS *Alert* and HMS *Discovery*, each carried about 60 officers and crew, and another Franklin search veteran, Captain George Strong Nares (1831–1915), was appointed to command it. Its objectives were wide-ranging. It was to approach the Arctic Ocean by the route explored by Kane, Hayes and Hall, and in addition to sending a sledge expedition to the Pole, it was to explore the area generally, and carry out an extensive scientific programme. It was not expected back until 1877.

When the expedition left Portsmouth on 29 May 1875, public enthusiasm and expectations were truly considerable, and just before sailing Nares received a telegram from Queen Victoria: 'I sincerely wish you and your gallant companions every success, and trust that you may safely accomplish the important duty you have so bravely undertaken.' Sadly, though, Sherard Osborn was unable to witness the final fruition of his plans, or the celebrations that hailed the expedition's departure: he had died three weeks earlier on 6 May.

The two ships successfully forced a passage through Kane Basin and Kennedy Channel, at the northern end of which *Discovery*, commanded by Captain Henry Stephenson, found a safe wintering site in Discovery Harbour. *Alert* forged on through the route pioneered by Hall, and at the beginning of September found a winter harbour at Floeberg Beach, near the northeastern extremity of Ellesmere Island. At 82°28'N, on the very shores of the Arctic Ocean, it was the highest latitude reached by any ship. The two crews wintered comfortably, and in early April three exploring parties set out with sledges, one heading east, one west, and one towards the Pole.

Their chosen method of travel was to man-haul their sledges, even though most other major expeditions were by this date using dog-sledges. Man-hauling had been pioneered by Parry in 1827. It had been much refined during the Franklin search but it was scarcely less agonizingly laborious for the men than it had been in Parry's day. The Royal Navy's tenacity in retaining the man-hauling tradition was one of the most outstanding reasons why, in 1911–12, Captain R.F. Scott was beaten to the South Pole by his Norwegian rival Roald Amundsen; while Scott's men wearily trudged to the Pole and back towards their meeting with death, Amundsen had raced ahead almost effortlessly and made a rapid safe return with his dog-teams.

The polar sledge party was led by Commander Albert Hastings Markham (1841–1918) with a sledge named *Marco Polo*, accompanied by Lieutenant Alfred Parr with the sledge *Victoria*. The two sledges had a total crew of 15 men. At the start, they were accompanied by three other sledges commanded by the medical officer, Edward Moss, and the engineer, George White, carrying extra provisions. Markham left the ship on 3 April, and on the 7th reached the point where he was to leave the land and set foot on the Arctic Ocean. As Sherard Osborn had predicted, there was no loose drifting ice here: the ice stretched in one solid, unbroken mass from shore to horizon. Nor was it the 'plain of smooth unbroken ice' described by Phipps; here, the immense power of the ocean current driving the floes in towards the shore ensured that it was a far less even surface, as Markham describes in his journal, published in Nares's narrative of the voyage.

The travelling today is a foretaste of what we are to expect; heavy floes fringed with hummocks, through and over which the sledges have to be dragged. Dr Moss was fortunate enough to shoot a hare on Depot Point, which is to be reserved as a *bonne bouche* for us when we attain our highest latitude. Land very much distorted by mirage. Camped for the night on a floe off Cape Hercules. Temperature remains extraordinarily low: minus 41°. Distance marched fourteen miles; made good four and a half.

8th [April]. – A charming day, although the temperature persists in remaining low. Care has to be taken in selecting the road so as to avoid the hummocks as much as possible; occasionally we are brought to a standstill by a belt of more than ordinarily large ones, through which we have to cut a road with pickaxes and shovels. Sledges double-banked as before. The large sledge, on which is the twenty-foot ice-boat, drags very heavily. This is caused by the overhanging weight at the two extremities. Glare from the sun has been very oppressive; the snow in places resembles coarse sand, and appears more crystallized than usual. A few of the party, including Parr and myself, suffering from snow-blindness. Distance marched ten miles. Temperature minus 30°.

9th. – Same system of double-banking the sledges continues. Parr's snow-blindness is no better, mine no worse. The snow goggles are worn by all, and certainly afford relief to the eyes. Moss is rendering valuable service by assisting me in the selection of a road – no easy task whilst going through hummocks. Although the temperature is minus 30°, the sun has sufficient influence to dry our blanket wrappers and other gear; the yards of the boats being very convenient for the purpose of tricing up our robes, etc. The snow is still very deep on the floes and between the hummocks, materially retarding our progress. Halted at seven, and encamped on a heavy floe. From its north-western edge the depot at Cape Joseph Henry was plainly visible; a great relief to our minds, as thoughts of its being buried in deep snow-drift would frequently occur to us. Distance marched thirteen miles; made good four.

In this and subsequent journal entries the distance travelled each day often greatly exceeded their actual northward progress (or 'distance made good'). This was because of the many deviations forced on them by the hummocks, and many trips backwards and forwards to advance their heavy loads little by little over the worst terrain. Later, other factors also contributed to the shortness of distances 'made good'. Less than a week later, their hardships were already increasing to the very limit of human endurance.

15th. – Blowing a north-westerly gale, with the temperature 35° below zero, and a considerable drift which rendered travelling quite out of the question. Extreme wretchedness and almost abject misery was our lot today. We derived no heat from our robes, they were frozen so hard, the temperature inside our tent being minus 22°. It is rather remarkable that we have this day experienced, during a gale of wind, a lower temperature than we have had during any gale the whole winter, which leads one to the conclusion that it is evident there can be no open water existing either to the northward or westward of us.

16th. – The wind this morning was still blowing fresh, though it had moderated considerably; it was, however, so cutting and piercing, and the drift was so dense, making it almost impossible for us to see our way through the hummocks, that it was deemed more prudent and advisable to remain encamped, however unpleasant and disagreeable such a course was to all concerned. We unanimously came to the conclusion that it was the most wretched and miserable Easter Sunday that any one of us had ever passed. Forty-eight hours in a bag, in a gale of wind off Cape Joseph Henry, with a temperature 67° below freezing point, is not a delightful way of passing the time – sleep was almost out of the question. In spite of the cold we did not omit the usual Saturday night's toast last evening; and as it was also the first anniversary of the Ships' commissioning we gave three cheers; this was taken up by the *Victoria*, and then we commenced to cheer each other, by way of keeping up our spirits.

At five struck the tents and commenced the march. Shirley being unable to walk, we were obliged to place him on one of the sledges, keeping him in his sleeping bag, and wrapping him well up in the coverlet and lower robe. This increases our weight to be dragged, besides diminishing our strength. Crossed the floe on which we were encamped, and cut our way through a hedge of hummocks, about one-third of a mile in breadth, on to another floe of apparently great thickness. These floes, although of stupendous size regarding their thickness, are unfortunately for us of no very great superficial extent, varying only from a quarter of a mile to a mile in north and south direction. The recent strong wind, blowing the snow from off the land to the floes, has made the travelling rather heavier than it was before. Between some of the large floes we occasionally meet small patches of young ice along which the sledges run smoothly; but, alas! they are never more than a few yards in extent. Encamped for the night on a large floe. Men appearing more done up, after lying so long idle in their bags, than if they had had a hard day's dragging. Beyond Cape Parry, which is at present the most distant land visible to the westward, can be seen two cloud-like objects that may be Aldrich's 'Cooper Key Mountains'; but again they may be clouds or mirage. Distance marched seven miles; made good one and a quarter.

17th. – Commenced the march at 11.30 a.m. Shirley has

again to be put on the sledge. Porter is rendered *hors de combat*, and is suffering a good deal of pain. He is just able to hobble after us. Our force is much weakened by the loss of these two men. A beautiful sunny day with the temperature as high as minus 24°. The men are taking kindly to their goggles, rarely taking them off whilst on the march, and quite willing to put up with a little inconvenience rather than be afflicted with snow-blindness. The snow being deep, we found the travelling on the floes very heavy indeed; the large boat comes along very slowly, and it is seldom we can advance many paces without resorting to 'standing pulls'. Arrived at the edge of a broad belt of hummocks, through which a road had to be cut, then on to a small floe, then through more hummocks, which again had to succumb before the strenuous exertions of Parr and his untiring road-makers; then more small floes and more hummocks and so it goes on.

And so it did go on: one day after another of immense labour but very little progress, and increasing sickness. Three weeks later:

8th. – The interiors of our tents in the evening have more the appearance of hospitals than the habitations of strong working-men. In addition to the 'cripples', four men belonging to the *Marco Polo* are suffering from snow-blindness, although in a mild form. At noon started all available hands under Parr, with pick and shovel road-making, as we are desirous of ascertaining if this apparently interminable line of hummocks is of great extent. To solve this is all we can now expect to do. A bright warm day. Aired and dried all tent gear, etc. Walked on with Parr towards the end of the day about a mile to the northward, selecting a route for the sledges. At our farthermost point from the summit of a high hummock we saw, about two or three degrees to the northward of Cape Aldrich, either land or the loom of it. The hummocks around us are of different heights and bulk, varying from small fragments of ice to huge piles over forty feet high.

9th. – We have at length arrived at the conclusion, although with a great deal of reluctance, that our sick men are really suffering from scurvy, and that in no mild form. Should our surmise be correct, we can scarcely expect to see any of the afflicted ones improve until they can be supplied with fresh meat and vegetables. We are unwilling for the men to suspect that they are really suffering from this terrible disease, but at the same time are issuing to those attacked a small quantity out of the very little limejuice we brought away with us. It is given to them in lieu of their grog, as being a better blood-purifier. We have only two bottles on each sledge of this excellent anti-scorbutic. It is another beautifully warm sunny day, with the temperature only a degree or two below zero. Made a start at half-past twelve by advancing with one sledge with half its load and two invalids upon it. This was dragged up to the extreme of yesterday's road-making, a distance of three-quarters of a mile, when the tent was pitched, the invalids placed inside, and the sledge taken back, again loaded, and again advanced with two more invalids; the men returning and bringing up the other two sledges, with the remainder of the gear and the fifth invalid, one at a time. It was past eight o'clock before the last sledge arrived, and though we had only made good three-quarters of a mile, so tortuous was our road, winding round and about the hummocks, that to accomplish this distance we marched between six and seven miles through very deep snow. After the tents were pitched, a party of road-makers were advanced to prepare a road through the hummocks.

10th. – There was a slight fall of snow during the day, when the temperature rose to 15°. Distance made good three-quarters of a mile.

After very serious consideration, I have arrived at the conclusion, though sorely against my inclination, that this must be our most northern camp. With five out of our little force totally prostrate, and four others exhibiting decided symptoms of the same complaint, it would be folly to persist in pushing on. In addition to which the greater half of our provisions have been expended. Tomorrow will be our fortieth day out; only thirty-one days' full allowance of provisions remain, so that prudence and discretion unite against our own desire of advancing, and counsel a return. A complete rest to the invalids of a couple of days may be productive of much good, during which time we may be usefully engaged in making observations in various interesting matters. With this we must be content, having failed so lamentably in attaining a high northern latitude. It is a bitter ending to all our aspirations.

After a day spent making scientific observations, they made one last march northward, without sledges, to attain the highest latitude possible, then, as a little temporary relief from the endless suffering, they had a party.

12th. – Breakfasted at 8.30, immediately after which, leaving the cooks behind at the camp to attend upon the invalids, the remainder of the party carrying the sextant and artificial horizon, and also the sledge banners and colours, started northwards. We had some very severe walking, struggling through snow up to our waists, over or through which the labour of dragging a sledge would be interminable, and occasionally almost disappearing through cracks and fissures, until twenty minutes to noon, when a halt was called. The artificial horizon was then set up, and the flags and banners displayed; these fluttered out bravely before a fresh SW wind, which latter, however, was decidedly cold and unpleasant. At noon we obtained a good altitude, and proclaimed our latitude to be 83°20'26"N, exactly 399½ miles from the North Pole. On this being duly announced three cheers were given, with one more for Captain Nares; then the whole party, in the exuberance of their spirits at having reached their turning point, sang the 'Union Jack of Old England', the 'Grand Palæocrystic Sledging Chorus', winding up, like loyal subjects, with 'God save the Queen'. These little demonstrations had the effect of cheering the men, who nevertheless enjoy good spirits. The instruments were then packed, the colours furled, and our steps retraced to the camp. On arrival the flags were hoisted on our tents and sledges and kept flying for the remainder of the day. A magnum of whisky that had been sent by the Dean of

Dundee, for the express purpose of being consumed in the highest northern latitude, was produced, and a glass of grog served out to all. It is needless to add his kindness was thoroughly appreciated, nor was he forgotten in the toast of 'absent friends'.

We all enjoyed our supper, for we had the hare shot by Dr Moss at Depot Point, equally divided between our two tents, cooked in our allowance of pemmican, making the latter uncommonly good and savoury. After supper a cigar, presented to us by May before leaving the ship, was issued to each man, and the day was brought to a close with songs, even the invalids joining in. All seemed happy, cheerful, and contented.

For the first three weeks of the return journey they had slightly easier going because they could still use the road they had cut on the journey out. But then at the beginning of June matters worsened.

2nd [June]. A sad list of sick this morning. Rawlings and Simpson completely done up, and utterly incapable of further work. It is marvellous how they have kept on so long. Lawrence is also attacked in his arms as well as his legs. We are now reduced to only six men, and they anything but healthy or strong, and two officers. Five men are carried on the sledges, and four can just manage to crawl after. Our routine is first to advance the heavy sledge, which is dragged by the whole available party, namely, eight; then return and bring up the other two sledges, single banked, four dragging each.

The weather has at last proved triumphant, and has robbed us of our road. The track was lost, despite our utmost efforts to adhere to it, shortly before lunch, and we have now to renew the arduous task of road-making. Unless the weather clears sufficiently to enable us again to pick up our track, our intention is to make straight for the land in the direction of the Snow Valley. Camped on a small floe completely surrounded by hummocks, through which we had to cut our way. Distance made good one mile and three-quarters.

A few days later:

> *8th.* – Poor Porter is no more! He expired at ten minutes
> past noon. He was sensible to within a few minutes of his
> death, and his end was calm and quiet. This is a sad calamity,
> although we were not totally unprepared for it, and I fear
> the depressing moral effect that this lamentable event
> will have on those who are very sick, and who consider
> themselves to be in nearly as precarious a condition.
>
> With the ensign half-mast, and the Union Jack as a pall,
> the funeral procession, attended by all but the four very
> bad cases, started at nine; and the burial service being read,
> the remains were consigned to their last icy resting-place in
> this world. Improvising a rude cross, formed with a boat's
> oar and a spare sledge-batten, it was placed at the head of
> the grave, with the following inscription:
>
> BENEATH THIS CROSS LIE BURIED THE REMAINS
> OF
> GEO. PORTER, RMA
> WHO DIED ON JUNE 8TH, 1876
> 'Thy will be done'
>
> Of all the melancholy and mournful duties I have ever
> been called upon to perform, this has been the saddest. A
> death in a small party like ours, and under the present
> circumstances, is a most distressing event, and is keenly
> felt by all. During the service all were more or less affected,
> and many to tears.

On the next day, the first of two relief parties arrived, and on
14 June they were back at the ship. But this was no triumphant
homecoming. Markham's last diary entry simply reports: 'Out of
my original party of fifteen men, three only – namely Radmore,
Joliffe and Maskell – were capable of dragging the sledge; the
remaining eleven having been carried alongside on the relief
sledges.' Markham also reported his opinion that it was utterly
impossible to reach the Pole over the ice of that region; he
believed that even with the very lightest equipped sledges, and
perfect health, the best that might be achieved would have been
about one degree farther. He was wrong, but it took another

30 years, and huge improvements in travelling equipment, to prove it.

The outbreaks of scurvy and three deaths (two men in the western party had died) brought the expedition to a premature end, and the plans for a second wintering were abandoned. They arrived back at Portsmouth on 2 November 1876 – to be greeted by widespread and bitter public disappointment. One newspaper that had reported its departure with wild enthusiasm, reported its return under the headline 'The Polar Failure', and found the vivid image that summed up the mood of the nation: 'Verily the expedition of 1875–6 has but little of which to boast. It went out like a rocket and has come back like the stick.'

The chief disappointment surrounded the failure of the polar party. Their final latitude, 83°20′26″N, was a new record, fought for with exceptional courage, but it was not spectacular enough; 399½ miles from the Pole cannot easily be portrayed as being close. But the detractors ignored both the dreadful hardships endured by Markham and his men, and the expedition's positive results in terms of exploration and discovery, and scientific work in fields including zoology, botany, geology and meteorology. They had not failed: too much had been expected of them in the first place. However, the perception that they had failed was sufficient yet again to dampen the nation's and the navy's enthusiasm for polar exploration. It was 25 years before the Royal Navy became involved in another polar expedition, and that was not to the Arctic: it was Captain Scott's first expedition to the Antarctic.

– 6 –

De Long and the *Jeannette*

1879–81

August Petermann died in 1878, but his zeal for new geographical knowledge lived after him. His *Geographische Mitteilungen* are published quarterly under his name even to this day. And in the year after his death, there was still one more explorer preparing earnestly to put his 'Open Polar Sea' theory to the test. This man was an American naval officer, Commander George Washington De Long (1844–81).

De Long had been in the Arctic once before, in 1873, when as a lieutenant he took part in a naval expedition to Baffin Bay to search for missing members of C.F. Hall's expedition. He had distinguished himself on that expedition by searching the shores of Melville Bay, northwest Greenland, with the ship's launch. Another interesting feature of the expedition was that two newspaper correspondents from the *New York Herald* also took part. It was one of the first attempts by any newspaper to participate directly in an Arctic expedition, and to exploit the expedition for its more sensational aspects in order to create news and sell newspapers. The man behind that idea was James Gordon Bennett, proprietor of the *Herald*, who had already used exploration to generate a sensational news story by sending Henry Morton Stanley to Africa to search for Livingstone. Immediately after he returned from the Arctic, in November 1873, De Long had contacted Bennett, attempting to interest him in supporting an expedition to the North Pole. Bennett had already thought of the idea, and although in 1873 he was not quite prepared for such a venture, he was soon convinced that, in De Long, he had found the ideal leader, and the two men remained in contact with each other. The event that finally persuaded Bennett that the time for a North Pole expedition had come, was a three-hour meeting between him and Petermann in Germany in March 1877. After the failure of his own expeditions to make substantial progress towards the North Pole, Petermann had modified his 'Open Polar Sea' theory; he had incorporated the theories of other oceanographers into his own, and concluded that the best chance of reaching the Pole was through Bering Strait, where a warm current known as Kuro Siwo entered the Arctic Ocean. He now believed that in the area where that current met the Gulf Stream, a warm polar sea would open the way to the Pole. Both Bennett and De Long willingly adopted that theory; Bennett agreed to finance an expedition and appoint De Long as leader. Soon after, De Long travelled to Britain and purchased the Arctic exploration vessel *Pandora*, which was subsequently re-named *Jeannette* after Bennett's sister.

An unusual feature of this expedition was that, although Bennett paid for it, the United States Navy took responsibility for crew, outfitting, and De Long's instructions. In addition to simply ordering him to 'proceed on your voyage toward the North Pole', the instructions ordered him first to search for the Swedish explorer Adolf Erik Nordenskiöld, who at that time was making the first successful navigation of the Northeast Passage. This was a piece of pure sensationalism on Bennett's part; Nordenskiöld was not lost, any more than Livingstone had been. He was in no need of rescue, and was known to be an outstandingly capable polar explorer; but finding him would still have created a marvellous news story. In the event, De Long paid little attention to this aspect of the instructions, and headed almost directly for the Pole.

Jeannette left New York on 8 July 1879, passed through Bering Strait at the end of August, and by 4 September was approaching the tiny Herald Island (Ostrov Geral'd) in the northern Chukchi Sea, where De Long planned to spend the winter. But they were now in dense ice, and progress was getting slower and slower. Two days later, De Long's journal records:

September 6th, Saturday. – This is a glorious country to learn patience in. I am hoping and praying to be able to get the ship into Herald Island to make winter quarters. As far as the eye can range is ice, and not only does it look as if it had never broken up and become water, but it also looks as if it never would. Yesterday I hoped that today would make an opening for us into the land; today I hope that tomorrow will do it. I suppose a gale of wind would break the pack up, but then the pack might break us up, and that is not to be desired. This morning shows some pools of thin ice and water, but as they are disconnected, and we cannot jump the ship over obstructions, they are of no use yet to us. A thick fog hangs over everything, even the island. A light northerly wind with a steady barometer, and a temperature ranging between 23° and 32°.

At one p.m. the fog lifted, and we saw a chance of making about a mile toward the island. Spread fires again and commenced forcing our way, ramming wherever we were opposed, and with good effect. Of course, ramming a ship through ice from ten to fifteen feet thick was impossible, but wherever a crack or narrow opening showed between two floes, even of that thickness, we could by judicious ramming, and backing and ramming again, shove them apart enough to squeeze through. Our steam-winch did good service, for we could easily snub the ship's head into a weak place when we did not have room to turn her with the helm. At 4.20, however, we had come to solid floes again, and as the thick fog again shut in we came to with our ice-anchor. Wishing to save even the coal we used with banked fires, until a good chance presented itself for going ahead, I let the fires die out. This evening three bears came down to about a mile from the ship, but fled upon being seen and chased by our hunters. Served out snow-goggles to all hands, with orders to wear them.

This inaction is most disagreeable, and it is even more disagreeable to see no chance for a change. The only hope of the pack breaking up is the occurrence of a gale of wind; and as the weather has been so uniformly calm and pleasant since our being beset that the ice has become well connected and solidified, it will require a heavy gale to make a change. Meanwhile, we are getting no nearer Herald Island, and are making no advance in any direction, unless we are really drifting, ice and all, to the NW. It is unpleasant to realize that our exploration for a whole year should come to a stop on the 6th September, and that at a point which a sailing ship, the *Vincennes*, reached in 1855 without any difficulty. And here we are in a steamer, and beset in the pack before we are two months out of San Francisco. My disappointment is great, how great no one else will probably ever know. I had hoped to accomplish something new in the first summer, and we have done nothing. While waiting for next summer we are consuming our provisions and fuel, and running the risk of the enfeeblement of the general health which a winter's confinement may produce.

In addition to being stuck fast in the ice, *Jeannette* had also begun an erratic drift. But at least, having resigned himself to a winter in the ice, De Long could reflect that their position appeared relatively safe.

This drift of ours is in no sense uniform or capable of being foreseen. It does not depend seemingly upon the wind, for it is different with the same winds at different times. That even light winds occasion drift and pressure is evident from the fact that the ice about a mile from the ship in all directions is constantly assuming new shapes. We seem to be held in the centre of a large floe, sufficiently strong to save a severe nip to the ship and to resist pressure on its edges. A mile from the ship in any direction new ice six inches thick is piled up in tables from six to twenty feet in height by the coming together of floes. One day we find large spaces of water, the next day we find the spaces narrowing, and the third day the spaces are closed and slabs of new ice six inches thick are piled up on end like a confused fence six, twelve, and eighteen feet high. We seem to move only in azimuth, remaining heeled over to starboard 5°. Our floe suffers no jar even, and immediately around the ship the conditions of ice do not change, except as snow-falls level all the projecting surfaces.

Their drift was a strange one, carrying the ship backwards and forwards in a triangular pattern, but in general they were moving slowly to the west and north, and by the end of the year they were to the north of Wrangel Island (Ostrov Vrangelya), a large island to the west of Herald Island. The trouble was, that after a winter of interminable monotony, they were still to the north of Wrangel Island.

There was still worse to come. The arrival of spring and summer 1880 failed to bring their expected release from the ice, and their triangular drift was now taking them nowhere. They had moved farther to the north of Wrangel Island, to around 73°N, but their erratic drift kept carrying them back to the same place. By 3 November 1880 they were again in about the same position as they had been on 26 April. They were helplessly stuck, clearly not moving towards open water, and facing yet another insufferably dreary and dark Arctic winter. On 31 October, De Long gave eloquent voice to his thoughts.

October 31st, Sunday. – Another week has come and gone, and with it ends the month. Uneventful, and, so far as any results obtained are concerned, a clear waste of life. It is hard to feel satisfied even with our being still alive. That, after all, seems such a negative kind of thing – a living with no purpose, an existence without present tangible results, a mechanical supplying the system with food, heat, and clothing, in order to keep the human engine running.

I have often wondered if a horse driving a saw-mill had any mental queries as to why he tramped over his endless plank, and what on earth there was accomplished by his so doing. The saw was generally out of his sight, he perceived no work accomplished, he never changed his position relatively, he worked on and on without advancing a foot, and ended his day's work in identically the same place at which he began it, and, as far as equine judgement could forecast, would do the same thing tomorrow, and every other day thereafter. If that horse had reasoning faculties, I pity him and appreciate now his thoughts and feelings. We are individually in that horse's position – we see no saw, we can detect no work accomplished, we move on without advancing a foot, we shall do tomorrow what we have done today and what we did yesterday, and we fill up with oats, so to speak, merely that the saw-mill may not have to suspend sawing. This kind of life is worse than Mr Mantalini and his mangle. With him life was 'one demnition grind', but with us it is 'one demnition blank'.

A man up here thinks a wonderful amount of nonsense, says many things which he would be surprised at remembering hereafter, and, if he writes, commits to paper many absurdities which he will laugh at afterwards. But to a physiologist, who could retain his own mental poise and strength under these circumstances, the study of human life and characteristics developed by a residence of white men in the Arctic regions would give materials for a very readable volume.

As De Long and his men settled down to the dull monotony of a second winter, they had at least one consolation: their drift had settled down to a more regular pattern, and began carrying them in a clear northwesterly direction. By May 1881 they were approaching the north of the New Siberian Islands. At the same time, they had the satisfaction of making some discoveries. What they found was only two very small islands, but De Long rejoiced.

May 16th, Monday. – LAND! There is something then besides ice in this world. About seven o'clock this evening Mr Dunbar, who usually winds his way aloft several times a day, could hardly believe his eyes when they rested on an island to the westward. He called Chipp to look at it, and Chipp saw it was land sure enough, and sent Ericksen to inform me. I had just finished working out our position when the extraordinary news came, and was writing out the result: Latitude 76°43′20″N, longitude 161°53′45″E, a drift since the 14th of five and a half miles to N, 16°E. Of course I dropped my books and ran up to the fore yard, and there, sure enough, I saw a small island one half point forward of our starboard beam, the first land that has greeted our eyes since March 24, 1880, nearly fourteen months ago. And our voyage, thank God, is not a perfect blank, for here we have discovered something, however small it may be. Some fog is resting over it, and to the right hand or northward of it, and we do not think we see all of our wonderful landfall.

De Long named their discoveries Jeannette Island and Henrietta Island (the latter after Bennett's mother). On 2 June, a sledge party landed on Henrietta Island to take formal possession in the name of the United States, and this, too, gave De Long some satisfaction.

> Thank God, we have at least landed upon a newly discovered part of this earth, and a perilous journey has been accomplished without disaster. It was a great risk, but it has resulted in some advantage.

De Long's satisfaction was short-lived. A week later, the ice began to loosen around the ship. At first, this appeared to be a good sign, and he reported, after a brief inspection of the ship's hull, 'No difficulty was anticipated in keeping the ship afloat and navigating her to some port, should she ever be liberated from the pack ice of the Arctic Ocean.' Within a day, however, the situation altered completely, and on 11 June De Long wrote:

> At four p.m. the ice came down in great force all along the port side, jamming the ship hard against the ice on the starboard side of her, and causing her to heel 16° to starboard. From the snapping and cracking of the bunker sides and starting in of the starboard ceiling, as well as the opening of the seams in the ceiling to the width of one and one-fourth inches, it was feared that the ship was about to be seriously endangered, and orders were accordingly given to lower the starboard boats, and haul them away from the ship to a safe position on the icefloe. This was done quickly and without confusion. The ice, in coming in on the port side, also had a movement toward the stern, and this last movement not only raised her port bow, but buried the starboard quarter, and jamming it and the stern against the heavy ice, effectually prevented the ship rising to pressure. Mr Melville, while below in the engine-room, saw a break across the ship in the wake of the boilers and engines, showing that so solidly were the stern and starboard quarters held by the ice that the ship was breaking in two from the pressure upward exerted on the port bow of the ship. The starboard side of the ship was

also evidently broken in, because water was rising rapidly
in the starboard coal bunkers. Orders were now given to
land one half of the pemmican in the deck-house, and all
the bread which was on deck, and the sleds and dogs were
likewise carried to a position of safety. At 4.30 there was
a lull in the pressure, and it was assumed for the moment
that the ice had united under the ship, and being as close
together as it could come would occasion us no further
injury, and that we might be able to take care of the ship
yet. The ship was heeled 22° to starboard, and was raised
forward 4' 6", the entire port bow being visible also to a
height of 4' 6" from the forefoot. (In the early morning we
had been able to see through the water down alongside
the stem on the starboard side, and we could see that the
forefoot was bent to starboard about a foot. This would
indicate that the pressure received on the 19th January
1880, was from port to starboard, instead of the other
way, as we then supposed.) But at five p.m. the pressure
was renewed and continued with tremendous force, the
ship cracking in every part. The spar deck commenced
to buckle up, and the starboard side seemed again on
the point of coming in. Orders were now given to get
out provisions, clothing, bedding, ship's books, and papers,
and to remove all sick to a place of safety. While engaged
in this work another tremendous pressure was received,
and at six p.m. it was found that the ship was beginning
to fill. From that time forward every effort was devoted to
getting provisions, etc., on the ice, and it was not desisted
from until the water had risen to the spar deck, the ship
being heeled to starboard about 30°. The entire starboard
side of the spar deck was submerged, the rail being under
water, and the water-line reaching to the hatch-coamings.
The starboard side was evidently broken in abreast of the
mainmast, and the ship was settling fast. Our ensign had
been hoisted at the mizzen, and every preparation made
for abandoning, and at eight p.m. everybody was ordered
to leave the ship. Assembling on the floe, we dragged all
our boats and provisions clear of bad cracks, and prepared
to camp down for the night.

At midnight piped down.

June 12th, Sunday (or Monday, June 13th). – At one a.m. were turned out by the ice opening in the midst of our camp. Transported all our gear and belongings to a place of safety, and again piped down at two a.m., leaving a man on watch. At one a.m. the mizzen mast went by the board, and the ship was so far heeled over that the lower yard-arms were resting on the ice.

At three a.m. the ship had sunk until her smoke-pipe top was nearly awash.

At four a.m. the *Jeannette* went down. First righting to an even keel, she slowly sunk.

The maintop-mast fell by the board to starboard, then the foretop-mast – and finally the mainmast, near the main truss – when she finally sank; the foremast was all that was standing.

Their predicament was not immediately precarious. The ship had sunk slowly enough, and De Long had acted promptly enough, to get all necessities out on the ice. They had provisions sufficient for a long journey to safety; they were in generally good health; and with both boats and sledges they were equipped for either ice or water. The region to the south of them was reasonably well mapped, and De Long was able to choose a route through the New Siberian Islands to the Siberian mainland. At first, the drift of the ice carried them northward, until on 25 June they reached the expedition's most northerly point at 77°46′N. At the same time they encountered difficult travelling conditions over rugged, broken ice, and on 27 June De Long recorded a familiar story.

June 27th, Monday. – one a.m., found us about a quarter of a mile farther, and we halted for dinner. Turned to at 2.15 a.m., and from this time to seven a.m. we had the hardest time we have yet had. We succeeded in advancing only half a mile farther south southwest, making one and a quarter miles in eleven hours' steady work. Just after leaving our halting place, we had another opening to cross twenty feet in width; and while we tried bridging it, it opened twenty feet more. After great exertion we succeeded in dragging in three large floes for bridges, and by herculean efforts got our sleds and boats over, launching first and second cutters. Drifting about one-eighth of a mile farther, we had another ice opening about sixty feet wide, and to bridge this we had literally to drag an ice-island thirty feet wide and hold it in place. Hardly had we done this when the lead widened, and we had to scour around for more huge blocks to make them serve our purpose. There seems to be general slackness to the ice, and a streaming away without any resistance. It is hardly late enough to find leads of any length, but there are openings enough to give us serious trouble.

To work like horses all day for ten or eleven hours, and to make only a mile, is rather discouraging; and the knowledge that we are very likely going three miles northwest to every mile we make southwest keeps me anxious.

Soon, however, applying the same unceasingly laborious effort as Parry, Markham and many others before them, they began to progress slowly south. In the middle of July they had a welcome break from their toil, when they discovered another new, small island, which De Long named after Bennett. There they stopped for a week to rest, enjoy a restorative diet of eggs, birds and other fresh food, and to make a scientific survey. Continuing south on 6 August, they were able to take to their three boats, and made fair progress through the New Siberian Islands, heading south-west for the Lena river delta. It was still not an easy journey – ice and weather were frequently against them – but they were able to land from time to time, and continued to enjoy a healthy diet of game. They were almost at the end of their voyage when, on 12 September, a fresh disaster hit them. De Long's record of it is concise and unemotional.

September 12th, Monday. – Called all hands at five; break-fasted at six. Fresh E wind; temperature 31°. Under way 7.30; course, south southwest (true); 8.40 abreast north end of Wassilewski Island; 9.40 abreast south end of Wassilewski Island; 11.30 came to alongside ice for dinner. Run by estimation, sixteen miles. Soundings, four and three-quarter fathoms. Under way at 12.30. Round to against ice at four. Whaleboat stove. Under way at 4.15; freshening east northeast breeze. At nine p.m. lost sight of whaleboat ahead; at ten p.m. lost sight of second cutter astern; wind freshening to a gale. Step of mast carried away; lowered sail and rode to sea anchor; very heavy sea and hard squalls. Barometer falling rapidly.

September 13th, Tuesday. – Very heavy northeast gale all day until six p.m., when it moderated; very heavy squalls; tremendous sea. Boat shipping a good deal of water, she kept sea anchor abeam. At ten a.m. got out the sail and attempted to ride under the lee of it. After doing so very well for an hour, the sheet parted and we lost sail and yard. Barometer fell to 29.35 at 35°. In the afternoon made a sea anchor of oars and mast, and managed to ride out gale under their lee. After six p.m. wind and sea moderated rapidly; clouds broke away; moon and stars appeared, and auroral flashes. At eight p.m. set a jury sail made of a sled cover, and kept the boat away to the westward before the sea.

September 14th, Wednesday. – Wind ahead; sea moderating rapidly. Rising barometer. Towards noon the wind settled to about south. Boat making about a west (true) course of about one knot per hour. Nothing seen of either second cutter or whaleboat. Soundings in ten fathoms. Served out eight and a half pounds of ham instead of the pemmican rations at dinner.

The three boats had been separated by the gale, and never came together again. The crews of all three experienced differing kinds of fate. One, commanded by Lieutenant Charles William Chipp, was never seen again; eight men were lost with it. Another, commanded by the chief engineer, George Melville, reached the eastern part of the Lena river delta, and the party on board was almost at once rescued by local hunters. All 11 men were saved. De Long's party of 14 men was unfortunate. They reached the Lena delta, but in its northern part, where there were no hunters. Their only hope was to walk south to the nearest settlement, Bulun, nearly 100 miles up the Lena river. By now, though, cold, hunger and exhaustion were weakening them too much for such a march, and on 21 September, when they had the good fortune to encounter two deserted hunters' huts, De Long decided on a change of plan.

When I saw these two huts – one evidently new, and both habitable and intended for a prolonged residence – I concluded that this was a suitable place to halt the main body, and send on a couple of good walkers to make a forced march to get relief. The two I selected were the doctor and Nindemann; and I had a preliminary conversation with the former on the subject, giving him my views. He is to push on until he does come to a settlement, and can get back relief to us. And we are to remain here and try to eke out an existence with two days' rations drawn out to their fullest extent, and such chance game as may offer. Though loth to do anything which seems like abandoning us, he is willing enough to do anything that may give a chance for relief, and by tomorrow morning I shall have his orders perfected and my plans made. Go on we cannot just now, and here we can have at least heat and shelter. Seeing something across the river and farther down that looked like a signal-post or a fish-frame, I sent Nindemann along to look at it; and some hut-like objects to the eastward being seen, I sent Alexey over to look at them. This was at four p.m. A flock of five small ducks had been swimming around in the river, and several rifle shots had been fired without effect. I had caused a strict search to be made around both huts for food of any kind, but nothing could be found. At six Nindemann returned. He found a gull in a trap and brought it in, but alas! it was rotten. The trap had been set for a fox or a goose, and baited with fish. We ate our supper and crawled under our blankets. Two good berths in the new hut gave bedsteads to the doctor, Collins, Nindemann, and myself; and ordering the fire to be thrown outside, and the house shut up to keep the heat in, I consigned myself to sleep. At 8.30 Alexey had not yet returned, and though I was anxious to have no one away from me, I could not doubt he would safely return. At nine p.m. a knock was heard outside, and Alexey's voice asking, 'All asleep inside?' and in an instant I was up. Sticking his head in the door, Alexey said, 'Captain, we got two reindeer'; and in he came bearing a hind quarter of meat. Sleep was at once forgotten. Fire was made, and cooking begun in both huts, and we consumed about one and one half pounds cooked meat each, finishing all that Alexey brought, except two tongues, before we cried enough.

At this stage, luck was certainly with them, and De Long's journal reflects a mood of growing optimism.

September 22nd, Thursday. – The hut remained warm until toward daylight, when it began to grow chilly. Called all hands at 5.30, and had a pemmican breakfast, and at 6.45 sent out Nindemann, Alexey, and five men to bring in our two deer. This, of course, changes my plans. We can now remain here a day or two to let our sick people catch up, and while living upon deer meat on hand can search for more to cook and carry with us. The two remaining days' pemmican is shut up tight during our use of other food. Looking around our hut we can see traces of Russians or other civilized beings. A rude checker-board, wooden forks, pieces of pencil, etc., and other evidences of the use of tools by somewhat skilled workmen. At noon light east breeze; temperature air 30°. Within the hut, at my berth in front of the fire, the thermometer stood at 70°.

At 1.50 Nindemann and his party returned, bringing in the two deer; seven hours' walking was necessary for them evidently. We immediately commenced getting dinner, and at three sat down to one and a half pounds each of fried steaks, liver, and heart. As soon as we were through dinner we had to commence preparing for supper, because, in our limited stock of cooking utensils, a pot, frying-pan, and pot cover, we can do but little at a time. Boiled down for two hours a lot of bones for soup, and served out one half pound meat for frying. At eight, therefore, we had soup, one and a half pints each, and a half pound fried meat, and at nine put out the fire and went to sleep, saving our candle-ends for some emergency. Tea was dispensed with also, because the pot was in use for soup. The sick seem to be improving. Boyd is on the rapid mend, Sam slowly, and Ericksen is no worse.

This rest, and food, and shelter will no doubt restore their feet at the earliest moment, and I must simply wait and hope. They cannot move now, and we are so well off for deer meat (probably one hundred pounds clear meat) that the necessity for separating our party seems not a pressing matter.

Prospects still looked good, but two days later De Long made what was almost certainly a premature decision to resume the march, before all the sick were fully recovered, and they set off again. In the first week of October their stock of food fell alarmingly and their situation in general worsened daily. On 6 October, as one of the seamen lay dying, he made the decision to send ahead his two fittest men, the ice-quartermaster William Nindemann, and seaman Louis Noros, to seek help in the nearest village.

October 6th, Thursday. – One hundred and sixteenth day. Called all hands at 7.30. Had a cup of third-hand tea with one half ounce of alcohol in it. Everybody very weak. Gale moderating somewhat. Sent Alexey out to hunt. Shall start Nindemann and Noros at noon to make the forced march to Ku Mark Surka. At 8.45 a.m. our messmate Ericksen departed this life. Addressed a few words of cheer and comfort to the men. Alexey came back empty-handed. Too much drifting snow. What in God's name is going to become of us – fourteen pounds dog meat left, and twenty-five miles to a possible settlement? As to burying Ericksen, I cannot dig a grave, for the ground is frozen and we have nothing to dig with. There is nothing to do but to bury him in the river. Sewed him up in the flaps of the tent, and covered him with my flag. Got tea ready, and with one half ounce alcohol we will try to make out to bury him. But we are all so weak that I do not see how we are going to move.

At 12.40 p.m. read the burial service and carried our departed shipmate's body down to the river, where, a hole having been cut in the ice, he was buried; three volleys from our two Remingtons being fired over him as a funeral honor.

A board was prepared with this cut on it:

IN MEMORY
H.H. ERICKSEN,
OCT. 6, 1881
USS Jeannette

and this will be stuck in the river bank abreast his grave.

While Nindemann and Noros walked on ahead, De Long and the remainder of the party tried to make progress as best they could. They were weakening rapidly now; almost without food, and on 10 October they made what proved to be their final march. De Long's journal records their last days.

October 10th, Monday. – One hundred and twentieth day. Last half ounce alcohol at 5.30; at 6.30 send Alexey off to look for ptarmigan. Eat deerskin scraps. Yesterday morning ate my deerskin foot-nips. Light SSE airs. Not very cold. Under way at eight. In crossing creek three of us got wet. Built fire and dried out. Ahead again until eleven. Used up. Built fire. Made a drink out of the tea-leaves from alcohol bottle. On again at noon. Fresh SSW wind, drifting snow, very hard going. Lee begging to be left. Some little beach, and then long stretches of high bank. Ptarmigan tracks plentiful. Following Nindemann's tracks. At three halted, used up; crawled into a hole in the bank, collected wood and built fire. Alexey away in quest of game. Nothing for supper except a spoonful of glycerine. All hands weak and feeble, but cheerful. God help us.

October 11th, Tuesday. – One hundred and twenty-first day. SW gale with snow. Unable to move. No game. One spoonful glycerine and hot water for food. No more wood in our vicinity.

October 12th, Wednesday. – One hundred and twenty-second day. Breakfast; last spoonful glycerine and hot water. For dinner we tried a couple of handfuls of Arctic willow in a pot of water and drank the infusion. Everybody getting weaker and weaker. Hardly strength to get firewood. SW gale with snow.

October 13th, Thursday. – One hundred and twenty-third day. Willow tea. Strong SW wind. No news from Nindemann. We are in the hands of God, and unless He intervenes we are lost. We cannot move against the wind, and staying here means starvation. Afternoon went ahead for a mile, crossing either another river or a bend in the big one. After crossing, missed Lee. Went down in a hole in the bank and camped. Sent back for Lee. He had turned back, lain down, and was waiting to die. All united in saying Lord's Prayer and Creed after supper. Living gale of wind. Horrible night.

October 14th, Friday. – One hundred and twenty-fourth day. Breakfast, willow tea. Dinner, one half teaspoonful sweet oil and willow tea. Alexey shot one ptarmigan. Had soup. SW wind, moderating.

October 15th, Saturday. – One hundred and twenty-fifth day. Breakfast, willow tea and two old boots. Conclude to move on at sunrise. Alexey breaks down, also Lee. Come to empty grain raft. Halt and camp. Signs of smoke at twilight to southward.

October 16th, Sunday. – One hundred and twenty-sixth day. Alexey broken down. Divine service.

October 17th, Monday. – One hundred and twenty-seventh day. Alexey dying. Doctor baptized him. Read prayers for sick. Mr Collins' birthday – forty years old. About sunset Alexey died. Exhaustion from starvation. Covered him with ensign and laid him in the crib.

October 18th, Tuesday. – One hundred and twenty-eighth day. Calm and mild, snow falling. Buried Alexey in the afternoon. Laid him on the ice of the river, and covered him over with slabs of ice.

October 19th, Wednesday. – One hundred and twenty-ninth day. Cutting up tent to make foot gear. Doctor went ahead to find new camp. Shifted by dark.

October 20th, Thursday. – One hundred and thirtieth day. Bright and sunny, but very cold. Lee and Kaack done up.

October 21st, Friday. – One hundred and thirty-first day. Kaack was found dead about midnight between the doctor and myself. Lee died about noon. Read prayers for sick when we found he was going.

October 22nd, Saturday. – One hundred and thirty-second day. Too weak to carry the bodies of Lee and Kaack out on the ice. The doctor, Collins, and I carried them around the corner out of sight. Then my eye closed up.

October 23rd, Sunday. – One hundred and thirty-third day. Everybody pretty weak. Slept or rested all day, and then managed to get enough wood in before dark. Read part of divine service. Suffering in our feet. No foot gear.

October 24th, Monday. – One hundred and thirty-fourth day. A hard night.

October 25th, Tuesday. – One hundred and thirty-fifth day.

October 26th, Wednesday. – One hundred and thirty-sixth day.

October 27th, Thursday. – One hundred and thirty-seventh day. Iversen broken down.

October 28th, Friday. – One hundred and thirty-eighth day. Iversen died during early morning.

October 29th, Saturday. – One hundred and thirty-ninth day. Dressler died during night.

October 30th, Sunday. – One hundred and fortieth day. Boyd and Görtz died during night. Mr Collins dying.

It can only be supposed that De Long himself died soon after. The dreadful irony was that Nindemann and Noros did encounter local inhabitants, but lost several maddeningly frustrating days to a seemingly impenetrable language barrier; Nindemann simply could not make them understand that a disaster had befallen them, and that there were men in urgent need of help. As their colleagues lay dying, the record of their journey relates:

> Another day was spent in an incessant but fruitless attempt to make themselves understood, and on Thursday morning, October 27th, Nindemann sitting alone on his berth and thinking of everything, of their terrible march, of their helpless companions, and of the hopelessness of carrying any aid to them, could contain himself no longer, and broke into sobs and groans. A woman in the hut took pity on him, and began talking earnestly to one of the men, who came to Nindemann and said something about a commandant. By this time Nindemann had picked up a few words, and he begged the man to take them on to Bulun, for he was in despair of doing anything in this place. The man in reply again said something about the commandant, and held up five or six fingers. Then he made Nindemann understand that he would take him to Bulun on the morrow.

So, when the only chance for the dying men was for Nindemann to get back with help immediately, he had to keep travelling south to find someone who would understand him. When he reached Bulun, on 29 October, it was already too late.

At Bulun, Nindemann met Melville who, on hearing his story, immediately organized a party to search for and rescue any survivors of De Long's party. This search lasted for most of November and he failed to find the De Long party's last camp; but it was only one of several search expeditions that were then either under way or in preparation.

The apparent disappearance of the De Long expedition, after its departure in 1879, had two contrasting effects on James Gordon Bennett and the *New York Herald*. On the one hand, the absence of news from his representative on *Jeannette*, the reporter Jerome Collins, deprived him of stories about the voyage, which were his main reason for organizing it. On the other hand, the expedition's disappearance was in itself a source of good news stories, and the search for it an even better one. When, in 1881, the US Navy sent the ship *Rodgers* to search for the missing men, Bennett partly sponsored it, and put on board another of his reporters, William Henry Gilder. In 1882, when Bennett learned of Melville's survival, he sent one more reporter, John P. Jackson, overland from St Petersburg to get the story. The activities of these two men illustrate the more unseemly aspects of newspaper involvement in exploration, and shows that, in some circumstances, the sensational press was no more inhibited then than it is now. Gilder, already an accomplished Arctic traveller, was presented with one first-rate story when the *Rodgers* was destroyed by fire in December 1881. He was presented with many more when the captain of *Rodgers* sent him on a 2,500-mile sledge journey across Siberia to alert the naval authorities to the loss of their ship from the telegraph office in Irkutsk. But also, in true popular-press fashion, when by chance he encountered a courier carrying Melville's confidential despatches to the US Navy, he gained access to them and used them to report the story of the *Jeannette* tragedy.

If Gilder's behaviour was in rather poor taste, it was a trivial matter by comparison with Jackson's. On arrival in Irkutsk, Jackson interviewed one of the survivors, John Danenhower. From him, he obtained a whole series of stories of bad relations, quarrelling and incompetence among the officers and crew of *Jeannette*, as well as some lurid stories of the sinking of the ship, and the intolerable agonies suffered by the survivors as they struggled towards safety. Worse still, Jackson then travelled to the Lena delta with his companion, an artist working for the *Illustrated London News*, and dug up the bodies (which a search party had earlier buried) to obtain sketches of them and to search the body of the reporter Collins for letters he may have written to Bennett.

Jackson's tasteless reporting caused a public sensation in the US, and outrage in government circles. Naval and Congressional investigations were held in attempts to negate the effect of his revelations. A tragedy had occurred. Twenty men from a total of 33 had died in the most distressing circumstances, yet those men were stripped of their dignity and their enterprise ended in a public squabble. The publication of De Long's journals in 1883 restored some of that dignity, as did the restoration of the bodies of De Long and his companions to their homeland early in the following year. But from this point on, newspapers, craving sensation, paid close attention to all major expeditions, and became a powerful influence on the course of Arctic exploration. The age of the 'Open Polar Sea' had finally passed into oblivion, and the 'heroic age' of polar exploration, when professional adventurers began to seek fame and wealth through courageous deeds, had begun.

In the year following the deaths of De Long and his colleagues, another American expedition established a new record farthest north almost by accident. In 1881, the United States International Polar Year Expedition of 1881–4 set up a scientific station in Lady Franklin Bay, Ellesmere Island, with the aim of taking part in an international project, extending throughout the Arctic, to make meteorological and magnetic observations for one full year. The leader was the US Army officer Adolphus Washington Greely. In April–June 1882, another expedition member, Lieutenant James Booth Lockwood, explored the north coast of Greenland eastwards to a point beyond the farthest achieved by the British Arctic Expedition of 1875–6. He reached a small island that is now named after him, lying at 83°24'N, so he just exceeded the record established by Markham. Sadly, though, Lockwood suffered the same fate as De Long. Successive relief expeditions failed over several years to reach the Greely expedition, and 19 men, including Lockwood, died before six survivors were finally saved in 1884.

– 7 –

Fridtjof Nansen

1893–6

The interventions of Petermann and Nordenskiöld had given an international dimension, and a pinch of nationalistic spice, to the quest for the Pole, which had previously been almost exclusively a preoccupation of the English-speaking world. During the last few years of the nineteenth century, the international perspective widened still further; the number of expeditions trying to reach the Pole began to increase rapidly, and the quest for the Pole showed signs of becoming an exciting race between explorers of several nations, fuelled by patriotic pride, and observed with intensifying interest by the newspaper-reading public throughout Europe and North America. With the De Long expedition and others of the same era, James Gordon Bennett had demonstrated that adventure stories sell newspapers; when the attainment of the North Pole became a competitive event, newspapers took notice as never before, reported each expedition in the minutest detail, and also sponsored expeditions seeking the Pole to ensure the race was run to the last.

It was not only glory-seeking adventurers who benefited from the growth of public interest in the Arctic Ocean and the North Pole. Some distinguished scientists were also able to benefit, especially if they could add a popular element of heroic adventure to their otherwise entirely serious work. One such was the Norwegian zoologist and explorer Fridtjof Nansen, who in 1893–6 commanded an expedition to study the marine currents of the Arctic Ocean. But the element of heroic adventure associated with this expedition was no mere sideshow: the whole expedition was so imbued with wild, reckless adventure, that by any reasonable reckoning he should never have survived it.

Fridtjof Nansen was born to a prominent Norwegian family on 10 October 1861. By the early 1890s he already had a solid reputation as an Arctic scientist and explorer, with two expeditions to his credit. He began modestly enough, as zoologist on the sealer *Viking* in 1882, but then in 1888 he announced his presence on the Arctic scene with a flourish, by leading the first expedition to cross the island of Greenland. He made the crossing from east to west using skis and man-hauled sledges, and by doing so proved beyond further doubt that the Greenland ice cap covers the entire interior of the island. That expedition demonstrated clearly enough that Nansen was one of those few explorers who could successfully blend scientific research with popular adventure. When he offered the public a similar blend in 1893–6, he showed beyond question that no explorer in the world could remotely match his ability to present a serious scientific experiment as a spectacular, death-defying, insanely courageous adventure.

At the heart of Nansen's North Polar expedition was the discovery, in 1884, that relics from the *Jeannette* expedition had drifted ashore on the southwest coast of Greenland. One of Norway's leading oceanographers demonstrated that the relics (which included a document signed by De Long and some clothing marked with the names of *Jeannette*'s crew members) could only have got there by drifting across the Arctic Ocean from the New Siberian Islands to the Greenland Sea. To demonstrate the existence of this trans-polar current, Nansen proposed that a suitably strengthened ship should be deliberately beset in the ice near the New Siberian Islands, and that its small crew should simply wait on board and pass their time as best they could for the three, four, five, or however many years it took to drift past the Pole and out into open water between Greenland and Svalbard. The hull of the ship was to be of a special egg-shaped design, so that, when squeezed between ice floes, the ship would simply rise up onto the surface of the ice. Large sections of the polar research community greeted his plan with a critical reaction ranging from gentle scepticism through accusations of recklessness and foolhardiness, to open derision – and certainly the plan seemed to offend against some of the most basic rules of survival. One of Nansen's fiercest critics was A.W. Greely, whose own expedition had ended in such horrific circumstances a decade earlier. In an article published in 1893, he foresaw the inevitability of shipwreck, ensuing accidents, disease and starvation, and the consequent mental, moral and physical breakdown of the crew. But not every commentator considered the idea so foolhardy, and in Norway it was generally very warmly received. The Norwegian government, King Oscar II of Sweden and Norway, Norwegian businesses and the public at large all contributed generously to the expedition's funds, enabling Nansen to build his 800-ton ship *Fram* (meaning *Forward*), and set out from Oslo with a crew of 12 on 24 June 1893.

The initial stages of the expedition passed entirely according to plan. Nansen took the *Fram* through the waters of the Northeast Passage – Barents Sea, Kara Sea, Laptev Sea – to a position north of the New Siberian Islands, near where *Jeannette* had sunk, and by 25 September 1893 the ship was firmly locked in the ice at about 78°50'N. *Fram* behaved exactly as he had predicted: when the ice squeezed her, as it often did, she rode safely upwards; and from the outset, a slow, and at first erratic northerly drift began. And the crew cheerfully settled down into a programme of scientific observations. So far, Nansen was vindicated.

However, there was one aspect of the expedition that Nansen had quite failed to take into account: his own restless, endlessly questing mind. A problem that faced this expedition more than any other was that the ship did most of the work. *Fram* drifted with the current as expected, resisted the ice as expected; she did all that was asked of her, and the crew could only watch and admire. The prospect of five years or more of playing second lead to his own creation clearly discomfited Nansen, and after barely five months in the ice, he began yearning for a more active role.

Up to this point, the North Pole had been mentioned only incidentally in relation to this expedition. It was assumed that *Fram* would pass over, or near to the Pole during the course of her drift, but that had always been incidental to the expedition's primary scientific aims: the expected proximity to the Pole had had surprisingly little influence on Nansen's planning and public presentation of the expedition. But after a few months in the ice, Nansen the hard-headed scientist began to yield without resistance to Nansen the adventurer. In January

1894 he recorded some of his deepest thoughts and longings, and the drift of those thoughts towards the North Pole.

Monday, January 15th. There was pressure forward both this morning and towards noon, but we heard the loudest sounds from the north. Sverdrup, Mogstad, and Peter went in that direction and were stopped by a large open channel. Peter and I afterwards walked a long distance NNE, past a large opening that I had skirted before Christmas. It was shining, flat ice, splendid for sledging on, always better the farther north we went. The longer I wander about and see this sort of ice in all directions, the more strongly does a plan take hold of me that I have long had in my mind. It would be possible to get with dogs and sledges over this ice to the Pole, if one left the ship for good and made one's way back in the direction of Franz Josef Land, Spitzbergen, or the west coast of Greenland. It might almost be called an easy expedition for two men.

But it would be too hasty to go off in spring. We must first see what kind of drift the summer brings. And as I think over it, I feel doubtful if it would be right to go off and leave the others. Imagine if I came home and they did not! Yet it was to explore the unknown Polar regions that I came; it was for that the Norwegian people gave their money; and surely my first duty is to do that if I can. I must give the drift plan a longer trial yet, but if it takes us in a wrong direction, then there is nothing for it but to try the other, come what may.

Thursday, January 16th. The ice is quiet today. Does longing stupefy one, or does it wear itself out and turn at last into stolidity? Oh, that burning longing night and day was happiness! but now its fire has turned to ice. Why does home seem so far away? It is one's all-life, without it is so empty, so empty — nothing but dead emptiness. Is it the restlessness of spring that is beginning to come over one, the desire for action, for something different from this indolent, enervating life? Is the soul of man nothing but a succession of moods and feelings, shifting as incalculably as the changing winds? Perhaps my brain is over-tired; day and night my thoughts have turned on the one point, the possibility of reaching the Pole and getting home. Perhaps it is rest I need, to sleep, sleep! Am I afraid of venturing my life? No, it cannot be that. But what else then can be keeping me back? Perhaps a secret doubt of the practicability of the plan? My mind is confused; the whole thing has got into a tangle; I am a riddle to myself. I am worn out, and yet I do not feel any special tiredness. Is it perhaps because I sat up reading last night? Everything around is emptiness, and my brain is a blank. I look at the home pictures and am moved by them in a curious, dull way; I look into the future, and feel as if it does not much matter to me whether I get home in the autumn of this year or next. So long as I get home in the end, a year or two seem almost nothing. I have never thought this before. I have no inclination to read, nor to draw, nor to do anything else whatever. Folly! Shall I try a few pages of Schopenhauer? No, I will go to bed, though I am not sleepy. Perhaps, if the truth were known, I am longing now more than ever. The only thing that helps me is writing, trying to express myself on these pages, and then looking at myself as it were from the outside. Yes, man's life is nothing but a succession of moods, half memory and half hope.

Nansen maintained his resolve to give the drift a longer trial, but by autumn 1894 his mind was made up. *Fram's* slow drift was taking her on the expected route towards Svalbard and Greenland, but over 400 nautical miles away from the North Pole on the Russian side. He thought she would get closer than that, but not sufficiently close to satisfy his curiosity: he decided that the following spring he would leave the ship with one companion, 28 dogs, sledges, kayaks, and provisions for 100 days, and attempt to reach the Pole.

It is almost impossible not to think of Nansen's proposed journey as a crazy, reckless, foolhardy, virtually suicidal act of bravado. He planned to leave a moving ship, knowing he had no hope of finding it again, in an uncharted area of the Arctic Ocean, sledge to the Pole, then return over unknown ice conditions to either Franz Josef Land or Svalbard, both uninhabited and over 500 miles away, and with only kayaks,

flimsy inshore vessels, to carry them over open sea, in the vague
hope of finding some explorer or hunter to rescue them. Such
terrible risks, just for the glory of priority at the Pole? Yet
Nansen chose not to think of it, or present it, as a quest for
glory, or as something particularly risky, but rather as a serious
and sober scientific investigation to determine the nature of the
Arctic Ocean in areas nearer the Pole than *Fram* would reach.
On 16 November 1894, he discussed his thoughts with *Fram*'s
captain, Otto Sverdrup.

Friday, November 16th. In the forenoon I went out with
Sverdrup on snow-shoes in the moonlight, and we talked
seriously of the prospects of our drift and of the proposed
expedition northwards over the ice in the spring. In the
evening we went into the matter more thoroughly in his
cabin. I stated my views, in which he entirely coincided.
I have of late been meditating a great deal on what is
the proper course to pursue, supposing the drift does
not take us so far north by the month of March as I
had anticipated. But the more I think of it, the more
firmly am I persuaded that it is the thing to do. For if it
be right to set out at 85°, it must be no less right to set
out at 82° or 83°. In either case we should penetrate into
more northerly regions than we should otherwise reach,
and this becomes all the more desirable if the *Fram* herself
does not get so far north as we had hoped. If we cannot
actually reach the Pole, why, we must turn back before
reaching it. The main consideration, as I must constantly
repeat, is not to reach that exact mathematical point, but
to explore the unknown parts of the Polar Sea, whether
these be near to or more remote from the Pole. I said
this before setting out, and I must keep it continually in
mind. Certainly there are many important observations to
be made on board during the further drift of the ship,
many which I would dearly like to carry on myself; but
all the more important of these will be made equally well
here, even though two of our number leave the ship; and
there can scarcely be any doubt that the observations we
shall make farther north will not many times outweigh in
value those I could have made during the remainder of

the time on board. So far, then, *it is absolutely desirable that we set out.*

Nansen's chosen companion was Hjalmar Johansen (1867–1913), another intrepid adventurer who, despite his naval reserve rank of lieutenant, joined the *Fram* as stoker, so keen was he to take part. In March 1895, with *Fram* at about 84°04′N, and after two false starts in February, they left *Fram* to begin their Pole journey.

AT last by mid-day, on March 14th, we finally left the *Fram*, to the noise of a thundering salute. For the third time farewells and mutual good wishes were exchanged. Some of our comrades came a little way with us, but Sverdrup soon turned back in order to be on board for dinner at 1 o'clock. It was on the top of a hummock that we two said goodbye to each other; the *Fram* was lying behind us, and I can remember how I stood watching him as he strode easily homewards on his snow-shoes. I half wished I could turn back with him and find myself again in the warm saloon; I knew only too well that a life of toil lay before us, and that it would be many a long day before we should again sleep and eat under a comfortable roof; but that that time was going to be so long as it really proved to be, none of us then had any idea. We all thought that either the expedition would succeed, and that we should return home that same year, or – that it would not succeed.

To begin with, they had good going and made distances of up to 20 miles a day; by 29 March they were already at 85°09′N, but also they had begun to experience some minor mishaps. On the 30th a team of dogs and a sledge fell into a deep crack in the ice and had to be hauled out; on the 31st, Johansen fell through the ice and froze both his legs; but most ominously, on 1 April, they walked for so long that they forgot to wind up their chronometers. Johansen's had stopped, but Nansen's was still ticking and they simply had to hope that it was still accurate. This could have been their undoing: without chronometers they would not have been able to calculate their longitude, and so would be unable to know in which direction to head for land. Also, just as depressing for Nansen, the ice conditions were getting worse; and, without apparently realizing it at first, he was beginning to experience the same phenomenon that had so frustrated Parry: the dreaded southerly drift.

Wednesday, April 3rd. Got under way yesterday about three in the afternoon. The snow was in first-rate condition after the southeast wind, which continued blowing till late in the day. The ice was tolerably passable, and everything looked more promising; the weather was fine, and we made good progress. But after several level tracts with old humpy ice, came some very uneven ones, intersected by lanes and pressure-ridges as usual. Matters did not grow any better as time went on, and at midnight or soon after we were stopped by some bad ice and a newly frozen lane which would not bear. As we should have had to make a long detour, we encamped, and Russen was killed (this was the second dog to go). The meat was divided into 26 portions, but eight dogs refused it, and had to be given pemmican. The ice ahead does not look inviting. These ridges are enough to make one despair, and there seems to be no prospect of things bettering. I turned out at midday and took a meridian observation, which makes us in 85°59′N. It is astonishing that we have not got farther; we seem to toil all we can, but without much progress. Beginning to doubt seriously of the advisability of continuing northwards much longer. It is three times as far to Franz Josef Land as the distance we have now come. How may the ice be in that direction? We can hardly count on its being better than here, or our progress quicker. Then, too, the shape and extent of Franz Josef Land are unknown, and may cause us considerable delay, and perhaps we shall not be able to find any game just at once. I have long seen that it is impossible to reach the Pole itself or its immediate vicinity over such ice as this, and with these dogs. If only we had more of them! What would I not give now to have the Olenek dogs? We must turn sooner or later. But as it is only a question of time, could we not turn it to better account in Franz Josef Land than by travelling over this drift-ice, which we have now had a good opportunity of learning to know? In all probability it will be exactly the same right to the Pole. We cannot hope to reach any considerable distance higher before time compels us to turn. We certainly ought not to wait much longer.

Nansen's decision came just five days later.

Monday, April 8th. No, the ice grew worse and worse, and we got no way. Ridge after ridge, and nothing but rubble to travel over. We made a start at two o'clock or so this morning, and kept at it as long as we could, lifting the sledges all the time; but it grew too bad at last. I went on a good way ahead on snow-shoes, but saw no reasonable prospect of advance, and from the highest hummocks only the same kind of ice was to be seen. It was a veritable chaos of ice-blocks, stretching as far as the horizon. There is not much sense in keeping on longer; we are sacrificing valuable time and doing little. If there be much more such ice between here and Franz Josef Land, we shall, indeed, want all the time we have.

I therefore determined to stop, and shape our course for Cape Fligely.

On this northernmost camping-ground we indulged in a banquet, consisting of lobscouse, bread-and-butter, dry chocolate, stewed 'tytlebær', or red whortleberries, and our hot whey drink, and then, with a delightful and unfamiliar feeling of repletion, crept into the dear bag, our best friend. I took a meridian observation yesterday, by which I see that we should be in latitude 86°10'N, or thereabouts.

Later, he corrected his latitude to 86°13'06" – a new record by nearly 3 degrees.

The first stages of the journey south were marked by surprisingly good travelling conditions, but they continued to experience minor setbacks, some of them self-inflicted.

Thursday, April 11th. Better and better. Found nothing but beautiful level tracts of ice yesterday, with a few ridges, which were easy to get over, and some lanes, with young

ice on, which gave us rather more trouble. They ran,
however, about in our direction (our course is now the
magnetic S. 22° W, or about the true WSW), and we could
go alongside them. At last, however, we had to make a
crossing, and accomplished it successfully, although the ice
bent under us and our sledges more than was desirable.
Late in the afternoon we came across a channel, which
we proposed to cross in the same way. We reached the
other side with the first sledge safely enough, but not so
with the other. Hardly had the leaders of the team got out
to the dangerous place where the ice was thinnest, and
where some water was on the surface, when they stopped
and warily dipped their paws in the water. Then through
went one of them, splashing and struggling to get out. The
ice began to sink under the weight of the other dogs and the
sledge, and the water came flowing up. I dragged dogs and
sledge back as quickly as possible, and succeeded in driving
them all on to the firm ice again in safety. We tried once
again at another place, I running over first on snow-shoes
and calling to the dogs, and Johansen pushing behind, but
the result was no better than the first time, as 'Suggen' fell
in, and we had to go back. Only after a long detour, and
very much fagged, did we finally succeed in getting the
two last sledges over. We were lucky in finding a good
camping-place, and had the warmest night and the most
comfortable (I might almost say cosy) morning – spent,
be it said, in repairs – that we have had on the trip. I
think we did the longest day's march yesterday that we
have yet achieved: about 15 miles. Two in the afternoon,
−17·6° Fahr. (−27·6°C).

Saturday, April 13th. We have traversed nothing but good
ice for three days. If this goes on, the return journey
will be quicker than I thought. I do not understand this
sudden change in the nature of the ice. Can it be that
we are travelling in the same direction with the trend
of the ridges and irregularities, so that now we go along
between them instead of having to make our way over
them? The lanes we have come across seem all to point
to this; they follow our course pretty closely. We had the

misfortune yesterday to let our watches run down; the time between our getting into the bag on the previous night and encamping yesterday was too long. Of course we wound them up again, but the only thing I can now do to find Greenwich mean time is to take a time-observation and an observation for latitude, and then estimate the approximate distance from our turning-point on April 8th, when I took the last observation for longitude. By this means the error will hardly be great.

This last comment was sheer wishful thinking. The problem of longitude was later to be a major source of worry. They continued south over the ice for nearly two more months, then at the beginning of June stopped for nearly a week to repair their kayaks, which would soon be needed as they approached open water. By then, there were increasing signs of the proximity of land, but they could not see land, and the longitude problem came to the fore. On 5–6 June, Nansen voiced his frustration.

I have just reckoned out our longitude according to an observation taken with the theodolite yesterday, and make it to be 61°16·5′E; our latitude was 82°17·0′N. I cannot understand why we do not see land. The only possible explanation must be that we are farther east than we think, and that the land stretches southwards in that direction, but we cannot have much farther to go now. Just at this moment a bird flew over us which Johansen, who is standing just outside the tent, took to be a kind of sandpiper.

Thursday, June 6th. Still on the same spot. I am longing to get off, see what things look like, and have a final solution of this riddle which is constantly before me. It will be a real pleasure to be under way again with whole tackle, and I cannot help thinking that we shall soon be able to use our kayaks in open water. Life would be another thing then! Fancy, to get clear for good of this ice and these lanes, this toil with the sledges, and endless trouble with the dogs, only oneself in a light craft dancing over the waves at play! It is almost too much to think of. Perhaps we have still many a hard turn before we reach it, many a dark hour; but some time it must come, and then – then life will be life again!

But there were still grave difficulties to overcome before life became life again. As they moved away from the smoother, continuous ice of the central Arctic Ocean, they approached much more difficult conditions on the fringes of the polar pack where lanes of open water added to the hazards. Nansen's frustration deepened.

Wednesday, June 12th. This is getting worse and worse. Yesterday we did nothing, hardly advanced more than a mile. Wretched snow, uneven ice, lanes, and villainous weather stopped us. There was certainly a crust on the snow, on which the sledges ran well when they were on it; but when they broke through – and they did it constantly – they stood immovable. This crust, too, was bad for the dogs, poor things! They sank through it into the deep snow between the irregularities, and it was like swimming through slush for them. But all the same we made way. Lanes stopped us, it is true, but we cleared them somehow. Over one of them, the last, which looked nasty, we got by making a bridge of small floes, which we guided to the narrowest place. But then a shameless storm of wet snow, or more correctly sleet, with immense flakes, set in, and the wind increased. We could not see our way in this labyrinth of lanes and hummocks, and were as soaked as ducked crows, as we say. The going was impossible, and the sledges as good as immovable in the wet snow, which was soon deep enough to cling to our snow-shoes underneath in great lumps, and prevent them from running. There was hardly any choice but to find a camping ground as soon as possible, for to force one's way along in such weather, and on such snow, and make no progress, was of little use. We found a good camping ground and pitched our tent after only four hours' march, and went without our dinner to make up.

Here we are, then, hardly knowing what to do next. What the going is like outside I do not know yet, but probably not much better than yesterday, and whether we ought to push on the little we can, or go out and try to capture a seal, I cannot decide.

Within ten days, though, Nansen's mood changed completely. The returning signs of wildlife about them, heralding the presence of land, became unmistakable. On 21 June, in an incident fraught with danger, they caught their first seal. In the frenzy of the hunt, with both men thinking of nothing but Nansen's pursuit of the seal, their two kayaks, lashed together with Johansen sitting in one of them, began to drift away from their floe, dragging the sledge with them. This caused Johansen's kayak to heel over, fill with water and begin to sink. For a moment, both men faced the catastrophic loss of all their most essential possessions: ammunition, powder, cooking apparatus, matches, and remaining food. But together they managed to bring the kayaks and their gear to safety, and they still had their seal. Nansen brightened greatly.

Saturday, June 22nd. Half-past nine a.m., after a good breakfast of seal's-flesh, seal-liver, blubber and soup.

Here I lie dreaming dreams of brightness; life is all sunshine again. What a little incident is necessary to change the whole aspect of affairs! Yesterday and the last few days were dull and gloomy; everything seemed hopeless, the ice impassable, no game to be found; and then comes the incident of a seal rising near our kayaks and rolling about round us. Johansen has time to give it a ball just as it is disappearing, and it floats while I harpoon it – the first and only bearded seal (*Phoca barbata*) we have yet seen – and we have abundance of food and fuel for upwards of a month. We need hurry no longer; we can settle down, adapt the kayaks and sledges better for ferrying over the lanes, capture seals if possible, and await a change in the state of the ice. We have eaten our fill both at supper and breakfast, after being ravenous for many days. The future seems bright and certain now, no clouds of darkness to be seen any longer.

That same day, the two men agreed to stay in camp in that same place to await better travelling conditions:

It is my opinion that for the time being we can do nothing
better than remain where we are: live on our catch without
encroaching on the sledge provisions, and thus await the
time when the ice shall slacken more or the condition of
the snow improve. Meanwhile we will rig up wooden grips
on our sledges, and try to make the kayaks watertight.
Furthermore we will lighten our equipment as much as we
possibly can. If we were to go on we should only be obliged
to leave a great deal of our meat and blubber behind us, and
this, in these circumstances, I think would be madness.

Their wait for improved conditions proved longer than expected;
the next month demanded the utmost patience; they yearned
to head for land and their campsite became known to them as
'Longing Camp'. Finally, on 23 July, they were able to start
moving again, both on foot and by kayak. On the next day:

Wednesday, July 24th. At last the marvel has come to pass —
land, land, and after we had almost given up our belief in
it! After nearly two years, we again see something rising
above that never-ending white line on the horizon yonder
— a white line which for countless ages has stretched over
this lonely sea, and which for millenniums to come shall
stretch in the same way. We are leaving it, and leaving no
trace behind us; for the track of our little caravan across
the endless plains has long ago disappeared. A new life is
beginning for us; for the ice it is ever the same.

It has long haunted our dreams, this land, and now it
comes like a vision, like fairyland. Drift-white, it arches
above the horizon like distant clouds, which one is afraid
will disappear every minute. The most wonderful thing is
that we have seen this land all the time without knowing
it. I examined it several times with the telescope from
'Longing Camp' in the belief that it might be snowfields, but
always came to the conclusion that it was only clouds, as I
could never discover any dark point. Then, too, it seemed
to change form, which, I suppose, must be attributed to
the mist which always lay over it; but it always came
back again at the same place with its remarkable regular
curves.

They still had several weeks of struggle before them, though; and in one incident, on 5 August, Nansen nearly lost his companion for good. Johansen, the victim, tells the story best.

Nansen had just brought his sledge to the edge of the water and stood holding it, as the ice inclined down towards the water. My sledge and kayak were standing a little way back, and I went across to fetch it. I leant down to pick up the drag-rope, when I suddenly observed an animal just behind the kayak. I thought at first that it was 'Suggen' [one of the dogs], but the next moment I discovered that it was not he, but a bear sitting in a crouching position ready to spring at me. Before I had time to get up from my stooping position, it was right upon me, pressing me backwards with its two legs down a slight incline to a fresh-water pool. The bear then dealt me a blow on the right cheek with one of its powerful fore-paws, making the bones rattle in my head, but fortunately it did not stun me. I fell over on my back, and there I lay between the bear's legs. 'Get the gun,' I shouted to Nansen, who was behind me, while at the same instant I saw the butt end of my own loaded gun sticking out of the kayak by my side, my fingers itching to get hold of it. I saw the bear's jaws gaping just over my head, and the terrible teeth glistening. As I fell I had seized the brute's throat with one hand, and held on to it for dear life. The bear was somewhat taken aback at this. It could not be a seal, it must have thought, but some strange creature to which it was unaccustomed – and to this slight delay I no doubt owed my life. I had been waiting for Nansen to shoot, and I noticed the bear was looking in his direction. Thinking that Nansen was taking his time, I shouted to him as I lay in the bear's embrace, 'Look sharp, or you'll be too late.' The bear lifted one of its paws a little, and strode across me, giving 'Suggen', who stood close by barking, and watching us, a blow which sent him sprawling and howling over the ice. 'Caiaphas' was served in the same way. I had let go my hold of the bear's throat and, taking advantage of the bear's inattention, I wriggled myself away from between its paws. Getting on my legs I seized my gun, when Nansen fired two shots and the bear fell down dead beside the pool.

Nansen had, of course, made haste to my assistance, but
when he saw me lying under the bear and went to get his
gun, which was lying in its case on the top of the kayak,
the sledge with the kayak slipped right out into the water.
There I lay under the bear, and there stood Nansen, and out
on the kayak lay the gun. His first thought was to throw
himself into the water and to fire from over the kayak, but
he soon gave up this idea, as he might just as likely hit
me as the bear. He had then to begin and pull the whole
concern up onto the ice again, which did not, of course,
take up much time, but to me, situated as I was, it was an
age. The bear fell down dead at the first charge.

Remarkably, Johansen survived the attack with only very trivial
superficial wounds.

Ten days later, on 14 August, they finally experienced the joy
of land beneath their feet, after fully two years at sea. But even
at the height of their celebration, the longitude problem came
again to the fore: they had no idea where they were.

In the evening we at last reached the islands we had been
steering for for the last few days, and for the first time for
two years had bare land under foot. The delight of the
feeling of being able to jump from block to block of granite
is indescribable, and the delight was not lessened when in
a little sheltered corner among the stones we found moss
and flowers, beautiful poppies (*Papaver nudicaule*), *Saxifraga
nivalis*, and a *Stellaria* (*sp*?). It goes without saying that the
Norwegian flag had to wave over this our first bare land,
and a banquet was prepared. Our petroleum, meanwhile,
had given out several days previously, and we had to
contrive another lamp in which train-oil could be used.
The smoking hot lobscouse, made of pemmican and the
last of our potatoes, was delicious, and we sat inside the tent
and kicked the bare grit under us to our hearts' content.

Where we are is becoming more and more incomprehensible. There appears to be a broad sound west of us,
but what is it? The island we are now on, and where
we have slept splendidly (this is written on the morning
of August 16th) on dry land, with no melting of the ice

in puddles underneath us, is a long moraine-like ridge running about north and south (magnetic), and consists almost exclusively of small and large – generally very large – blocks of stone, with, I should say, occasional stationary crags. The blocks are in a measure rounded off, but I have found no striation on them. The whole island barely rises above the snow-field in which it lies, and which slopes in a gradual decline down to the surrounding ice. On our west there is a bare island, somewhat higher, which we have seen for several days. Along the shore there is a decided strand-line (terrace). North of us are two small islets and a small rock or skerry.

As I mentioned before (August 13th) I had at first supposed the sound on our west to be Rawlinson's Sound, but this now appeared impossible as there was nothing to be seen of Dove Glacier, by which it is bounded on one side. If this was now our position, we must have traversed the glacier and Wilczek Land without noticing any trace of either; for we had travelled westwards a good half degree south of Cape Buda-Pesth. The possibility that we could be in this region we consequently now held to be finally excluded. We must have come to a new land in the western part of Franz Josef Land or Archipelago, and so far west that we had seen nothing of the countries discovered by Payer. But so far west that we had not even seen anything of Oscar's Land, which ought to be situated in 82°N and 52°E? This was indeed incomprehensible; but was there any other explanation?

They were lost, but nonetheless they were experiencing a measure of good fortune seldom granted to polar explorers. They had been foolish to leave the ship; they had been recklessly careless in letting their chronometers wind down and stop; when killing their seal, they had nearly lost Johansen's kayak; and Johansen had been extremely lucky to survive the bear attack with scarcely a scratch. It was pure chance that they had found land at all. In ordinary circumstances, any other explorer would have been dead by now; but Nansen appeared to live a singularly charmed life; the luck was always on his side, and much more was to come.

Nansen had guessed correctly that they were in Franz Josef Land, though they were not in the western part, but in the far northeast on an unknown island that Nansen subsequently named after his wife and daughter, Eva and Liv. Later, he changed his mind, and decided they were in the unexplored far northeast of Svalbard; in either event, their best course would be to the south and west, hoping to reach either Eira Harbour, in the southwest of Franz Josef Land, where he knew there was a hut left by an earlier British expedition, or Spitsbergen, where there were many huts and, in summer, many ships.

During the next few days they paddled their kayaks south-westward through the Franz Josef Land archipelago with those hopes in mind, but on 28 August, with autumn rapidly approaching, Nansen chose to stop and build a comfortable winter hut on an island in the central northern part of the archipelago, which he later named 'Jackson Island' (Ostrov Dzheksona). There, he and Johansen built a hut of stone plugged with moss and earth, and covered with a roof of walrus-hide, supported by driftwood. There, they spent an uncomfortable winter, with bear meat as their staple food and walrus blubber for fuel. The high point of their enforced detention was Christmas, which they celebrated as best they could; but for them the festivities extended to little more than a wash, a change of shirt, a brief change of diet, and a dream of home.

Tuesday, December 24th. At 2 p.m. today −24°C (11.2° below zero Fahr.). And this is Christmas Eve, cold and windy out of doors, and cold and draughty indoors. How desolate it is! Never before have we had such a Christmas Eve.

At home the bells are now ringing Christmas in. I can hear their sound as it swings through the air from the church tower. How beautiful it is!

Now the candles are being lighted on the Christmas trees, the children are let in and dance round in joyous delight. I must have a Christmas party for children when I get home. This is the time of rejoicing, and there is feasting in every cottage at home. And we are keeping the festival in our little way. Johansen has turned his shirt, and put the outside shirt next him; I have done the same, and then I have changed my drawers, and put on the others that I had wrung out in warm water. And I have washed myself, too, in a quarter of a cup of warm water, with the discarded drawers as sponge and towel. Now I feel quite another being; my clothes do not stick to my body as much as they did. Then for supper we had 'fiskegratin', made of powdered fish and maize-meal, with train-oil to it instead of butter, both fried and boiled (one as dry as the other), and for dessert we had bread fried in train-oil. Tomorrow morning we are going to have chocolate and bread.

Wednesday, December 25th. We have got lovely Christmas weather, hardly any wind, and such bright, beautiful moonlight. It gives one quite a solemn feeling. It is the peace of thousands of years. In the afternoon the northern lights were exceptionally beautiful. When I came out at six o'clock there was a bright, pale yellow bow in the southern sky. It remained for a long time almost unchanged, and then began to grow much brighter at the upper margin of the bow behind the mountain crests in the east. It smouldered for some time, and then all at once light darted out westwards along the bow; streamers shot up all along it towards the zenith, and in an instant the whole of the southern sky from the arc to the zenith was aflame. It flickered and blazed, it whirled round like a whirlwind (moving with the sun), rays darted backwards and forwards, now red and reddish-violet, now yellow, green, and dazzling white; now the rays were red at the bottom, and yellow and green farther up, and then again this order was inverted. Higher and higher it rose; now it came on the north side of the zenith too, for a moment there was a splendid corona, and then it all became one whirling mass of fire up there; it was like a whirlpool of fire in red, yellow, and green, and the eye was dazzled with looking at it. It then drew across to the northern sky, where it remained a long time, but not in such brilliancy. The arc from which it had sprung in the south was still visible, but soon disappeared. The movement of the rays was chiefly from west to east, but sometimes the reverse. It afterwards flared up brightly several times in the northern sky; I counted as many as six parallel bands at one time, but they did not attain to the brightness of the former ones.

And this is Christmas Day. There are family dinners going on at home. I can see the dignified old father standing smiling and happy in the doorway to welcome children and grandchildren. Out of doors the snow is falling softly and silently in big flakes, the young folk come rushing in fresh and rosy, stamp the snow off their feet in the passage, shake their things and hang them up, and then enter the drawing-room, where the fire is crackling comfortably and cosily in the stove; and they can see the snowflakes falling outside, and covering the Christmas corn-sheaf. A delicious smell of roasting comes from the kitchen, and in the dining-room the long table is laid for a good, old-fashioned dinner with good old wine. How nice and comfortable everything is! One might fall ill with longing to be home. But wait, wait, when summer comes . . .

Oh, the road to the stars is both long and difficult.

On 19 May 1896 they were able to start out again, hauling sledges (the sledge-dogs had long since been killed as fodder for each other), heading southwest. They now believed they were on 'Gillies Land' (also known as 'White Island'; now Kvitøya), an island in the extreme northeast of Svalbard, and they thought they were walking towards Spitsbergen. Later they were able to take to their kayaks, but after doing so they committed yet another act of carelessness that should have meant the end of them. On 12 June, Nansen recorded:

In the evening we put in to the edge of the ice, so as to stretch our legs a little; they were stiff with sitting in the kayak all day, and we wanted to get a little view over the water to the west, by ascending a hummock. As we went ashore the question arose as to how we should moor our precious vessel. 'Take one of the braces,' said Johansen; he was standing on the ice. 'But is it strong enough?' 'Yes,' he answered; 'I have used it as a halyard on my sledge-sail all the time.' 'Oh, well, it doesn't require much to hold these light kayaks,' said I, a little ashamed of having been so timid, and I moored them with the halyard, which was a strap cut from a raw walrus-hide. We had been on the ice a little while, moving up and down close to the kayaks. The wind had dropped considerably, and seemed to be more westerly, making it doubtful whether we could make use of it any longer, and we went up on to a hummock close by to ascertain this better.

As we stood there, Johansen suddenly cried: 'I say! the kayaks are adrift!' We ran down as hard as we could. They were already a little way out, and were drifting quickly off; the painter had given way. 'Here, take my watch!' I said to Johansen, giving it to him; and as quickly as possible I threw off some clothing, so as to be able to swim more easily: I did not dare to take everything off, as I might so easily get cramp. I sprang into the water, but the wind was off the ice, and the light kayaks, with their high rigging, gave it a good hold. They were already well out, and were drifting rapidly. The water was icy cold, it was hard work swimming with clothes on, and the kayaks drifted farther and farther, often quicker than I could swim. It seemed more than doubtful whether I could manage it. But all our hope was drifting there; all we possessed was on board; we had not even a knife with us; and whether I got cramp and sank here, or turned back without the kayaks, it would come to pretty much the same thing; so I exerted myself to the utmost. When I got tired I turned over, and swam on my back, and then I could see Johansen walking restlessly up and down on the ice. Poor lad! He could not stand still, and thought it dreadful not to be able to do anything. He had not much hope that I could do it, but it would not improve matters in the least if he threw himself into the water too. He said afterwards that these were the worst moments he had ever lived through. But when I turned over again, and saw that I was nearer the kayaks, my courage rose, and I redoubled my exertions. I felt, however, that my limbs were gradually stiffening and losing all feeling, and I knew that in a short time I should not be able to move them. But there was not far to go now; if I could only hold out a little longer, we should be saved — and I went on. The strokes became more and more feeble, but the distance became shorter and shorter, and I began to think I should reach the kayaks. At last I was able to stretch out my hand to the snow-shoe, which lay across the sterns; I grasped it, pulled myself in to the edge of the kayak – and we were saved. I tried to pull myself up, but the whole of my body was so stiff with cold, that this was an impossibility. For a moment I thought that after all it was too late; I was to get so far, but not be able to get in. After a little, however, I managed to swing one leg up on to the edge of the sledge which lay on the deck, and in this way managed to tumble up. There I sat, but so stiff with cold, that I had difficulty in paddling. Nor was it easy to paddle in the double vessel, where I first had to take one or two strokes on one side, and then step into the other kayak to take a few strokes on the other side. If I had been able to separate them, and row in one while I towed the other, it would have been easy enough; but I could not undertake that piece of work, for I should have been stiff before it was done; the thing to be done was to keep warm by rowing as hard as I could. The cold had robbed my whole body of feeling, but when the gusts of wind came they seemed to go right through me as I stood there in my thin, wet woollen shirt. I shivered, my teeth chattered, and I was numb almost all over; but I could still use the paddle, and I should get warm when I got back on to the ice again.

Two auks were lying close to the bow, and the thought of having auk for supper was too tempting; we were in want of food now. I got hold of my gun, and shot them with one discharge. Johansen said afterwards that he started at the report, thinking some accident had happened, and could not understand what I was about out there, but when he saw me paddle and pick up two birds he thought I had gone out of my mind. At last I managed to reach the edge of the ice, but the current had driven me a long way from our landing-place. Johansen came along the edge of the ice, jumped into the kayak beside me, and we soon got back to our place. I was undeniably a good deal exhausted, and could barely manage to crawl on land. I could scarcely stand, and while I shook and trembled all over Johansen had to pull off the wet things I had on, put on the few dry ones I still had in reserve, and spread the sleeping-bag out upon the ice. I packed myself well into it, and he covered me with the sail and everything he could find to keep out the cold air. There I lay shivering for a long time, but gradually the warmth began to return to my body.

The magic charm that had followed Nansen from the very beginning of *Fram*'s ice drift, and throughout his journey with Johansen, had shown itself yet again in this incident. His gift was not that he could do no wrong; rather that he could repeatedly do wrong, make fatal mistakes, and get away with it. But nothing that had gone before could remotely match the miracle that occurred a few days later, as their fight for survival reached its climax.

It was past midday on June 17th when I turned out to prepare breakfast. I had been down to the edge of the ice to fetch salt water, had made up the fire, cut up the meat, and put it in the pot, and had already taken off one boot preparatory to creeping into the bag again, when I saw that the mist over the land had risen a little since the preceding day. I thought it would be as well to take the opportunity of having a look round, so I put on my boot again, and went up on to a hummock near to look at the land beyond. A gentle breeze came from the land, bearing with it a confused noise of thousands of bird-voices from the mountain there. As I listened to these sounds of life and movement, watched flocks of auks flying to and fro above my head, and as my eye followed the line of coast, stopping at the dark, naked cliffs, glancing at the cold, icy plains and glaciers in a land which I believed to be unseen by any human eye and untrodden by any human foot, reposing in arctic majesty behind its mantle of mist – a sound suddenly reached my ear, so like the barking of a dog, that I started. It was only a couple of barks, but it could not be anything else. I strained my ears, but heard no more, only the same bubbling noise of thousands of birds. I must have been mistaken, after all; it was only birds I had heard; and again my eye passed from sound to island in the west. Then the barking came again, first single barks, then full cry; there was one deep bark, and one sharper; there was no longer any room for doubt.

At that moment, I remembered having heard two reports the day before, which I thought sounded like shots, but I had explained them away as noises in the ice. I now shouted to Johansen that I heard dogs farther inland. Johansen started up from the bag where he lay sleeping, and tumbled out of the tent. 'Dogs?' He could not quite take it in, but had to get up and listen with his own ears, while I got breakfast ready. He very much doubted the possibility of such a thing, yet fancied once or twice that he heard something which might be taken for the barking of dogs; but then it was drowned again in the bird-noises, and, everything considered, he thought that what I had heard was nothing more than that. I said he might believe what he liked, but I meant to set off as quickly as possible, and was impatient to get breakfast swallowed. I had emptied the last of the Indian meal into the soup, feeling sure that we should have farinaceous food enough by the evening. As we were eating we discussed who it could be, whether our countrymen or Englishmen. If it was the English expedition to Franz Josef Land which had been in contemplation when we started, what should we do? 'Oh, we'll just have to remain with them a day or two,' said Johansen, 'and then we'll have to go on to Spitzbergen, else it will be too long before we get home.' We were quite agreed on this point; but we would take care to get some good provisions for the voyage out of them. While I went on, Johansen was to stay behind and mind the kayaks, so that we should run no risk of their drifting away with the ice. I got out my snow-shoes, glass, and gun, and was ready. Before starting, I went up once more to listen, and look out a road across the uneven ice to the land. But there was not a sound like the barking of dogs, only noisy auks, harsh-toned little auks, and screaming kittiwakes. Was it these, after all, that I had heard? I set off in doubt.

Then in front of me I saw the fresh tracks of an animal. They could hardly have been made by a fox, for if they were, the foxes here must be bigger than any I had ever seen. But dogs? Could a dog have been no more than a few hundred paces from us in the night without barking, or without our having heard it? It seemed scarcely probable; but whatever it was, it could never have been a fox. A wolf, then? I went on, my mind full of strange thoughts, hovering between certainty and doubt. Was all our toil, were all our troubles, privations, and sufferings, to end here? It seemed incredible, and yet . . . Out of the shadowland of doubt, certainty was at last beginning to dawn. Again the sound of a dog yelping reached my ear, more distinctly than ever; I saw more and more tracks which could be nothing but those of a dog. Among them were foxes' tracks and how small they looked! A long time passed, and nothing was to be heard but the noise of the birds. Again arose doubt as to whether it was all an illusion. Perhaps it was only a dream. But then I remembered the dogs' tracks; they, at any rate, were no delusion. But if there were people here, we could scarcely be on Gillies Land or a new land, as we had believed all the winter. We must after all be upon the south side of Franz Josef Land, and the suspicion I had had a few days ago was correct, namely, that we had come south through an unknown sound and out between Hooker Island and Northbrook Island, and were now off the latter, in spite of the impossibility of reconciling our position with Payer's map.

It was with a strange mixture of feelings that I made my way in towards land among the numerous hummocks and inequalities. Suddenly I thought I heard a shout from a human voice, a strange voice, the first for three years. How my heart beat, and the blood rushed to my brain, as I ran up on to a hummock, and hallooed with all the strength of my lungs. Behind that one human voice in the midst of the icy desert, this one message from life, stood home and she who was waiting there; and I saw nothing else as I made my way between bergs and ice-ridges. Soon I heard another shout, and saw, too, from an ice-ridge, a dark form moving among the hummocks farther in. It was a dog; but farther off came another figure, and that was a man. Who was it? Was it Jackson or one of his companions, or was it perhaps a fellow-countryman? We approached one another quickly; I waved my hat: he did the same. I heard him speak to the dog, and I listened. It was English, and as I drew nearer I thought I recognized Mr Jackson, whom I remembered once to have seen.

I raised my hat; we extended a hand to one another, with a hearty 'How do you do?' Above us a roof of mist, shutting out the world around, beneath our feet the rugged, packed drift-ice, and in the background a glimpse of the land, all ice, glacier, and mist. On one side the civilized European in an English check suit and high rubber water-boots, well shaved, well groomed, bringing with him a perfume of scented soap, perceptible to the wild man's sharpened senses; on the other side the wild man, clad in dirty rags, black with oil and soot, with long, uncombed hair and shaggy beard, black with smoke, with a face in which the natural fair complexion could not possibly be discerned through the thick layer of fat and soot which a winter's endeavours with warm water, moss, rags, and at last a knife had sought in vain to remove. No one suspected who he was or whence he came.

Jackson: 'I'm immensely glad to see you.'

'Thank you, I also.'

'Have you a ship here?'

'No; my ship is not here.'

'How many are there of you?'

'I have one companion at the ice-edge.'

As we talked, we had begun to go in towards land. I took it for granted that he had recognized me, or at any rate understood who it was that was hidden behind this savage exterior, not thinking that a total stranger would be received so heartily. Suddenly he stopped, looked me full in the face, and said quickly:

'Aren't you Nansen?'

'Yes, I am.'

'By Jove! I am glad to see you!'

And he seized my hand and shook it again, while his whole face became one smile of welcome, and delight at the unexpected meeting beamed from his dark eyes.

'Where have you come from now?' he asked.

'I left the *Fram* in 84°N lat., after having drifted for two years, and I reached the 86°15' parallel, where we had to turn and make for Franz Josef Land. We were, however, obliged to stop for the winter somewhere north [of] here, and are now on our route to Spitzbergen.'

'I congratulate you most heartily. You have made a good trip of it, and I am awfully glad to be the first person to congratulate you on your return.'

Once more he seized my hand, and shook it heartily. I could not have been welcomed more warmly; that handshake was more than a mere form. In his hospitable English manner, he said at once that he had 'plenty of room' for us, and that he was expecting his ship every day. By 'plenty of room' I discovered afterwards that he meant that there were still a few square feet on the floor of their hut that were not occupied at night by himself and his sleeping companions. But 'heart-room makes house-room,' and of the former there was no lack.

As soon as I could get a word in, I asked how things were getting on at home, and he was able to give me the welcome intelligence that my wife and child had both been in the best of health when he left two years ago. Then came Norway's turn, and Norwegian politics; but he knew nothing about that, and I took it as a sign that they must be all right too. He now asked if we could not go out at once, and fetch Johansen and our belongings; but I thought that our kayaks would be too heavy for us to drag over this packed-up ice alone, and that if he had men enough it would certainly be better to send them out. If we only gave Johansen notice by a salute from our guns, he would wait patiently; so we each fired two shots. We soon met several men: Mr Armitage, the second in command, Mr Child, the photographer, and the doctor, Mr Koetlitz. As they approached, Jackson gave them a sign, and let them understand who I was; and I was again welcomed heartily. We met yet others: the botanist, Mr Fisher, Mr Burgess, and the Finn Blomqvist (his real name was Melenius). Fisher has since told me that he at once thought it must be me when he saw a man out on the ice; but he quite gave up that idea when he met me, for he had seen me described as a fair man, and here was a dark man, with black hair and beard. When they were all there, Jackson said that I had reached 86°15′N lat., and from seven powerful lungs I was given a triple British cheer, that echoed among the hummocks.

No chance meeting in history, no Livingstone and Stanley even, could ever match this one for pure serendipity. Nansen was by no means sure where he was, despite his growing conviction that he was in Franz Josef Land. There are hundreds of islands in Franz Josef Land, many that are tiny, and also about 50 large ones where finding another occupant would be a major task. Most were still undiscovered in 1895. On only one of those islands were there any human residents: at Cape Flora on Northbrook Island. Cape Flora had already been the scene of one remarkable story of survival. It was there, in 1881, that the British explorer Benjamin Leigh Smith (1828–1913) saw his ship *Eira* crushed by the ice, managed to salvage only a fraction of their equipment and provisions, and yet managed to live through the winter on a diet of bear and walrus meat, in a primitive hut of stones and turf, with sailcloth for a roof. In 1882, he and his crew sailed in the ship's boats to safety. Frederick Jackson (1860–1938) was the next explorer to visit the cape. He and a small team of scientists had been established there since 1894, exploring, mapping and making a scientific survey. That Nansen should stumble accidentally on their tiny camp on that one inhabited island amid a great maze of other islands, is nothing short of miraculous.

Jackson, too, gave an account of that joyful meeting.

Just after dinner Armitage came rushing in to tell me that through his field-glass he could see a man on the floe to the SSE of Cape Flora, about four miles off. I could hardly believe it, such a thing seemed utterly impossible, and thought he had mistaken a walrus on the ice for a man; but having got a glass I could see he was correct. I could also make out somewhat indistinctly a staff or mast, with another man apparently standing near it close to the water's edge. It occurred then to me that it might be one of my own men, although they had all been at dinner a few minutes before, but I however found that all were present. I got a gun with all speed and firing off a shot on the bank to endeavour to arrest the stranger's attention, I started off to meet him coming across the ice, having placed Armitage on the roof of the hut to direct my course, as the high hummocky ice hid him from me when I got down upon the floe. On nearer approach I shouted to him and waved my cap. I thought at first that some accident had happened to the *Windward*, which had started earlier than I expected, and that this man had come off in a boat from her to communicate with us.

On our approaching each other about three miles distant from the land, I saw a tall man on ski with roughly made clothes and an old felt hat on his head. He was covered with oil and grease, and black from head to foot. I at once concluded from his wearing ski that he was no English sailor but that he must be a man from some Norwegian walrus sloop who had come to grief, and wintered somewhere on Franz Joseph Land, in very rough circumstances.

His hair was very long and dirty, his complexion appeared to be fair, but dirt prevented me from being sure on the point, and his beard was straggly and dirty also.

We shook hands heartily and I expressed the greatest pleasure at seeing him. I inquired if he had a ship? 'No,' he replied, 'my ship is not here' – rather sadly I thought – and then he remarked, in reply to my question, that he had only one companion who was at the floe edge.

It then struck me that his features, in spite of the black grease and long hair and beard resembled Nansen, whom I had met once in London before he started in 1893, and I exclaimed:

'Aren't you Nansen?'

To which he replied:

'Yes, I am Nansen.'

With much heartiness I shook him warmly by the hand and said: 'By Jove I'm d——d glad to see you,' and congratulated him on his safe arrival. Then I inquired:

'Where have you come from?'

He gave me a brief sketch of what had occurred, and replied: 'I left the *Fram* in 84° north latitude and 102°

east longitude after drifting for two years, and I reached the 86°15′ parallel and have now come here.'

'I congratulate you most heartily,' I answered; 'you have made a deuced good trip of it and I am awfully glad to be the first person to congratulate you.'

Soon after, Johansen, too, waiting patiently to learn what Nansen had found, experienced his own emotional reception.

I was becoming more and more anxious about the solution of it all; my shirt was waving high on a long pole fixed on the top of the hummock, and could be seen a good way off, black as it was, against the white snow. At last I saw a black spot appearing now and then among the uneven ice in the direction of the interior. I thought at first it was Nansen coming back, but I soon discovered that the person who was approaching me had no ski, and when he came nearer I saw the long barrel of a gun over his shoulder. He was a stranger – the first strange man I had seen for three years. I hastened to fetch one of our small flags, which I fixed up beside the pole with the shirt, so that he could see what nationality I belonged to.

I next noticed that he had clean, modern clothes, and that his face, too, was clean and washed. I could hear him breathing heavily, and see him sink through the snow now and then; his long boots reached high up over his thighs. I ran towards him; he waved his cap and I my old greasy hat, and soon we were shaking each other by the hand.

'English?' he asked.

'No,' I answered; unfortunately, I could not speak his language. I tried German and French; but no, we could not make ourselves understood to each other. Yet there was already an understanding – that which comes from the heart. Mr Child – that was his name – had set out at once, when he heard from Nansen that he had left his comrade out by the edge of the ice. Nansen had not time to tell him that I did not understand English.

I conducted him to our encampment, and when he saw our sledges and kayaks, our miserable tent, our cooking utensils, with bear's flesh and blubber, I saw his fine, dark eyes wander from me to all these things, while he seemed to be struck with surprise. I used the 'finger-language' as best I could.

Shortly, others of Jackson's party appeared, including the doctor, Reginald Koettlitz, who spoke German and served as interpreter. Once they understood each other, they gave Johansen a simple but moving welcoming ceremony.

Mr Armitage took out his pocket-flask and filled a cup with port wine, which he offered me. All took off their caps, and with uncovered heads they gave a cheer for Norway, while they looked up at our little flag. My feelings at this moment may be more easily imagined than described; there I stood, in the midst of these brave men, a horrible, blackened savage in rags, and with long hair, suddenly restored to civilization; among a crowd of strange people, who brought with them the fragrance of soap and clean clothes, surrounded by the ice with which we had been struggling for the last three years, while above my head waved the flag which I felt I represented; never have I felt as I did then, that I had a 'fatherland', and with uplifted head I drank the cup of welcome, while the Englishmen's cheers rang out across the icefields.

The warmth of their welcome, contrasting so strongly with their long ordeal on the ice and their spartan winter, clearly overwhelmed them, and Nansen wrote a few days later:

Tuesday, June 23rd.

> Do I sleep? do I dream?
> Do I wonder and doubt?
> Are things what they seem?
> Or are visions about?

What has happened? I can still scarcely grasp it. How incessant are the vicissitudes in this wandering life! A few days ago swimming in the water for dear life, attacked by walrus, living the savage life which I have lived for more than a year now, and sure of a long journey before us, over ice and sea, through unknown regions, before we should meet with other human beings – a journey full of the same ups and downs, the same disappointments, that we have become so accustomed to – and now living the life of a civilized European, surrounded by everything that civilization can afford of luxury and good living, with abundance of water, soap, towels, clean, soft woollen clothes, books, and everything that we have been sighing for all these weary months.

A few weeks later, Jackson's support ship *Windward* arrived, and took Nansen and Johansen to Tromsø in northern Norway, where they landed on 21 August and experienced a joyful reception from the first of many welcoming crowds. By yet another of those tricks of fate that seemed so often to favour Nansen, they were able to share that welcome with their colleagues on the *Fram*, who had reached Tromsø just one day before them, after successfully and safely completing their three-year ice drift off Svalbard a week earlier. Together, for the next three weeks, they sailed on a triumphal voyage from celebration to celebration in one town after another along the Norwegian coast, climaxing on 9 September in Nansen's home town of Oslo.

Nansen's exploring career did not end there, but it was his last great adventure. *Fram* still had two more major polar adventures to come, exploring with Otto Sverdrup in the Canadian Arctic in 1898–1902, and with Roald Amundsen in the Antarctic in 1910–12. Then she returned home to Oslo for good and is still there, with a museum built around her.

Nansen's fate could so easily have been very different from that ecstatic tour of welcome; he offered Nature so many opportunities to dispose of him that one wonders why none was accepted. It is sometimes difficult to avoid thinking that there was some divine purpose in saving Nansen from his own folly. In later life he devoted himself to lofty humanitarian causes: in 1917, towards the end of the First World War, he was responsible for maintaining a supply of American foodstuffs to Norway, which was neutral. From 1920 to 1922, he was High Commissioner of the League of Nations, and in that capacity organized the repatriation of over 400,000 prisoners of war. In 1922, he was awarded the Nobel Peace Prize. Through all that he maintained an active interest in encouraging polar research, right up to his death in 1930. He was, in very many ways, a truly great man.

Johansen's future proved very different and poignant. After a few years of celebrity he began to meet financial and family problems and took to drink. At Nansen's request, Roald Amundsen took him on his South Pole expedition of 1910–12, but in the Antarctic Amundsen shunned and humiliated him for expressing divergent views. On his return home he drifted back into alcoholism and on 3 January 1913 he shot himself.

– 8 –

Salomon August Andrée

1896–7

Nansen's attempt to reach the North Pole from *Fram* may have been reckless in the extreme, but in comparison with the next two attempts on the Pole it appears almost sensible. In 1895, the Swedish engineer Salomon August Andrée (1854–97) unveiled his plan for an aerial expedition to the North Pole, using an unpowered hydrogen-filled balloon made of Chinese silk. Even to a layman, some of the flaws in this are almost immediately obvious. Without power, Andrée's success depended heavily on a consistent southerly wind to reach the Pole, then a consistent northerly wind to carry the balloon back to civilization. Accumulation of ice on the surface of the balloon might easily add so much excess weight as to force the balloon down to a crash landing on the ice. No balloon had ever before stayed aloft for as long as Andrée's expedition required. Despite such basic obstacles, Andrée argued that 'an air balloon is ... capable of carrying the explorer to the Pole and home again in safety; with such a balloon, the journey across the waste of ice *can* be carried out.'

Andrée persuaded himself that he could gain sufficient control over the direction and altitude of his balloon by the use of three drag ropes, each over 1,000 feet long, and three small sails mounted over the gondola. More importantly, in lectures before the Swedish Academy of Sciences and the Swedish Anthropological and Geographical Society, he persuaded his country's scientific community that this technical impossibility was possible. His plans were endorsed by Sweden's foremost polar explorer, Adolf Erik Nordenskiöld; and he won financial support from King Oscar II of Sweden/Norway, and Alfred Nobel (1833–96), the explosives manufacturer, philanthropist, and founder of the Nobel Prize. There are echoes here of the patriotic fervour that had accompanied Nansen's proposals for the *Fram* expedition; he found healthy support within Sweden, but most of the rest of the world considered his scheme to be pure folly. Unlike Nansen, he lacked a sound scientific basis for his ideas – his belief in being able to control the direction of the balloon's flight was always exaggerated, and his plans for survival in the event of a crash were always inadequate. And as an Arctic explorer he was almost a novice; he lacked Nansen's genius for turning disaster into triumph. From the very outset, Andrée's plans were dogged by misfortune, and the misfortune rapidly turned to tragedy. The venture destroyed him, but it provided one of the most extraordinary and most moving stories in the history of exploration.

Andrée intended to use northern Svalbard as the base for his polar flight, and he first attempted the flight in 1896. This expedition achieved little. He spent about six weeks erecting his balloon house, a huge, hangar-like structure, in Virgo Harbour (Virgohamna) on Danes Island (Danskøya), off the northwest coast of Spitsbergen. After that, he spent the next two weeks waiting for a favourable wind. The wind remained unsuitable, so on 20 August he left for home.

In 1897, with support from the same willing sponsors, Andrée tried again. This time, the wind was more favourable, and in the early afternoon of 11 July, he and two companions, Nils Strindberg and Knud Frænkel, boarded their balloon the *Örnen* (*Eagle*) and took off.

From the very first moment, the flight of the *Eagle* was doomed to failure. The only decipherable record of the incident by any of the three men is a terse note by Strindberg.

Good-bye is said 1h 50m GMT.
Enter car 1 52m GMT.
Start 1 55
Guide-rope is lost

A more detailed account of this early disaster was assembled from the accounts of eye-witnesses on the ground.

The balloon rises slowly, with rather erratic movements,

some 50–100 m, (150–300 ft), and drives in a north-easterly direction across Virgo harbour, drawing after it the guide-lines which glide over the water, leaving behind them a broad, sharp furrow like that made by a vessel. Over the middle of the harbour the balloon begins to sink lower and lower; then comes a sharp jerk which, according to one statement, forces the car halfway down below the water, though according to another witness it merely sweeps the surface. Then the balloon at once rebounds like a vast ball and continues to rise, while the travellers empty eight of the bags of sand, thereby losing 207 kg (450 lbs) of its invaluable ballast at the very start.

Immediately after this dipping, one of the sailors on shore is heard to cry: 'Why! the drag-lines are lying here on the shore!' This causes a great sensation, for the intention was, of course, to make the whole of the journey at a height of 150–200 m (about 500–660 ft) by means of the drag-lines, whereby a certain steering-power could be obtained. At first it was thought that the ropes had broken off, but on reaching the spot where they lay, and examining them closely, it was found that the screwing-on section had come unscrewed. The lines had been laid out along the shore below the balloon-house in an easterly direction, in order, if possible, to give the balloon a turn towards that quarter from the very start, thus enabling it to clear the highest part of Amsterdam Island. When they were being laid out, they had evidently got a kink here and there, and when the balloon rose these began to twist themselves, this, in its turn, causing the screws, which had only a very few threads, to come unscrewed, so that the lower two-thirds of the three ropes fell to the earth together. This had evidently taken place at the instant when the balloon was seen to give a jerk. The loss of these ropes meant that the ballast had become further diminished by some 530 kg (1,160 lbs).

Various opinions have been expressed as to the actual cause of this mishap. One thing is certain, however, and that is, that the loss of the guide-lines caused the whole of the balloon journey to take place altogether in another way than had been intended, for the travellers now found themselves in an almost ordinary free balloon which would be compelled to obey the direction of the wind.

The most detailed surviving account of the departure by any of the three aeronauts, and the most vivid revelation of their highly optimistic mood, is contained in a long letter from Nils Strindberg to his fiancée Anna Charlier, but surprisingly he told her nothing of the loss of the guide ropes.

I went ashore and packed a few articles in the car of the balloon and arranged some things here and there. The work of removing the front side of the house went on briskly, and one plank after the other was thrown down. The balloon stood there steady and secure protected against . . .? the winds by the canvas on the fourth and fifth floors. I took some photographs of the work. Then I went on board again with Svedenborg for a moment to fetch some things that had been forgotten, and then I compared chronometers for the last time. When we came on board breakfast was just being served, and we were persuaded to sit down to table in company with the chief and the doctor. The chief took in a bottle of champagne and a toast was drunk to a prosperous journey for us. Everyone enjoyed the breakfast, and when I went on shore again, time did not allow of the others getting anything to eat before the start. We had to satisfy ourselves with sandwiches and ale in the car. When I came on land again the work had made good progress and the balloon was being allowed to lift a little. Some small balloons were let go to test the direction of the wind, which proved favourable. It was quite an inspiring sight when the balloon had been lifted to such a height that the carrying-ring of the gondola left the ground. Andrée gave orders; everyone was willing and helpful and everything went well. I walked about taking photographs up to the last minute.

The balloon had now risen to such a height that the carrying-ring was a good distance above the ground, and was held fast by three ropes. The moment had come to attach the car. When this had been done and a sufficient number of bags of ballast had been taken on board, the time had come to say goodbye. This was done heartily and touchingly but without any signs of weakness. Then Andrée cries: 'Strindberg and Fraenkel, are you ready to get into the car?' Yes! and so we got in. Now my thoughts turned for a moment to you and my dear ones at home. How would the journey succeed? And how fast my thoughts came, but I had to restrain them. I asked Machuron, who stood nearest and whom I had found most congenial, to give my love to you. I wonder if a tear did not tremble on my cheek at that moment. But I had to see that the camera was in order and to be ready to throw out ballast, etc. And now all three of us stand there on the top of the car. There is a moment's solemn silence. Machuron says: 'Attendez un moment! Calme.' The right moment comes. 'Cut away everywhere!' comes Andrée's voice. Three knives cut the three lines holding fast the carrying-ring and the balloon rises amid the hurrahs of those below; we answer with a: 'Hurrah for old Sweden!' and then we rose from out the balloon-house. A peculiar sensation, wonderful, indescribable! But one has no time for much thought. I photographed for a while and then we see that we are descending. Ballast is thrown out, but we dip into the sea a moment. Then we rise again. And now everything seems to be going all right. We can still hear the hurrahs at a distance. I take one or two more photographs and then prepare the last card to you, which I intended to throw down on Hollander Naze. But forgot it. Good-night!

One of the most remarkable aspects of this expedition, given the many setbacks that befell it, was the remarkably buoyant mood that the three men were able to sustain. One of the few episodes of self-doubt was expressed on the second day of the flight by Andrée, who, having told his companions to get some sleep, reflected in solitude on their predicament.

Although we could have thrown out ballast, and although the wind might, perhaps, carry us to Greenland, we determined to be content with standing still. We have been obliged to throw out very much ballast today and have not had any sleep nor been allowed any rest from the repeated bumpings, and we probably could not have stood it much longer. All three of us must have a rest, and I sent Strindb. and Fr. to bed at 11.20 o'cl., and I mean to let them sleep until 6 or 7 o'cl. if I can manage to keep watch until then. Then I shall try to get some rest myself. If either of them should succumb it might be because I had tired them out.

It is not a little strange to be floating here above the Polar Sea. To be the first that have floated here in a balloon. How soon, I wonder, shall we have successors? Shall we be thought mad or will our example be followed? I cannot deny but that all three of us are dominated by a feeling of pride. We think we can well face death, having done what we have done. Is not the whole, perhaps, the expression of an extremely strong sense of individuality which cannot bear the thought of living and dying like a man in the ranks, forgotten by coming generations? Is this ambition?

Not long after, their situation worsened. The wind changed direction and started carrying them west, then east. At the same time, the balloon was accumulating ice and leaking air so much that they began bumping along the surface of the ice; all they could do to maintain a margin of altitude above the ice was to throw out all disposable ballast: sandbags, buoys, a rope-ladder, some provisions; even, on one occasion, as much urine as they could collectively muster. But by then, the flight was already doomed; their height and direction were simply too erratic, and on 14 July, Andrée recorded briefly

6.20 o'cl. the balloon rose to a great height
but we opened both valves and were
down again at 6.29 o'cl.

8.11 o'cl. p.m. we jumped out of the balloon.
The landing . . .
Worn out and famished but 7 hours' hard work had
to be done before we could recreate ourselves.

They had landed on the ice of the Arctic Ocean at 82°56'N, 29°52'E, about 200 miles north of the nearest part of northeast

Svalbard, and a little farther from the nearest point of Franz Josef Land.

It was at this time that the contrast between Andrée's luck and Nansen's was starker than ever. Where Nansen had been repeatedly careless but astonishingly lucky, Andrée was careful and reflective but could do virtually nothing right. Like Nansen, he chose to head over the ice to Franz Josef Land, where Cape Flora had become a widely known rallying point for both exploring and hunting expeditions. But the drift of the ice was against them, and soon after they chose instead to head for northern Svalbard, where a small depot of provisions awaited them. As a further misfortune, as they walked south, the island to which the ice carried them was virtually undiscovered and never before landed upon. This was White Island (Kvitøya) in the extreme and seldom visited northeast of the Svalbard archipelago. In those circumstances, the spirit of the party remained quite remarkably lively. The beginning of their ice-walk is recorded in the remainder of Strindberg's letter to Anna. Parts of the letter were illegible by the time it was found, so there are gaps.

Well, now your Nils knows what it is to walk on the Polar ice. We had a little mishap at the start. When we were crossing from our ice-floe with the first sledge it went aslant and fell in. It was with difficulty we succeeded in getting it up. I climbed down up to the knees and held fast the sledge so that it should not sink. Andrée and Fraenkel crossed over to the other ice-floe and then suddenly we managed to get the sledge up, but I expect that my sack which was on the sledge is wet inside. And it is there that I have all your letters and your portrait. Yes, they will be my dearest treasure during the winter. Well, my dear, what will you be thinking in the winter? That is my only anxiety. Well, after we had got the sledge up again we piloted ourselves across some floes with channels of water between. The way we did it was by making the ice-floes move quickly so that they came near each other. This was slow work with the large floes of course. At last we came on to a large field of ice across which we wandered with our sledges two or three kilometres. Each is loaded with about 160 kg, so that they are very heavy, and during the last hour what we did was that all three of us helped with one sledge at a time. Now we have encamped on a picturesque bit of ice and have pitched our tent. In the tent we have our sleeping-sack, in which all three of us are now lying side by side. It is a squeeze, but the fellowship is good. Well, there is much I should write about, but now I must sleep. Good-night.

Woke up at 11.30 o'cl.
    Cooking and tidying.
    Start 2.15 o'cl.
    Difficult leads in the ice. Andrée and I of different opinions respecting the crossing of the channel. Scanty dinner. After the midday meal we covered some km (one or two). Night-camp by a large hummock (4 m high). I made soup with pease, rusks, soup-tablets and Rosseau meat-powder . . .

24 July, 12.5 o'cl. GMT (25 . . .) We have just stopped for the day after drudging and pulling the sledges for ten hours. I am really rather tired, but must first chat a few words. First and foremost I must congratulate you, for on this day your birthday begins. Oh, how I wish I could tell you now that I am in excellent health and that you need not fear anything for us. We are sure to come home by and by . . . yes, how very much all this occupies my thoughts during the day, for I have plenty of time to think, and it is so delightful to have such pleasant memories and such happy prospects for the future as I have, to think about!

(Later) Now we have camped for the night and had coffee and eaten our sandwiches with cheese and h . . . biscuits and syrup and . . . Just now we are putting up the tent and Fraenkel is making the meteorological observations. Just now we are enjoying a caramel, it is a real luxury. You can fancy we are not over-delicate here. Yesterday evening I gave them (for it is I that attend to the housekeeping) a soup which was really not good, for that Rousseau meat-powder tastes rather bad, one soon becomes tired of it. But we managed to eat it in any case . . .

Well, we have stopped for the night on an open place;

round about there is ice, ice in every direction. You saw from Nansen's pictures how such ice looks. Hummocks, walls, and fissures in the sea alternating with melted ice, everlastingly the same. For the moment it is snowing a little, but it is calm at least and not especially cold. At home I think you have nicer summer weather.

Yes, it is strange to think that not even for your next birthday will it be possible for us to be at home. And perhaps we must winter here for another year more. We do not know yet. Now we are moving onwards so slowly that perhaps we shall not reach Cape Flora this winter, but, like Nansen, we shall be obliged to pass the winter in a cellar in the earth. Poor little Anna, in what despair you will be if we should not come home next autumn. And you can think that I am tortured by the thought of it, too, not for my own sake, for now I do not mind if I suffer hardships as long as I can come home at last . . .

Now the tent is in order and we are going to our berths. We are all rather tired but in good humour. We discuss our mental characteristics and our faults, a very educative . . . I chat with . . .

The (2) 5,7 at 9 o'cl. GMT. We awoke today about 12 o'clock, but as it was rain and . . . we remained in the tent and slumbered till three. Then we rose and I cooked a little food – cocoa and condensed milk and biscuits and sandwiches. At 4.30 o'cl. we started, and now we have drudged and pulled our heavy sledges for four hours and a half. The weather is pretty bad: wet snow and fog; but we are in good humour. We have kept up a really pleasant conversation the whole day. Andrée has spoken about his life, how he entered the Patent Bureau, etc. Fraenkel and Andrée have gone forwards on a reconnoitring tour. I stayed with the sledges, and now I am sitting writing to you. Yes, now you have evening at home and you, like I, have had a very jolly and pleasant day. Here one day passes like another. Pull and drudge at the sledges, eat and sleep. The most delightful hour of the day is when one has gone to bed and allows one's thoughts to fly back to better and happier times, but now their immediate goal is where we shall winter. We hope to be in a better position. Now the others are coming back and we shall continue the drudging with the sledges. Au revoir . . .

31 July, 10 o'cl, a.m. Now it is a long time since I chatted with you. Since then the situation has . . . the evening . . . me . . . large channel . . . we determined to alter our equipment the next day so that each of us could pull his own sledge. The method we had hitherto employed of all three pulling one sledge and then going back and fetching the other sledges took too much time. On the 26th July we crossed the lead and then on the other side we unloaded our goods, and then we began to unpack in order to leave some of the provisions and equipment here.

By mid-September, they were in sight of White Island, but, as Andrée recorded, 'There is no question of our attempting to go on shore for the entire island seems to be one single block of ice with a glacial border.' He still hoped to drift west towards more habitable and more frequently-visited land. Even in that perilous situation, the mood of optimism prevailed, or at least any sense of pessimism was masked. They still had plenty of provisions, and were able to supplement that with the meat of bears, seals and birds. Strindberg kept a record of their meals, which read, typically:

12 Aug. 1.30 o'cl. p.m.	Morning. Bear's-meat (0.7 kg) and ivory gull (lact Mellin's food gruel).
12 Aug. 8.30 p.m.	Dinner. Bread butter biscuit cheese.
13 Aug. 2 o'cl. a.m.	Supper. Bear's-meat (½ kg) 2 pieces of bread per man Potage au Cerfeuil Stauffer and biscuits (6 each).
13 Aug. 2 o'cl. p.m.	Morning. 0.6 kg bear's-meat (the last of the old bear) 2 pieces hard bread Coffee and biscuits.

His final report of their meals, on the 25th anniversary of King Oscar II's accession, records a veritable feast.

Banquet 18 *Sept.* 97
on an ice-floe immediately east of . . .
Seal steak and ivory gull fried in butter and seal-blubber,
seal liver, brain and kidneys. Butter and Schumacher bread.
Wine.
Chocolate and Mellin's-food flour with Albert biscuits
and butter.
Gateau aux raisin.
Raspberry syrup sauce.
Port-wine 1834 Antonio de Ferrara given by the King.
Toast by Andrée for the King with royal Hurrah:
The national anthem in unison.
Biscuits, butter, cheese.
A glass of wine.
Festive feeling.
During the day the union-flag waved above the camp.

Two weeks later, their situation became even more difficult,
but they continued to face it courageously. Andrée's last fully
intelligible diary entry reads:

1 Oct. was a good day. The evening was as divinely beautiful
as one could wish. The water was alive with small animals
and a bevy of 7 black-white 'guillemots youngsters' were
swimming there. A couple of seals were seen too. The work
with the hut went on well and we thought that we should
have the outside ready by the 2nd. But then something else
happened. At 5.30 o'cl. (local time) in the morning of the
2 we heard a crash and thunder and water streamed into
the hut and when [we] rushed out we found that our large
beautiful floe had been splintered into a number of little
floes and that one fissure had divided the floe just outside
the wall of the hut. The floe that remained to us had a diam.
of only 24 metre (80 ft) and one wall of the hut might be
said rather to hang from the roof than to support it. This
was a great alteration in our position and our prospects.
The hut and the floe could not give us shelter and still we
were obliged to stay there for the present at least. We were
frivolous enough to lie in the hut the following night too.
Perhaps it was because the day was rather tiring. Our

belongings were scattered among several blocks and these were driving here and there so that we had to hurry. Two bear-bodies, representing provisions for 3–4 months, were lying on a separate floe and so on. Luckily the weather was beautiful so that we could work in haste. No one had lost courage; with such comrades one should be able to manage under, I may say, any circumstances.

A few days later, these new circumstances broke their resolve not to land on White Island, and Strindberg noted tersely on 5 October 'Moved to land'. That was almost his last diary entry. His last, three lines later and written on 17 October records simply 'home 7.5 o'cl. a.m.' From that point on, the expedition fell forever silent.

In the next few years, expeditions searched for Andrée and his companions from Greenland to Siberia, but found nothing. Carrier pigeons and buoys carrying messages from them had been released during the flight, and some were found, but they gave not the slightest indication of where the three men had landed. For decades, their fate remained an absolute mystery. Gradually it was acknowledged that they were dead; but otherwise the expedition seemed utterly, irretrievably and inexplicably lost.

The most astonishing thing of all about the Andrée expedition is that we now know almost exactly what happened to them. Over 30 years later, in 1931, something almost miraculous occurred. By then, White Island had come within the range of hunters and explorers, and on 5–6 August a combined scientific and hunting expedition on the ship *Bratvaag*, led by the Norwegian geologist Gunnar Horn (1894–1947), visited the island. On the 6th, a hunting party, supervised by the skipper Peder Eliassen, went ashore to hunt for walruses. Horn tells the story.

As the day went on, the skipper returned to the ship. He neared us calmly and quietly and told us that they had made a great find. *They had found Andrée!* And they had also found the canvas boat of the expedition, filled with all kinds of equipment.

Eliassen had in his hands a book which had lain in the boat. The book was wet and heavy, and the leaves stuck

A dangerous incident during the Barentsz expedition of 1596-7

The *Racehorse* and the *Carcass* force their way through the ice during the Phipps expedition, 1773

The 14-year-old Horatio Nelson, a junior member of the phipps expedition, attacking a bear (see p.24)

Parry's sledge boat and sledges, used in the laborious trek across the ice,1827

Payer reaches Cape Saulen during his northerly explorations, on his and
Weyprecht's 1872-4 expedition

The Pole party manhauling their sledge on Nare's expedition, 1876

The sinking of the ice-bound *Jeannette* on De Long's expedition, 1881

Fridtjof Nansen, outside Jackson's hut at Cape Flora, 1896

Photographs taken at the time, of Salomon Andree's ill-fated balloon expedition
Above, the departure, 11 July 1897
Below, immediately after landing on the ice, 14 July 1897

Otto Sverdrup, Captain of Nansen's
ship *Fram* during their 1893-6
expedition

Robert E. Peary, 1856-1920

Frederick Cook, 1865-1940

Roald Amundsen, 1872-1928

The departure of the airship *Italia,* 1928 (*photo courtesy of* Gertrude Nobile)

The Russian icebreaker *Yamal* at the North pole, 1993 (*photo:* Darius Wampler)

together, but it could be opened in one or two places, and we saw that it was the expedition's observation-book with detailed calculations of the astronomical observations. There was side after side with figures, with here and there a list of the supply of provisions, a bill of fare for the week, together with other memoranda. We were astonished to see how neatly and orderly everything was written. It was just as if the notes had been put down in a warm room, and yet the calculations had been made and written during the course of a death-march across the ice. We were aware that Nils Strindberg had been the scientific member of the expedition, so that it must have been he who had made the memoranda. And he must have been a man of the right sort. On the first page we were able to read a part of the title: 'The sledge journey 1897'. There could be no doubt but that this was the expedition's observation-book, used after they had left the balloon, probably far northwards among the ice. The news of the discovery made a deep impression on us all. Here on White Island, here where we now stood, consequently, was the place where the boldest of all Polar expeditions had come to a tragic close. We sat still a moment ere we thought of rising again. Our words were very few, overwhelmed as we were by the discovery that had just been made.

They had found Andrée's last camp, the bodies of the three men, and their still partially legible notes and journals. More remarkable even than that, exposed but still undeveloped photographic film was discovered with them, and it later proved possible to print good images from this ancient film stock; we can not only read, we can *see* what happened to them.

The one great mystery that still hangs over the expedition is how and when they died. It was probably not long after Strindberg's last diary entry, and we know that Strindberg was the first to die, for he alone had been buried. According to Horn, Andrée and Frænkel 'seem to have sunk into their last slumber side by side within the tent, and, to judge by all appearances, simultaneously.'

The cause of death will never be known for certain. It is most unlikely that they starved; by their own account they had meat for several months; they also had firearms and plenty of ammunition. The initial theory was expressed by one of the hunters who found them: 'I think they died in their sleep! – that the cold finished them! In any case, they did not die of hunger!' Horn added, too, that their predicament of absolute isolation, with little hope of being found, must have caused some mental deterioration; additionally so since the three were obliged to share the same sleeping bag, with Andrée and Frænkel 'obliged to witness the death struggles of Strindberg just in that one sleeping-sack'. In other words, the two men might just have died of cold compounded by grief. More recently, it has been suggested that they might have died of carbon-monoxide poisoning from a faulty cooking stove, or that their plentiful diet of bear meat might have been the cause: trichinosis, a parasitic disease caused by inadequate cooking of certain kinds of meat, has not infrequently killed polar explorers.

In September 1931, in solemn ceremony, the bodies of the three men were returned to Stockholm, and after a funeral service in the great church of St Nicholas, on 9 October they were, together, cremated.

The Andrée story is full of saddening, moving incidents, and one of the most moving of all is the story of Strindberg's intended wife, Anna Charlier. After his death, she eventually married, but she never lost her love for him. Before she died in England in 1947, she asked for her heart to be taken to Stockholm and buried beside his remains.

The Italian Quest

1899–1900

In the two or three years before and after the turn of the century, there were often several North Pole expeditions out in the field at the same time. One of the more unusual attempts was led by Luigi Amedeo di Savoia, Duke of the Abruzzi. He was an Italian nobleman, third son of the King of Spain, who had abdicated just 18 days after Luigi's birth on 24 January 1873. He was an adventurer and mountaineer, who began climbing in the Alps when still young.

The unusual aspect of Luigi's expedition was not that he had an elevated aristocratic status. Since the 1850s, the Arctic regions between Greenland and Novaya Zemlya had been a favourite resort among certain members of the European nobility, and the very rich, who had a taste for big-game hunting. Some Arctic game was very big, very easy to kill, and certain to impress the neighbours back home. There were honourable exceptions, including the Prince of Monaco and the Duke of the Abruzzi, who used their voyages to the Arctic for the advancement of knowledge. The unusual thing about Luigi's expedition was that it was Italian. To that date, Italy had absolutely no Arctic exploring tradition. Southern European explorers in general tended to look south, not north. Nonetheless it was a competently organized, competently conducted expedition, which trod new ground. Most of Luigi's senior officers were Italian, but, as was common on Arctic expeditions at the time, the captain and crew were Norwegian.

His plan was to reach the North Pole by dog-sledge from Franz Josef Land, preferably from the northernmost island in the group, Rudolf Island (Ostrov Rudol'fa). The expedition set sail from Oslo on the ship *Stella Polare* on 12 June 1899, and

managed to find a harbour for the winter in Teplitz Bay, which
they discovered and named, on the west coast of Rudolf Island.
They experienced a difficult winter. In September, *Stella Polare*
was badly damaged by the pressure of the ice, and developed a
leak that forced the party to put their most essential equipment
and provisions on shore. Part of the winter was spent in repairing
the leak. In January, Luigi's fingers became so badly frostbitten
that parts of them had to be amputated. That misfortune caused
a major change of plans, for he was no longer able to lead the
main assault on the Pole, and had to hand over the task to his
second-in-command, Captain Umberto Cagni.

Cagni first set out on 21 February 1900, but had to return to
base after only two days because of an accident in which he fell
into a channel of open water and nearly froze to death. On 11
March he set out again. His party now consisted of ten men,
102 dogs, and 13 sledges. The party was divided into three
detachments, of which two, carrying extra supplies, were to
return to base when they were of no further use. Luigi followed
them for a short way, and recorded their parting.

Captain Cagni was at the head with the sledges which
formed his detachment; he was followed by Lieutenant
Querini and Dr Cavalli, who came last. We marched thus
in file for a distance of about twenty yards over ice which
was continually moving under our feet. A man walked
before the dogs of the first sledge; others walked beside the
sledges which followed and pushed them on. On reaching
the old ice, we had to turn to the south-west to find a spot
where it would be easy to get on it, and I assisted at this
first struggle with difficult ice. If the whole ice-pack were
similar to that we had already crossed, it would be an easy
matter to reach the Pole, both on account of the speed with
which the journey could be performed, and because the
smooth ice would not damage the sledges. On the rugged
ice-pack, however, two guides armed with ice-axes had to
precede us, to level the surface where it was most broken
up, and we were forced to follow a winding path to avoid
the places where it was impracticable. The sledges were
often overturned while crossing those uneven stretches
of ice, and the men obliged to raise them up, or else

the runners remained caught among the sharp points of the ice. The sledges were, therefore, frequently and easily damaged, and our way was lengthened by the continual zig-zags our guides were obliged to make in order to find the best places. It was then that I left my companions, bidding them good-bye one by one.

Captain Cagni and I took leave of each other with heart-felt words, which expressed our sincere and mutual good wishes of soon meeting again after a successful expedition. I felt that this time our parting was definite, and that I could not see him again until many weeks had elapsed, on his return from the most severe trial he would have to undergo in all his life. If it had not been always easy to live together in the limited space of the same tent, at that solemn moment no memory of slight misunderstandings ruffled the tranquillity of our minds, or rendered the last clasp of our hands less affectionate.

The sledges then went on; the doctor was the last to salute me, and the convoy disappeared among the tall hummocks. Gini and I climbed a mound of ice to see the convoy once more as it proceeded on its way. Just now it was they who had saluted us; this time we saluted them, and from far away the cry of 'Evviva', three times repeated, replied to our cheer. It was the last farewell. We lost sight of the convoy shortly after.

From then on, for Luigi and the men left behind, 'Our daily life . . . was filled with a single thought – the return of our comrades.' Cagni, meanwhile, pressed on across the ice, experiencing the familiar problems of those who had gone before him: bad weather, bad ice conditions, the need to keep going, however exhausted the party became. As he approached and reached his farthest north, he recorded:

Sunday, April 22nd. — We rose this morning at five, feeling a slight heaviness, as often happens after coming to important decisions. I reflected much last night, and renounced one of my golden dreams which still survived, and did not seem to me quite impossible to realize. 'To reach the 87th degree' we should have to do about a hundred miles in a week, which would be difficult. But even supposing that we succeeded, we would not be certain of covering the same distance on our return. It would be such an unusual and extraordinary feat that we could not be sure of it. And if, while we were eighty miles farther to the north, we should be surprised by bad weather, what would become of us? Today we can reckon on forty-four days' provisions, but at reduced rations, on which no sort of saving can be effected without weakening the men. And in the silence of the night, lit up by a bright and unclouded sun, this argument always came back to my mind more clearly, more precisely, more powerfully, and overcame little by little all the resistance offered by my ardent wishes, my ambition, and the highest ideals of all of us. I decide that I shall return as soon as I reach 86°30', even if I were to get there in a very few days. I have hardly come to that decision when I am assailed by a doubt; shall we reach even 86°30'?

We start at nine and cross some ice sprinkled with blocks and small hillocks, which do not oblige us to deviate much from our path. At half-past ten we are on the edge of a large expanse of water, which we call the Lake of Como. It is well frozen, and we take more than an hour walking quickly to cross it. There is not much saline efflorescence on it, and it is not sticky; the dogs cross over it without stopping, and oblige us to run to keep up with them. While they are resting on the other shore, I take a meridian altitude, although this morning I had resolved to take no observation, so as to avoid a loss of time. But the sun is unclouded, the horizon clearly defined, and the opportunity is favourable. When we are again on the march, I make the calculations mentally. Since noon yesterday, and also this morning, we must have travelled more than I had reckoned. We are at 85°48'N lat.

As soon as I overtake the guides, who are getting ready a crossing over a pressure-ridge, I announce to them this good news, and Petigax replies with more. On account of the large expanse of water and of some ridges on its banks, we thought that the ice-pack would be uneven, but, beyond these ridges, it appears as it did yesterday. This intelligence, in the state of suspense which we are in, is very consoling. On account of it, and of the latitude, we resolve to take a short rest about two o'clock, and then to try to reach the 86th degree this evening. Fenoillet showed his joy by the shout which he gave to send the dogs on their way.

We stop at ten minutes past two, to take coffee, and at ten minutes to three we are again on the march. We have never succeeded in making it so quickly; even the cooking-stove shares our enthusiasm!

We feared that the dogs might be weary, but they travel very well; they make stages of an hour and even an hour and a half, without stopping for a moment; then they have five minutes' rest, which I time with my watch, and start off again as fresh as when they set out. It is true that the sledges are lightly laden; the heaviest, which is always that which carries the sleeping-bag, does not weigh more than 440 lb including the vehicle; but it is certain that, as shown by our daily performances, all the dogs we now have are excellent; they are for the most part well trained, and know by experience that when they slacken their pace through laziness, our shouts are followed by blows.

We proceed thus towards the north until six, at which hour we approach a very long ridge running from east to west, and as it seems broad, our hearts beat in dread of delay. We cross it, however, without having to work with the axe, in a few minutes. Beyond the ridge is level ice, with a sprinkling of blocks and small hillocks, which, as they partly conceal each other, have in the distance the appearance of forming serried lines; they seem to be more pressure-ridges; this idea, repeated several times, irritates our nerves, and we hasten our steps.

We only stop at half-past seven; we must have done fully the thirteen miles which separated us from the 86th degree. We encamp close to a hillock, in order to have shelter from the south-west wind which rose at midday. The sky is overcast, but the temperature remains low, and this makes us hope that the weather will continue to be fine. We feel very nervous, in spite of our fatigue, and have reason to be; we speak of reaching 86°16' tomorrow if the ice will allow us, and Nansen more than ever is the chief subject of conversation this evening. The state in which we have found the ice-pack in these last three days shows us now, how two men with three sledges were able to travel eighteen miles a day.

It must have been the expanse of water, stretching to the east and the west as far as the eye could see, we crossed yesterday, which reflected on the sky the long broad dark stripe which we saw on the 20th. I believe that if we had reached it forty-eight hours sooner, instead of serving us as an excellent road it would have stopped us, hesitating and disconsolate; and who knows whether we might not have refrained from making our supreme effort, which is on the point of being victorious?

Monday, April 23rd. – We were astounded at our success. The tent having been pitched, I carried the cooking-stove into it, whilst Petigax hung up the pots to fill them with snow. We had not exchanged a word for several hours; I held out my hand to him and we clasped each other's warmly. I thanked him for all that he had done to help me; I wished to tell him that the hand he clasped was that of a grateful friend, but I do not remember what I said to him, nor do I know if he heard me. He replied, stammering, that he had only done his duty, but his voice, like mine, was choked by emotion and, as in mine, tears shone in his eyes.

'The flag!' I said to him, and we left the tent without further thought of the cooking-stove. We searched hastily in the kayak for our little flag; tied it to a bamboo pole and I waved it to the cry of 'Long live Italy! Long live the King! Long live the Duke of the Abruzzi!' And to each of my cries the others answered with a shout which expressed all the exultation of their souls.

Resound on, sacred words, resound throughout these regions of pure and eternal ice, this sparkling gem! For never shall a conquest won by the sword, nor by the favours of fortune, adorn the Crown of the House of Savoy with one of greater lustre!

We had set out at nine, by a cloudy sky and northerly breeze which had risen in the early hours of that morning. We had made good progress until half-past ten, when, in crossing a ridge, the trace of one of Canepa's sledges broke. I was luckily ahead, and succeeded in stopping the six dogs before they were able to pass my sledges and follow the track of Petigax and Fenoillet. This accident, however, made us lose half an hour. As compensation, we found a large tract of level ice, where I stopped for a quarter of an hour to take a meridian altitude, and at ten minutes past twelve we were marching across recently formed ice, now beginning to move.

A little later we were in the midst of pressures, which seemed to come from every direction. The ice was creaking on all sides and overlapping, and raising up pressure-ridges with a loud noise; winding channels were opening, and, where other channels were closing, new ridges were rising. I had never seen the ice so full of life, or so agitated, or threatening. The dogs were terrified, they howled and stopped; we urged them forward with our shouts, and hastily helped now one sledge and then another. We overtook the guides at last; they had stopped on a small tract of very old and level ice, which seemed very solid in comparison with the thin ice around it, and there we breathed freely. After a quarter of an hour the pressures ceased, and nothing more was to be heard beyond slight creaking noises, the last palpitations of that great convulsion.

We resumed our march. I had never felt so weary. I could hardly stand; the dogs refused to go on and we had to beat them every minute. At half-past two we found a channel which we crossed, and climbed up on a large block of ice which from the other side of the channel seemed to be attached to the ice-pack, but which was really surrounded by water. At that moment, both ice-fields began to move, and we remained imprisoned on this floating island, which seemed as though it would be shattered to bits by the first strong pressure. For some minutes we felt very uneasy; we had to escape from thence at any price. Luckily, the channel closed up slightly towards the north. Petigax and Fenoillet lost no time, and by working with admirable cleverness and coolness in the midst of falling blocks, and on ice-floes which seemed about to sink, they made a passage, across which the sledges were quickly dragged to a place of safety.

We sought for some shelter from a fresh south-west wind which had risen, and made our luncheon with coffee. The meridian altitude gave us 86°4'. We still wanted ten miles to reach Nansen's farthest latitude, and in four hours at most we ought to be able to cover them. We resolved at all costs to attempt to reach 86°16' that evening.

At half-past three we set out again. We had at first wide expanses of level ice, then new ice, and then a frozen lake. The dogs seemed to have felt great relief from the short rest, and pulled willingly without stopping. I, too, was completely freed from the strange and sudden fatigue of this morning. We twice crossed the lake, which was curved in the shape of a gigantic horseshoe, with its convexity turned towards the east, and came upon a level and smooth ice-pack, sprinkled over with blocks of ice, at the beginning, and then without any elevation or ruggedness.

Petigax and Fenoillet walked singly, about a hundred steps ahead of the convoy, which went on in silence, leaving behind it two furrows, which faded away in the distance. Every now and then I looked at the time; in spite of the rapidity of our march, we advance for more than an hour, or an hour and a half, without the briefest halt, then, after five minutes' rest, on again. Seven o'clock passed, eight o'clock passed, and still we went on. We must have covered much more than ten miles, but at that moment I hardly took note of this. I did not even think of it. The absence of all obstacles, the sameness, the monotony of the march had stupefied my brain, and I followed my sledges, which did not require my help, as though I were asleep. My thoughts wandered far away — far from ice and cold. I was among green trees and in a warm climate . . . I was dreaming . . .

During our short stoppages we looked at each other, smiling, but none of us spoke; it seemed to us as though our voices might break the charm which was leading us on to victory.

Nine o'clock passed; Petigax had taken the leading place, and, walking with long strides, had left the convoy behind; the sledges sometimes drew nearer to or fell back from each other, but never stopped. The sky had become clear, the wind had again shifted to the north, and here and there were heaps on the ice.

It was a quarter to ten. My mind came back to the present, and I remembered that tomorrow we should have to travel again. I called out to Petigax and made signs to him to stop to encamp. To our left was a small hillock; we brought the sledges near to it so as to shelter them from the north wind, and drew them up in line; the tent was untied and spread. We did all this mechanically, like automata.

When beneath the tent, at that first moment of repose, when all the fibres of the body seem to unbend and relax after long fatigue, the clear idea of things came back to me. We have conquered! We have surpassed the greatest explorer of the century.

We planted our flag before the tent. I prepared a special soup, made up from all the stores we had; half a biscuit apiece was served out over and above the usual ration; it was a feast worthy of Lucullus. Then we made punch — real punch, with cognac — and drank to the Duke of the Abruzzi, to the prosperity of our country and to those who were absent.

At one o'clock we were not in bed; we talked about our families, our friends and our comrades; of the satisfaction that they, and still more our Prince, would feel with the work we had performed. More than ever did we feel profoundly grateful towards Him who had opened for us a path to glory. For that evening, after so many privations and so much anxiety, our enterprise seemed glorious to us. The temperature had fallen to −39°, but we only perceived the cold was so intense when we looked at the thermometer.

Tuesday, April 24th. — We awoke very late this morning. The thermometer indicates −37°. It must have fallen last night below −40°. The weather is fine, and there is still a north wind, which pierces the skin.

I decided yesterday evening that I would go on all day and tomorrow until noon; then take the meridian altitude, have our meal, and afterwards try by a single march to return to encamp in this place. I calculate that thus I shall certainly reach 86°30′.

The men were pleased with my plan, though their eyes showed the desire they felt in their hearts of reaching the 87th degree. But I resist this general wish; I try to persuade all, including myself, that it is merely vanity to want to make up the round number; to the 250 miles from our farthest point north to Prince Rudolph Island we should have to add sixty, almost a fourth of the amount, and that would be too much!

We are not ready to start till a quarter to twelve. I wait till I have again taken the meridian altitude. We travelled yesterday even more than we thought, and performed a really wonderful march. We are in 86°18′20″N lat., and the magnetic variation is zero.

At ten minutes past twelve we are on our way to the north. The ice is like that of yesterday, level and smooth, and, later on, undulating. At first the dogs are not very willing to pull, but encouraged by our cries and a few blows, they advance at a rapid pace, which they keep up during the whole march. At five we meet with a large pressure-ridge, which almost surprises us, as it seems to us a century since we have seen any; we lost a quarter of an hour in preparing a passage through and crossing it. Beyond it the aspect of the ice changes; the undulations are more strongly marked, and large blocks of ice and small ridges indicate recent pressures, but luckily they do not stop us or obstruct our way.

Soon after six we come upon a large channel running from east to west; we must stop. Beyond the channel is a vast expanse of new ice, much broken up and traversed by many other channels. Even if I were not prevented from doing so, I would now think twice before risking myself in the midst of them; I have too lively a remembrance of my anxiety yesterday morning. On the other hand, after the good march we have made today, we consider that we are in 86°31'N lat., and if we did push forward on that ice, even for half a day, we would gain very few miles and besides run the risk of losing a sledge. The dogs are much tired, and we, too, feel the effects of yesterday's strain. I therefore consider that it is more prudent to definitively stop here, and both the guides are of the same opinion.

The sun is quite unclouded. I bring out the sextant and take altitudes of the sun to calculate the longitude, while Fenoillet and Canepa put the sledges in order and spread the tent in a sort of small amphitheatre of hillocks, which shelter us from the north wind. On that farthest to the north, which is almost touched by the water of the channel, we plant the pole, from which our flag waves.

We had a repetition of yesterday's feast, followed by a hearty toast to the Duke of the Abruzzi; while pronouncing it, I feel agitated, and perceive that my emotion is strongly shared by my companions; after a short silence, our conversation begins again with an animation it never attained before under this poor ragged tent. The idea which recurs most often, and amuses us most, is that of our arrival at the cabin – the surprise the Prince and our companions, who, after the details of our first march, must have lost all hope of our ever succeeding in doing anything, would feel. It is suggested that we should make a great placard, with a piece of the tent, and write upon it 86°30', so that they should see it from afar on our arrival. We talk about our homes, and our return to our country. Oh, how the future smiles on us!

We go out into the open air. The thermometer indicates −35°; but, nevertheless, I see, for the first time, the guides walking up and down after the soup. They are talking of *their* country! Of their Courmayeur, where at this moment the meadows appear covered with verdure, after their long rest under the white mantle of winter. We all remain outside for a long time, our minds enchanted by our great happiness. We have reached the end of all our fatigues; our return seems to us now like an excursion, our eyes turn no more with eagerness towards the north, but to the south, where, beyond so much ice, beyond a cold sea, and the rugged mountains of Scandinavia, and farther on again, our loved ones are waiting for us.

The air is very clear; between the north-east and the north-west there stand out distinctly, some sharply pointed, others rounded, dark or blue and white, often with strange shapes, the innumerable pinnacles of the great blocks of ice raised up by the pressure. Farther away, again, on the bright horizon, in a chain from east to west, is a great azure wall, which from afar seems insurmountable. It is our 'Terræ ultima Thule'!

To the south, however, stretches away the level expanse of ice, white and sparkling, lit up by the midnight sun.

Wednesday, April 25th. – I was not able to close my eyes last night, either on account of the cold or of my state of nervous excitement; and the men, also, slept little. We rose at seven; we ate only pemmican, and set to work to get the sledges ready. I have decided on leaving one, and we must unload them all; for a part of the pemmican, which has hitherto formed the foundation of the loads, must be taken away, to have at hand when required. When all the loads are made up, the heaviest sledge weighs 418 lb, and the lightest, from which nothing is to be taken for some time, 374 lb.

I place in the snow three tin tubes, hermetically closed with wax, each containing one of the usual papers addressed to the Hydrographic Office of the Royal Navy. I have written on the paper 'April 25th, 1900. 86°31'N lat. 68°E long. (I believe that this is correct within a couple of miles.) Having reached this my farthest point to the north, I begin my return journey with provisions for thirty days, 200 rations of pemmican, four sledges, and thirty-four dogs, with 300 rations. We are all in excellent health. – CAGNI.'

At eleven we have everything quite ready, and we take our coffee and milk; while the men are packing up the tent and harnessing the dogs, I take the meridian altitude, both with the artificial horizon and the natural horizon, which is very distinct. It is easy to do so on account of the very slight elevation of the sun in this latitude. We are at 86°32'N lat. [He later corrected this to 86°34'49"N.]

The convoy is ready to start; I photograph it, and give the signal of departure.

Petigax goes forward, following the tracks made yesterday, and our hearts beat quickly as we take the first steps of our return to our country.

Cagni had achieved a record farthest north at about 86°34′N, but at a price. One of his three-man support parties, led by the scientist Francesco Querini, failed to arrive back at the base. Despite a search for them, they were never found; three lives had been lost in pursuit of a 20-mile advance beyond the previous record.

After returning home in September 1900, the Duke of the Abruzzi returned to naval service and to mountaineering around the world, but he did not return to the Arctic.

– 10 –

Peary Enters the Arena

1898–1906

The most obsessive of all seekers of the North Pole, and one of the first to claim to have attained it, was the American explorer Robert Edwin Peary.

Peary was born to a poor family in Pennsylvania on 6 May 1856. After service in the US Coast and Geodetic Survey and the US Navy (of which he remained an officer throughout his career), he began to dream of achieving greatness as an explorer. His first expedition was a relatively modest trip to central west Greenland, during which he ascended onto the ice cap to a distance of about 150 km inland. The depth of his driving ambition is revealed in a rather chillingly intense passage in a letter to his mother a few months later. His Greenland journey had brought him some recognition, but he wanted more.

> I *must* have fame, and I cannot reconcile myself to years of commonplace drudgery and a name late in life when I see an opportunity to gain it now and sip the delicious draughts while yet I have youth and strength and capacity to enjoy it to the utmost. And I am not entirely selfish, mother. I want my fame *now* while you too can enjoy it.

This quotation, along with several others later on, is taken from the British explorer Wally Herbert's excellent biography of Peary, *The Noose of Laurels*, published in 1989.

Peary began his quest for fame with a series of more ambitious expeditions to the northern part of the Greenland ice cap. On his expedition of 1891–2, he crossed the ice cap from west to east, discovering what is known as Peary Land. Frederick Cook served as surgeon on that expedition, and the experience showed him something of the dark side of Peary's ambition: despite his remark to his mother, it was utterly selfish. He was so single-mindedly determined to fulfil his own chosen destiny that he was prepared to humiliate his subordinates, virtually enslave an entire band of Eskimos (whom he called 'my natives'), and he harboured a consuming hatred for anyone he considered a rival. Already, he showed a conviction that north Greenland belonged to him alone, just as he was later to claim ownership of the North Pole. He crossed Greenland again on his expedition of 1893–5, and he returned to north Greenland in 1896 and 1897, with the object of removing a meteorite that the Eskimos of the region had used as a source of iron for generations. It was on his next expedition, in 1898–1902, that he made his first attempts to attain the Pole. All Peary's North Pole expeditions used the route explored by Kane and Hall, and were usually launched from the north coast of Ellesmere Island.

An incident in his preparation for the first attempt indicates the absolute obsession that had taken hold of him. In the winter of 1898–9, he and his black servant, Matt Henson, made a journey to northern Ellesmere Island in atrocious weather. At one point, Peary began to suspect his feet were frozen. Henson's biographer reports the story.

> Matt handed a bucket to Ahnidloo and told him to fill it with snow. Then he inserted the blade of his knife under the top of Peary's sealskin boots. He ripped the boots from both feet, and gently removed the rabbit-skin undershoes. Both legs were bloodless white up to the knee, and, as Matt ripped off the undershoes, several toes from each foot clung to the hide and snapped off at the first joint.
>
> 'My God, Lieutenant! Why didn't you tell me your feet were frozen?'
>
> 'There's no time to pamper sick men on the trail,' Peary replied tersely. Then he added thoughtfully, 'Besides, a few toes aren't much to give to achieve the Pole.'

After the subsequent surgical removal of more frostbitten flesh, Peary was left with no more than two little toes. His 'stumps', as he called what was left of his feet, gave him occasional discomfort for the rest of his exploring career.

Despite that heroic determination, his first two attempts were poor failures; in 1900 he reached only 83°50′N, and in 1902 84°17′27″N. He returned home despondently reflecting that, at the age of 46, he was already too old for journeys of that kind. However, he retained the loyalty of his supporters, a powerful group who had organized themselves in 1899 as the Peary Arctic Club, and before long he was planning another effort. He also began to revise his travelling techniques into what he called the 'Peary System', which was essentially a combination of long-distance sledging methods developed by other explorers during the nineteenth century. A main Pole party was preceded over the ice by a trailblazing party, which in addition to preparing a route through the hummocks, also built igloos for the main party to sleep in. Other supporting parties followed the trailblazers planting depots of provisions along the route. So, the main party, freed of as much weight and as many time-consuming chores as possible, could travel fast and light towards the Pole. Eskimos served as dog drivers, and Peary was always accompanied also by Matt Henson. Thus prepared, Peary set out for the Arctic again on the ship *Roosevelt* on 16 July 1905. He wintered at Cape Sheridan in extreme northeast Ellesmere Island, and in February 1906 he travelled west along the island's north coast where he started out onto the ice.

March 6th. I left Point Moss and headed northward from the land over the Polar pack.

In 1902 it was just a month later that I left Hecla going north. And four years previous, on the 6th of March, I left Payer Harbour with eighteen sledges on a journey which took me to 84°17′ north latitude; a great march as regards distance and latitude covered.

I quote from my Journal: 'If I can do as well this time we shall win. God and all good angels grant it, and let me seize this great trophy for the Flag.'

We were rather late in getting started and it was noon when we left the edge of the ice some two miles north of the land. Here the sun was visible for a few moments through a notch in the southern mountains. Was it a good omen? I thought that it must be.

An ideal day, clear and calm and bitter cold, the southern sky vivid yellow, the northern rose-coloured like my dreams.

The going was good at first though our trail was tortuous, but later became extremely arduous.

Reaching Henson's first igloo, Marvin, Ryan and I remained and began working upon an additional igloo, while I sent my Eskimos ahead with half-loads to form an advance cache and reconnoitre the ice. They returned with a report that the ice was heavily rafted since yesterday's party passed and the trail faulted. Two sledges were considerably damaged by the day's work. My supper and breakfast of tea and raw frozen, musk-ox steak were more than enjoyable.

Again I quote from my Journal: 'The battle is on at last. We are straightened out on the ice of the Polar Sea heading direct for our goal.'

He made swift progress at first, but on 26 March, at 84°30'N, his luck changed.

After striking Henson's trail we kept on over large old floes of hard surface interrupted by not particularly difficult pressure ridges, and after a good long march reached Henson's igloo.

His record said that he was here during the storm of the 22nd and had left on the 23rd. A postscript undated said there was an igloo just ahead and a lead beyond. The Captain's record of the 25th said he was leaving about noon to join Henson.

I had noticed in coming up to the igloos a dark object on the northern edge of the floe, and now assumed it to be an empty tin, or cast off clothing on top of an igloo.

When my men came up we fed the dogs, put our gear inside, and began making tea, when Ahngmalokto said he could hear dogs up ahead of us. I turned the tea making over to him, and went out to investigate.

I soon met the Captain coming out to me, and found three parties banked up here, by a broad open lead extending east and west across our course, farther than we could see. I immediately started to investigate the lead and from a pinnacle it looked as if there might be a chance to cross during the night. The northern ice was slowly moving west.

I told Henson to have his men stand watch and watch, and if the chance came to notify everyone so that a quick crossing could be effected. I then went back to my igloo.

After my tea I sent a note to the Captain telling him if there was a chance to cross, to travel with Henson for two days and then return, and a note to Henson to get across the lead at the first possible moment and push on.

Early in the morning of the 27th I went up to see how things were going, and met the Captain coming to report that Henson had started to try and get across to the west, and he was about to follow.

When he got away I climbed a pinnacle to reconnoitre and was not encouraged. The lead was evidently widening. Came down and sent a note to the Captain that if he could not get across to return with everyone and I would send him and Clark and their men back for more supplies. I could not afford to feed all these teams and people here during what might be a several days' wait.

The Captain and Clark got away before noon with seven sledges, and I moved up beside the lead. At night the lead was still widening and the ice slowly moving west.

The open water caused a long delay, and he was still camping by the lead on 1 April.

It was a shame to be wasting such weather in idleness, and yet it could not be helped, nor was it possible to be seriously downhearted in such sunshine. In the morning the centre of the lead had closed so that a man 'walking wide' as the polar bear does, could cross it, but an easterly movement of the northern ice during the night had opened a place some 200 feet wide on the northern side of the lead which effectually barred crossing. The set of the current was still to the west. A light air from NEN and NW during the day might I hoped shut the lead up by morning.

We continued drying our clothing in the sun and doing odd jobs to pass away time and keep from thinking. It was wearing to be held from one's work and object so many days, and yet there were many chances yet. It was still early in the season, dogs and men were in good condition, and I could not help believing that once across this lead (the 'Hudson River?') which is undoubtedly the tidal crack between the land ice of Lincoln Sea and the central polar pack, we should have good going and little interruption from water.

I had two beacons made of empty pemmican tins and placed one on the summit of Observatory Pinnacle, and the other on a high pinnacle to the west.

I quote from my Journal:

April 2nd. – Across the 'Hudson River' at last, thank God, after a loss of seven days of fine weather.

Ryan came in about nine last evening with his three men Ahngodoblaho, 'Teddy' and Itukashoo.

He brings a story of delay from open leads at the igloos where the Doctor turned back; again this side of cache number two, and in his last march here, which makes my men's faces very long. The Captain was also bothered by open water and was three days getting to the cache. Ryan met him just this side.

On the other hand he says from the 'Dr's igloos' in to the land the ice has not moved, and that there was no wind in near the land on the 22nd.

Further setbacks followed, and soon frustration began to emerge as the weather took a turn for the worse.

The ten days' delay of Henson's party, and seven of mine, in fine weather, had been a terrible set-back. Without that we should have been beyond Abruzzi's highest now. As it was I was two degrees ahead of four years ago, when I left Cape Hecla.

The wind and snow continued all night of the 6th and the forenoon of the 7th, then the sun broke through and showed that it was no longer snowing, though the wind continued unabated accompanied by a furious and blinding drift.

On this date Nansen reached his highest, and but for the accursed lead, I should now have been ahead of him. As it was I was behind him and stalled again. Came on thick again during the night and continued blowing and drifting without abatement. It seemed as if it *must* clear off some time, but as yet there were no signs of it.

The wind continued its infernal howling past the igloo and among the pinnacles of the rafter close by all night. I was so comfortable physically, however (barring my stumps which were always cold when I was not walking, and sometimes even then), that there was nothing to distract me from its hell-born music, or keep me from thinking of the unbearable delay. It seemed as if I had been here a month. The wind which had been a little south of true west swung more to the south, the drift was less dense, as if the bulk of the snow were packed, and I fancied there was less weight in the wind in the evening. I hoped to God it would clear soon. I was curious also to see if the continued blow had materially changed our position to the east. There had been no detectable disturbance in the ice since the morning of the 6th. This could be accounted for in two ways; one that the ice was already jammed to the eastward, and the old floes too heavy (and with no young ice between) to permit any compacting or shutting up; the other that the central pack (detached from the land ice along the big lead) was moving eastward as one mass. I could not help thinking that in the latter case, the differences of wind pressure and water resistance of the different floes would cause more or less motion among them, or at least cause strains that would be more pronounced. It would be surprising if the 'Hudson' was not wide open now, and I hoped Marvin and Clark were across it with their supplies, and the former near enough to overtake me in a march or two from here. If the 'Hudson' was open and they the other side of it, it would necessitate a decided modification of my plans, for the season was too late now for me to wait for them to come up. I must push on with what I had here, and take the chances of good going, long marches, and the certainty of eating dog again before I got back to land.

April 10th was another miserable day. The wind not quite so violent, but still continuing with a heavy drift that made travelling out of the question.

Temporarily at least I had got past chafing at the delay and simply longed for the cessation of the infernal music, and to see the bright sun glinting on the ice-fields again, as a thin-blooded invalid in winter longs for the soft breath of summer.

I cheated as much of the time away as possible, planning what I would do when I got back, and then I ran against the black wall, unless I win *here*, all these things fall through. Success is what will give them existence. Then I went over again what I should do in the various contingencies, if it ever cleared, but that did not take long. I knew what I should do in every contingency I could think of.

And always through the black shadow of impending failure showed the steady light of so many days nearer my island and its people.

I quote from my Journal:

Another day, the sixth of the interminable gale. Will it never end?

Soon after, it did end. Ironically, it also improved the going for him; the wind had driven hard-packed snow into the hummocks of the pressure ridges, evening out his trail. But the delays caused by the open lead and the gale had been too great; also, his dogs were becoming exhausted. All he could hope to achieve now was a new record surpassing Abruzzi's, but it gave him no pleasure.

Hurrying on between these leads a forced march was made. Then we slept a few hours, and starting again soon after midnight, pushed on till a little before noon of the 21st.

I should have liked to leave everything at this camp and push on for the one march with one empty sledge and one or two companions, but I did not dare to do this owing to the condition of the ice, and was glad as we advanced that I had not attempted it. I do not know if any of my Eskimos would have remained behind. In this last spurt we crossed fourteen cracks and narrow leads, which almost without exception, were in motion.

When my observations were taken and rapidly figured, they showed that we had reached 87°6' north latitude, and had at last beaten the record, for which I thanked God with as good a grace as possible, though I felt that the mere beating of the record was but an empty bauble compared with the splendid jewel on which I had set my heart for years, and for which, on this expedition, I had almost literally been straining my life out.

It is perhaps an interesting illustration of the uncertainty or complexity of human nature that my feelings at this time were anything but the feelings of exultation which it might be supposed that I should have. As a matter of fact, they were just the reverse, and my bitter disappointment combined perhaps with a certain degree of physical exhaustion from our killing pace on scant rations, gave me the deepest fit of the blues that I experienced during the entire expedition.

As can perhaps be imagined, I was more than anxious to keep on, but as I looked at the drawn faces of my comrades, at the skeleton figures of my few remaining dogs, at my nearly empty sledges, and remembered the drifting ice over which we had come and the unknown quantity of the 'big lead' between us and the nearest land, I felt that I had cut the margin as narrow as could reasonably be expected. I told my men we should turn back from here.

My flags were flung out from the summit of the highest pinnacle near us, and a hundred feet or so beyond this I left a bottle containing a brief record and a piece of the silk flag which six years before I had carried around the northern end of Greenland.

Then we started to return to our last igloo, making no camp here.

On the return journey, he again had to face difficulties, suffer hardship, negotiate the big lead. The only joy remaining to him was to get back safely to the ship. Late in May, he finally reached

Cape Union, on the Ellesmere Island coast, a short march south of the ship.

I think I never shall forget the march from there to the *Roosevelt*. At risk of being regarded as imaginative I may say that it actually seemed to us as if we had arrived in God's country once more. It was a perfect night, clear and calm, the sunlight softly brilliant and the rich warm colours of the cliffs offering to our eyes a very decided contrast to the savage pinnacles of the sea ice and the snow-covered Greenland coast.

From where we landed the hard level ice-foot presented the best of walking, and we made good time to Cape Rawson. As we rounded it the slender spars of the *Roosevelt* looked very, very beautiful in the yellow midnight May sunlight.

Long before we reached the ship some of the Eskimos in the shore settlement spied us, I saw them scurrying across the ice-foot to the ship, and a few moments later several figures came out from the ship to meet us.

Arrived on board I immediately sent two Eskimos and teams back with food and stimulants to bring in the three stragglers. I learned that Marvin and Ryan and some Eskimos had left for the Greenland coast in search of Clark, and that Captain Bartlett and Dr Wolf were still pegging away at the work north of Hecla. I sent a messenger to recall Marvin, and another with a letter to Hecla to reach Captain Bartlett as soon as he arrived.

Then to my room where I quickly ripped my rank fur clothing from myself, and threw it out on the quarter-deck; then to my bath. After that, my dinner, a real dinner with real food such as civilized men eat; and then to my blankets and to sleep, unmindful of the morrow.

I quote from my Journal of the next day:

What a delicious thing rest is. With Jo's picture on the wall above my head, with my face buried in Ahnighito's pillow of Eagle Island fir needles, and its exquisitely delicious fragrance in my nostrils, I for the moment echo from the bottom of my heart Ootah's remark, 'I have got back again, thank God!' Yet I know that a little later I shall feel that I might have done more and yet got back, and yet again still deeper down I know that we went to the very limit and that had we not got across the 'big lead', when we did, we should not have returned.

Since reaching the ship I have had an aversion to pencil and paper, and have only cared to lie and think and plan. To think after all the preparation, the experience, the effort, the strain, the chances taken, and the wearing of myself and party to the last inch, what a little journey it is on the map and how far short of my hopes it fell. To think that I have failed once more; that I shall never have a chance to win again.

It is understandable that at that point Peary should have been deeply depressed, deprived of hope. But after his return home in December 1906, his despondency slowly began to lift. Many of his supporters remained willing to back him, and before long he found himself planning one more attempt, which was eventually scheduled for 1908. In the meantime, there was at least one rival still in the ring.

– 11 –

The American Onslaught

1898–1909

The 1890s had seen the quest for the North Pole become an international race. In the first decade of the twentieth century it was still a race, but became almost exclusively an American preserve. In addition to Peary, several other American explorers and adventurers mounted an intensive assault on the Pole: Walter Wellman, Evelyn Briggs Baldwin, Anthony Fiala, and Frederick Albert Cook.

Of these, the most persistent was Walter Wellman (1859–1934), a journalist who mounted no fewer than five attempts. All were spectacularly unsuccessful in terms of approaching the Pole, but some were imaginative and innovative, and achieved success in other respects.

Wellman also expressed as lucidly as any explorer the reasons that compelled him to seek the Pole.

The quest of the North Pole – and the South Pole – is a law of gravity within man. It is the all-compelling instinct to know all of the unknown; it matters not where – in the depths of the sea, high in the air, in the mystery of the origin of life, in the greater puzzle of the hereafter, in the whisperings from the occult world, in the geologic records of ages past, in the minutiae of chemistry, in the vastness of the solar and stellar systems, in the infinitude of space – everywhere and as to everything, from the planets to atoms, man wants to know, feels that he must know.

The North Pole stood as the centre and symbol of a vast, unknown region. To make this unknown known was one of the highest ambitions of man. The utilitarian value of that knowledge is perhaps nothing. Its scientific value is a matter of opinion and discussion. But the true scientific spirit is: 'Wherever in all the realm of physics there exists an unknown, a missing link, a dark spot, go find what is there, and discuss its value afterward in the light of the knowledge gained.'

Wellman's first attempt was in 1894, when he made a relatively conventional journey north by dog-sledge from Svalbard. This attempt was thwarted when his ship, *Ragnvald Jarl*, was crushed by ice off Walden Island (Waldenøya), a small island in northeast Svalbard. He tried to set off for the Pole after the ship had been wrecked, but the lateness of the season and deteriorating ice conditions stopped him before he reached 81°N. He tried again in 1898–9 on an expedition to Franz Josef Land. This time, a month after setting off for the Pole from the southern part of the archipelago, and just as he prepared to leave the northernmost island of the group, and to set out, full of optimism, across the Arctic Ocean, his plans were ruined.

But pride goeth before a fall. On this very morning which marked the end of the Arctic night and the dawn of the brighter day, a little accident happened. It was a trivial thing in itself, tremendous in its consequences. My sledge, carrying 500 pounds of weight, had stuck in a rough place. As usual, I called to the dogs and threw my weight into the harness. A lunge forward, and down into a little crack in the ice – a tiny little crack such as we had crossed every day by the scores – went my right leg. The momentum threw me forward upon my face, and my shin bone received the full force of the thrust. At first I thought the leg was broken in two or three places, so great was the pain. For a few moments I felt faint. But when I had picked myself up and found that I had nothing worse than a bruise and sprain, I counted myself very lucky, and went on my way as contented as if nothing had happened.

Next morning of course I was sore and lame, and the prudent thing would have been to stop for a week or ten days and get all right again. But I kept going, the leg getting worse and worse, and I suppose I should have been rash enough to go so far that I never could have gotten back had not something else happened.

Fortunately, this other thing did happen, and it came down upon us like a thief in the night, in the shape of an ice-pressure which acted just like an earthquake under our camp and destroyed sledges, dogs, stores and instruments in the twinkling of an eye, and came within an ell of getting all of us.

After these two incidents, he had no option but to turn back with his Pole journey scarcely begun. His leg was far more badly damaged than he chose to think; after returning to his base, he spent the next 15 weeks lying flat on his back on the floor of the hut, waiting for it to mend. Despite that, the expedition did not fail completely. The party carried out a scientific programme and made some important geographical discoveries in the archipelago.

After his two failures to reach the Pole over the ice, Wellman decided upon a radically different approach to the problem, and elected to use an airship. This was a courageous decision. He had first thought of a balloon flight during his first expedition in 1894, about the same time as Andrée, but the fate of Andrée's second expedition discouraged him from pursuing the idea. As a journalist, he had also gained insights into the terrible pressures that the world's press was, by then, capable of placing on the shoulders of explorers, especially if they announced an intention to reach the North Pole. From that moment on, everything the explorer did came under the gaze of the public. He had seen it happen to Andrée.

Andrée, it will be remembered, was unable to make his flight in 1896, and was attacked by the yellow press of his own and other countries as a bluffer and fakir because he had sense enough not to start before the conditions were favourable. Brave as he was in ignoring the cowards who love to throw printer's ink and other nasty stuff at a man who tries to do something and doesn't do it quickly enough to suit the mob – the mob that always howls to have the gladiator kill the beast or the beast eat the gladiator the first half hour or damns it as a poor show – he at last fell victim to their goadings.

By the following year he had learned that his balloon was a poor one; that it did not hold gas well. He realized it was not fit for such a voyage, even if the plan itself was sound. But Andrée knew if he failed to start, the yellow press would hound him into his grave, and he preferred death in the Arctics.

I know from men who were with him that Andrée said, just before he sailed, in July, 1897, that he was committing suicide. He did not dare abandon his effort and go home to face the newspapers. He did start.

A dirigible, powered airship was less vulnerable than a powerless balloon, but even so it was a new technology, still untried in polar exploration, and the first airship that Wellman tried could summon only a meagre 70 horse-power, generating a top speed of just 18 miles per hour. He found sponsorship for an aerial attempt on the Pole from the *Chicago Record-Herald*, but his first airship expedition, in 1906, experienced much the same fate as Andrée's first, ten years previously. Tempting fate, he chose a take-off site very close to Andrée's, on Danskøya, northwest Svalbard. There, all the ground facilities for his flight were installed, but it was soon found that the airship's mechanical equipment was defective. Like Andrée on his first attempt, he never took off; the main body of the airship, named *America*, was never even unpacked.

After that failure, Wellman took his airship back to Paris for major modifications. Its balloon was enlarged to increase the lift; the 'car' underneath was redesigned; and the power was increased by the use of two 80 horse-power engines providing a top speed of 26 miles per hour. It was by then the second largest airship in the world, surpassed only by one of the early models of the famous zeppelins, but this was still not enough to cope with strong headwinds, so again, like Andrée, Wellman had to rely on ideal weather conditions. The airship also had another weakness in that, rather like Andrée's balloon, it had a long dangling leather rope that Wellman called an 'equilibrator'. This had fuel cans attached to it, intended to stabilize the airship and control its height.

The expedition arrived back at the base used in 1906 on 8 June 1907. The preparations were completed by the end of July, but then Wellman found the weather against him. He had to wait for over a month before contrary winds moderated. On 2 September the conditions were right and Wellman, the engineer Melvin Vaniman and the navigator Felix Riesenberg, started their flight. By this time, the season was late, and Wellman preferred to call it a trial flight rather than an attempt on the Pole. Nevertheless, it had its exciting moments.

The engine was started, and the *America* leaped forward. With a thrill of joy we of the crew felt her moving through the air. Looking down from our lofty perch, we could see the equilibrator swimming along in the water, its head in the air, much like a great sea-serpent. We soon ran away from the steamer, and could hear the men upon her cheering us as we lost sight of her. Soon the wind freshened from the northwest, accompanied by snow. We were in danger of being driven upon the mountainous coast, which would mean the destruction of the ship and probably the loss of our lives as the steel car went tumbling down the cliffs into the sea.

Everything depended upon the engine. Vaniman kept it running, and increased its effective output as the danger of shipwreck became most pressing. Inch by inch we fought our way past the mountains, one after another, clearing the last by only a few rods. The open Arctic Ocean was before us; and well satisfied with the work-ing of engine and ship up to this time, it was with great satisfaction I gave the order to Riesenberg at the wheel to 'head her north!' We should have a try at it, at least.

But we had not run far before the snow-squall increased in violence. Just then we learned our compass had been deranged by an accident. The air was so thick with flying snow we could not see the mountains, and were lost in a snowstorm threatening to drive us to destruction upon a lee coast. Three times we came up so near the mountains, looming suddenly ahead out of the thick air, that we thought all was over, but each time the motor and propeller brought us round to temporary safety, with the helm thrown hard over.

At last, after some two hours of this, during which we must have covered 35 miles, we realized there was but one thing to do, and that was to try to land the ship where she could be saved. In a momentary break in the thickness of the weather we saw before us a glacier – a mass of ice filling a valley between two mountains – and decided to make an effort to bring the *America* down upon its smooth surface.

But before we could descend upon the glacier we must drag our equilibrator, and also the retarder (which we had now let down into the sea) up the face of the great ice-wall – a vertical cliff of ragged, rugged ice rising nearly 100 feet sheer from the sea. Was it possible for our serpents to climb this frightful barrier? We should soon see, for now the wind was driving us straight toward the frightful precipice. As the *America* swept over the glacier the two serpents crawled up the wall without getting foul and apparently without injury. Arriving at the top, they wound between and around giant rocks of the moraine. As we moved inland the serpents fell into deep crevasses in the ice, and then crept out again.

Finally, by pulling the valve-cord and letting out gas we brought the airship down near to the surface of the glacier. At the right moment the ripping knife was run into the sides of the huge envelope overhead, the gas rushed out; with a sigh the *America* gave up her life-breath, and settled down upon the ice. The descent was made so gently that our clockwork registering instruments ran right along as if nothing had happened. As we stepped out of the car the cloth of the balloon lay in a great heap alongside, and we saw that the America lay across two crevasses. And there, still attached to the ship, were the two serpents, virtually uninjured after their rough experience.

The three men survived; it was the first flight by an airship over the Arctic Ocean, however brief; and Wellman remained confident enough in his chosen means of transport to try it again. In 1908 his commitment, as a journalist, to the

Presidential election of that year prevented a further attempt, but in 1909, he was again ready with an improved and more powerful airship, *America II.*

Wellman, although an admirable innovator, was not one of the luckiest of polar explorers. Even before he began his fifth attempt on the Pole, he learned that one of the two men appointed to look after his airship hangar during his absence had drowned on a hunting trip. The hangar had been destroyed in a storm. The rebuilding of the facilities took several weeks and delayed his start, but finally, by mid-August, he was ready.

August 15, 1909, we started on the second voyage the *America* had made over the polar sea. In the crew were Vaniman and I, cool-headed, resourceful Louis Loud, who is Vaniman's brother-in-law, and Nicholas Popoff, a daring and clever young Russian, who later took up aviation, and won the cup at Nice by a fine flight out over the Mediterranean and back.

Again we carried the leather equilibrator which had been so severely tested in the flight of 1907, when, in making our descent upon the Spitzbergen mainland through a snowstorm, the serpent climbed the rugged vertical glacier face, a hundred feet of sheer ice, wound in and out among the great boulders brought down in the moraine of the glacier, plumped deep into crevasses and crawled out of them again, and was with us practically uninjured when the ship finally came to rest in the valley of ice.

This second voyage began propitiously. The weather was fine, a light breeze blowing from the south. At the wheel I steered her several times around the strait which lay in front of our camp to learn if everything was in good order. All going well I headed her north. We passed out over Smeerenburg point of Amsterdam Island, where the Dutch whalers had a blubber-boiling station two centuries past. The equilibrator just touched the sands where the summer town reeked with whale oil and rum in the long ago.

One look back to our camp showed the men there waving their hats in excited glee and running for the hilltops, the better to see the airship as she moved toward the northern horizon. It was with inexpressible joy we of the crew noted how strong and fast we were going north. The engine was running steadily. The ship was not pitching or rolling. The equilibrator seemed to be riding well. Helped a little by the breeze, we were making close to twenty-five knots per hour, northward, toward the Pole.

At last our three years of arduous work, our long vigil of worry and planning, our weeks and months of struggle against gales and all sorts of obstacles, seemed in a fair way to be rewarded. The ship we had so painstakingly built and perfected was giving a splendid account of herself.

We had made a fine start. To the east the icy mountains and huge glaciers of the Spitzbergen coast glistened in the sunlight. To the north the ice-pack's white was looming in view. Far to the southwest our steamer, the *Arctic*, was headed our way, a dot on the waters, moving with such clumsy slowness compared with our ship of the air. Below us the dark green waters of the polar sea glided past, our equilibrator's lower end thirty or forty yards above them.

So elated were we, one and all, that we hallooed to one another, and laughed, and cracked our jokes, Vaniman and Loud in the engine room smiling up at Popoff and me at the wheel.

I gave the helm to Popoff and prepared to take my 'departure' from the land, as the basis of our dead reckoning. The whole north coast of Spitzbergen, with its sharp-pointed black peaks, its valleys filled with gleaming ice-fields, was rising to our vision, a wondrous Arctic panorama.

At the rate we were going we could reach the Pole in less than thirty hours! It is no wonder we were happy.

In a pause I looked over the side at the waters far below, now flecked with small fields of floating ice, the main pack being but a few miles farther north. At that instant I saw something drop from the ship into the sea. Could one believe his eyes? Yes — it was the equilibrator.

The leather serpent, so thoroughly tested two years before, had played us false. It parted within a yard of the top, and plump down into the ocean went 1,200 pounds of our balancing device and its contents of reserve provisions. Relieved of this load, the *America* shot into the clouds.

Instantly we all knew the voyage was at an end, that

without the equilibrator the ship would soon become unmanageable. The provisions we could do without in a pinch, because we had more in the car. But the equilibrator was indispensable.

Vaniman sang out to me, 'We'll have to fight our way back to Spitzbergen!' And seeing the look on my face, he added, 'There is no help for it — you'll have to do it.'

Our ears were ringing with the rapidity of our ascent. It was growing colder at this great altitude. Vaniman jumped for the valve line and pulled it far down to let enough hydrogen out of the top of the balloon to prevent us going to still greater heights. Before the *America* stopped climbing we had the whole northern part of Spitzbergen spread out in one great frozen picture before our eyes, and I imagined that away in the east I could see Walden Island where the old *Ragnvald Jarl* had been crushed in the ice in 1894. Would the Arctics never bring me anything but bad luck?

And whilst Vaniman was working to stop our flight into the cloud I sat there wondering if I had the right to take the lives of my crew in my hand by holding her head to the north, equilibrator or no equilibrator. My own life, yes; theirs, no. And in bitterness inexpressible, I told Popoff at the wheel to turn her around and steer for Spitzbergen.

Then ensued a struggle which none of us engaged in it will ever forget. At the higher altitude the wind was strong from the southwest. We were carried so far over the ice-pack that the Spitzbergen coast began to fade away in the distance, sixty or seventy miles away. At the lower altitude to which the *America* was presently brought down by letting out gas, the wind was not so strong, and, the motor still working well, we were able to make headway to the southward.

In addition to her equilibrator the *America* carried a similar serpent of leather covered with steel points designed to serve as a retarder or drag-anchor against adverse winds. I asked Vaniman and Loud to let this down to take the place in part of the lost equilibrator when the ship was to descend to the earth. With almost infinite trouble they managed to effect the manoeuvre, and we had the weight of the retarder, 400 pounds, to protect the ship from touching the ice.

Unfortunately, this improvised equilibrator had a loop of steel cable dragging from its lower end, and every ten or fifteen minutes this loop caught fast upon the sharp edge of an ice floe. Popoff and I soon became quite expert in swinging the ship about with her helm, describing full or half circles, till that pesky steel loop would slide off the ice hook in which it had made fast.

Thus we fought our way south, mile by mile and hour by hour, often delayed by the cable loop fouling anew in the ice below, but still making headway, the *America* giving a right good account of herself as a ship of the air under unfavourable circumstances.

Once we heard strange, uncanny sounds from the aft of the ship, near where the sledge dogs lay in their kennel. We recognized Popoff's voice, and knew he was there. But the sounds were unearthly. Afterward, we three compared notes and found all had had the same experience. The blood had seemed to run cold and clammy from our hearts, for each of us felt sure our comrade from Russia had lost his reason and become a jibbering maniac up there in the air over the polar sea.

Ten minutes later the mystery was explained. Popoff had gone back to feed the dogs. One had snapped at him, and the unearthly sounds we had heard with dismay were only Popoff's remonstrance in his native tongue, talking to the dogs, trying to quiet them.

Soon we saw a little steamer working her way out from the coast of Spitzbergen, headed toward us. We knew she was the *Farm*, a Norwegian government vessel, which Captain Isachsen had at Red Bay, where he was carrying on survey work.

For several hours the *Farm* steamed toward us, and we motored toward the *Farm*. We met at the edge of the ice-fields, beyond which line, of course, the *Farm* could not come.

Without much doubt the *America* could have made her way back to our camp under her own power, but we wished to do everything prudence could suggest to make sure of saving our ship. So we gave a tow line to the *Farm*, and the remainder of the afternoon was spent in steaming homeward in this strange manner, a little steamer towing our airship twenty times her size, we up aloft hallooing down to the men on the boat as if they were pigmies of the earth.

But the *America* did not tow well. She ran up alongside of the *Farm*, now on one side, now on the other, and then came around with a jerk and shock which threatened to tear in pieces the steel framework of our car.

An hour or so of this and then the wind strengthened. The danger of a smashup of the car was so great we resolved to let the airship down till it just touched the surface of the sea, hoping she would tow more easily and safely there. So we let out more gas, and soon were wallowing about in the trough of the sea. The *Farm* sent her boats to us, and we managed to get the instruments and dogs over to the steamer. The dogs had been quiet during their voyage in the air. The moment they were put in the boat they fell to fighting one another. Captain Isachsen has written in a Norwegian magazine that he and his officers were every moment expecting to see the frail car of the *America* break up in the sea, and were wondering if it would be practicable to save the crew.

'We were reassured,' he writes, 'when we saw Mr Wellman take out a big cigar, light it, and sit there calmly smoking while he gave orders to his men, which were as calmly obeyed.'

After a great deal of trouble we saved all valuables from the *America* and then the *Farm* towed her back to camp. Here she got away from us. In putting her up on the beach a gust of wind upset the gas bag, spilled off the car and engines, while the envelope, relieved of the weight, blew high in the air and then exploded. It was recovered, not seriously damaged. The steel car was partly destroyed; but that was small loss, as we should not have used it again in any event. All the motors, machinery, and instruments were saved.

Within a week of Wellman's return home in autumn 1909, both

Peary and Cook announced their rival claims to have attained the North Pole, and the attention of the world's press was fixed upon them. Wellman's exploits sank into oblivion. He continued to be enthralled by airships and aviation, and to undertake pioneering flights, but he withdrew from the Arctic. It was to be 17 years before other explorers, with better airships, demonstrated their effectiveness in the exploration of the Arctic Ocean.

In between two of Wellman's early attempts to attain the Pole, his expeditions of 1898–9 and 1906, two other American explorers entered the race, both using the same sponsor. The explorers were Evelyn Briggs Baldwin (1862–1933) and Anthony Fiala (1869–1950), and the sponsor was William Ziegler (1843–1905).

This was a curious episode, for the collaborations of Baldwin and Ziegler in 1901–2, and Fiala and Ziegler in 1903–5, resulted in two of the most lavishly equipped expeditions ever to seek the Pole; they were also two of the most completely unsuccessful.

By 1901, Baldwin already had a modestly impressive record as a polar explorer. He had served as meteorologist on Peary's expedition of 1893–5, and on Wellman's expedition of 1898–9. On the former, he was described by Peary as 'ingenious and perseverant', and on the latter he discovered several islands in Franz Josef Land, including one of the largest in the group, which he named after Alexander Graham Bell. In 1897 his obsession with the Arctic drove him to hasten to Svalbard after hearing of Andrée's expedition, in the hope of securing a place on the balloon. Luckily for him he was too late: the balloon had already left.

It was a chance meeting between Baldwin and Ziegler that brought Baldwin's own expedition to life. Ziegler was a multimillionaire business magnate with interests in real estate, food manufacture and traction. He had observed with interest the development of the race for the Pole during the 1890s, but would probably not have thought of mounting his own expedition had he not been won over by Baldwin, whose impressive record, obvious enthusiasm, and absolute conviction that the Pole could be reached from Franz Josef Land, persuaded him to give Baldwin his chance.

Baldwin must have been amazed by his own good fortune. In Ziegler, he had found the sort of multi-millionaire who believes that any problem can be solved if enough money is thrown at it; in this case he thought $250,000 (about £50,000 at that time) might suffice. So, when Baldwin's palatially outfitted ship *America* headed north in summer 1901, the vessel could barely float under the huge weight of provisions, equipment and coal on board. Much of the equipment appears to have been randomly selected and randomly stored. Baldwin was strong on luxuries: electric lighting, telephones and communications balloons; weak on essentials: he forgot to take dog harnesses. There were also two other ships, the supply ship *Frithjof*, and the *Belgica* which took an emergency depot of supplies for the Pole party to east Greenland. In Archangel, Baldwin completed his arrangements with the purchase of 420 dogs and 15 ponies. He found a suitable base for his expedition on Alger Island (Ostrov Aldzher), one of Wellman's discoveries, and also managed to lay 18 depots of provisions in readiness for the Pole journey. From that point on, however, nothing went right. During winter, Baldwin's popularity among his men plummeted, and it is not difficult to understand why. His novel schemes for keeping his men fit during the winter included sending them over to the other side of the island to bring back a depot of supplies that they had only recently placed there. Nobody liked that. He refused to let them take camping equipment on the grounds that it was only a one-day trip. This nearly backfired on him, when one party got lost – they were travelling entirely in the dark – and were found suffering from frostbite. Some of the most discontented of all were his scientists, who were ordered to take part in this pointless exercise alongside all the others; as a result, they were unable to conduct their research, their sole reason for being there. When the exercise was over their work was again stopped when they were required to occupy much of the winter moving supplies 50 miles north to an advance camp. Baldwin also managed to infuriate the Norwegian captain, Carl Johansen, who quarrelled with him and was promptly relieved of his command. There were many other arbitrary decisions that caused anger among the party: they were not permitted to keep diaries; the artist Russell Porter was ordered to hand over all his paintings and sketches. When, with the return of the sun in

1902, Baldwin started moving several tons of goods north to Rudolf Island, he again made the scientists take part, so their work stopped again; in all they achieved very little during this expedition. Baldwin would not even let them explore during these northern journeys, even though they were surrounded by unknown land.

There was one more supreme folly to come. Having made all his preparations for the journey over the ice, Baldwin suddenly panicked about the low level of his coal stocks – even though the expedition plan included the despatch of a supply ship carrying coal in 1902. So, just as he was poised for his great journey, he ordered the whole expedition back on the ship, and on 1 July (the day the supply ship started out to meet them) they all headed back to Norway. Baldwin's aim was to resume the expedition in 1903, but Ziegler was so dissatisfied with Baldwin's conduct that the leadership was taken from him, and given instead to the expedition's photographer, Anthony Fiala.

Baldwin's failure as a polar explorer ultimately destroyed him as a person. After 1902, his life lapsed into a sad decline. He tried to arrange further expeditions, but his reputation accompanied him everywhere. Eventually he faded to obscurity as a minor government clerk in Washington, DC. In 1933, he lost that job, too, in a round of government economies. During his last months he was supported only by the charity of his friends. On 25 October 1933 he was killed in a motor accident in Washington.

Anthony Fiala was a journalist, newspaper artist and photographer. He had no polar experience before the Baldwin expedition, but during it he had made a good impression as the expedition's photographer, and he had used the opportunity to make the first motion pictures ever recorded in the Arctic. After Ziegler had selected him to replace Baldwin, he still had large sums of money at his disposal, but he used it less extravagantly and more thoughtfully. He left Norway for the Arctic on the ship *America* in June 1903, and despite difficult ice conditions managed to force his ship through the Franz Josef Land archipelago to 82°04′N, a record for a ship in that region. Returning south a little, he reached Abruzzi's old base at Teplitz Bay, Rudolf Island, and established his own base there, naming it 'Camp Abruzzi'. He was lucky enough to find supplies left by Abruzzi still in good condition, and he also retrieved a large quantity of food left on the island by Baldwin. As winter approached, the expedition was snug, comfortable, settling down to its scientific work, and all seemed well. Then, however, Fiala's luck turned against him. In November, the pressure of ice around the ship increased alarmingly, and the expedition's members, most of whom were based on the ship, spent a frantic ten days transporting all their supplies on shore before *America* sank on 21 November. From then on, 39 men had to winter in a hut designed for 15.

Fiala made two attempts on the Pole in 1904, but achieved little. He began his first on 7 March, but the intense cold drove him back after only four days. On a second attempt on 25 March, an early failure of the sledges made him turn back even sooner. After that, his chief responsibility was to escort men who wanted to go home to the south of the archipelago to await the relief ship *Frithjof*. The ship failed to arrive because of bad ice conditions, so Fiala left these men to winter at Cape Flora, while he returned to Rudolf Island. Now, with his expedition worryingly split into two camps at opposite ends of the archipelago, Fiala's determination to lead a sledge party to the Pole began to waver. In the end, his worry about the welfare of the men at Cape Flora overcame him. He set out for the Pole once more on 15 March 1905, but his heart was no longer in it. He turned back only eight days later at 82°N, and from then on his sole concern was to get all his men to safety before the relief ship arrived; the ship, *Terra Nova*, turned up at the end of July, and the whole party sailed for home.

Although he had scarcely been more successful than Baldwin, Fiala's subsequent fate could not have been more different. He was spared the ignominy experienced by his predecessor, and he later worked successfully as a travel photographer, war correspondent, lecturer, and owner of a New York company that specialized in outfitting expeditions to all parts of the world. He died in 1950.

Ziegler, mercifully, was at least spared the embarrassment of another expensive but dismal failure; he died in 1905, before Fiala's return.

– 12 –

The Cook/Peary Feud

1. Cook's Story: 1907–9

As in most aspects of life, the history of Arctic exploration is full of jealousies, rivalries, disputes, hatreds, chicanery, fraud. But nothing in the world of exploration can ever match the sheer depth of nastiness, or the passionate intensity of the feud between supporters of Frederick Albert Cook and Robert Edwin Peary over which of them first attained the North Pole. The two men announced their claims to priority within a week of each other, in September 1909, and within days a bitter quarrel was under way. The dispute has never ended. Even now, well over 80 years after the event, tempers are still simmering, and the arguments are still carried on with a vehemence that appears almost deranged. There are also those who hold more temperate, scholarly views, yet are still unable to agree. When, in 1989, the British polar explorer Wally Herbert published a thoughtful and carefully researched biography of Peary suggesting he had not reached the Pole, he was swiftly rebutted by the National Geographic Society of Washington, DC. The Society, which stood by Peary in 1909, still stands loyally by him today, and will if necessary commission a scientific inquiry to repudiate any serious challenge to his priority.

The beginning of the dispute was such a spectacular piece of theatre that it appears contrived – which it very probably was. On 2 September 1909 Cook, returning south from northwest Greenland on a Danish supply vessel, announced to the world, from a telegraph office in the Shetland Islands, that on 21 April 1908 he had attained the Pole. Just four days later, on 6 September, Peary telegraphed from Indian Harbour, Labrador, that he had reached the Pole on 6 April 1909. The shock-waves that reverberated around the world after those two announcements

were of an immensity never before witnessed in the history of
exploration, not least because each had the backing of rival
American newspapers of enormous influence. Gordon Bennett's
New York Herald had invested in Cook, while the *New York Times*
supported Peary. For once, Bennett backed the wrong man.
Cook's claim was widely accepted in the beginning, but after a
prolonged and vicious smear campaign from the powerful Peary
clan, Peary gained the upper hand, which he retains to this day.
Damaging episodes in Cook's life appeared to expose him as a
practised fraud. That, plus the sheer impossibility of the feats that
he claimed to have accomplished in reaching the Pole, cost him
the race. It was not difficult to fake a journey to the North Pole.
The navigational observations could be worked out beforehand
because the location of the Pole was known. Provided there
was no undiscovered land along the route, it could simply be
recorded as a long, difficult march across the sea ice. Part of
Cook's undoing was that there *was* a little bit of land along the
route he claimed to have taken, and he did not report seeing it.
Nevertheless, Cook still has his supporters, and it is not difficult
to understand why. He was widely acknowledged to be a good,
kind, gentle and compassionate man – in the starkest contrast
to Peary, who was none of these. For many, it is simply more
agreeable to think that he reached the Pole ahead of Peary, but
all the evidence suggests he did not. He is a most difficult man
to understand, but there are hints in his career as to why he
might have chosen to fake the journey.

Frederick Albert Cook was born in the state of New York
in 1865. He trained as a medical doctor, and it was in that
capacity that he began his career as a polar explorer. In
1891–2, he was surgeon and ethnologist on Peary's first expedition to north Greenland. It is ironic to reflect, considering
their later relations, that Peary recorded during the expedition that

> To Dr Cook's care may be attributed the almost complete
> exemption of the party to even the mildest indispositions,
> and personally I owe much to his professional skill, and
> unruffled patience and coolness in an emergency. In
> addition to his work in his special ethnological field, in
> which he has obtained a large mass of most valuable

material concerning a practically unstudied tribe, he was always helpful and an indefatigable worker.

On the other hand, Cook was already forming an entirely different view of Peary. He witnessed Peary's enslavement and abuse of the Eskimos, his inclination to humiliate expedition members who served under him. As a man of compassion, a medical man, he took note of those things. This was the beginning of the deterioration of relations between Cook and Peary. Later, Cook was to attribute the apparent suicide of one of Peary's subordinates, John Verhoeff, to 'Peary's injustice', remarking that he had been 'treated with about the same consideration as that accorded the Eskimo dogs'. When another of Peary's men, Eivind Astrup, died by suicide, Cook again attributed it to Peary's 'injustice and ingratitude' and his 'narrow and intolerant brutality'. Both men were Cook's friends; the death of both clearly poisoned Cook's attitude to Peary; they are substantial clues as to Cook's later behaviour.

These experiences were damaging enough, but relations between the two men were probably soured forever by a later occurrence, in 1901, when Peary's Arctic Club sent Cook to northeast Greenland to examine Peary's physical condition. Noting the absence of Peary's toes, he told him he was 'through as a traveler on snow on foot'. Noting also that he was suffering from malnutrition, he told him to eat raw meat and liver, to which Peary replied 'I would rather die.' Altogether Cook found Peary 'wrecked in ambition, wrecked in physique, wrecked in hope . . . Peary was worried, anxious, discouraged as I have never seen him before.' Cook was meeting Peary at one of the lowest points in his life, and all the news he brought to him was unpleasant. There was already bad feeling between the two men, and this encounter must have sharpened it. These, too, are important clues as to why Cook decided to set himself up as Peary's rival in the quest for the Pole.

Apart from his work with Peary, Cook was trying throughout the 1890s and early 1900s to forge his own career as adventurer and explorer. In 1893 and 1894, he led two minor expeditions to Greenland. In 1897–9, he served on the Belgian Antarctic Expedition, led by Adrien de Gerlache de Goméry – the first exploring expedition to winter in the Antarctic. A colleague on that expedition was Roald Amundsen, who also featured later in the story of the North Pole.

By this time, Cook was establishing a modest but good reputation as an explorer and doctor, and he could have gone on to enhance it still further by legitimate means. But then just a few years later, something went strangely wrong. In 1906, he claimed to have made the first ascent of Mount McKinley in Alaska, North America's highest mountain. The achievement was widely publicized and his book about it became a best-seller. However, after his feud with Peary broke out in 1909, one of the most damaging pieces of evidence brought against him was that he had faked the ascent; he had been nowhere near the top of the mountain. Other members of the expedition had known it all along, but had been silenced by a threat from Cook of libel action.

Cook's attempt on the North Pole began on 3 July 1907, when he departed from the United States on the ship *John R. Bradley*, supposedly on a hunting expedition to the Smith Sound region north of Baffin Bay. He had occasionally attempted on previous expeditions to establish himself as an Arctic travel guide for wealthy Americans, and on this occasion he was sponsored and accompanied by the wealthy big-game hunter J.R. Bradley, after whom the ship was named. But he also harboured a secret desire to claim the North Pole, and when the *Bradley* returned home in September 1907, he remained behind to winter at the tiny Eskimo settlement of Anoritoq, on the Greenland shore of Smith Sound. When winter ended, his movements displayed a pattern which can now be interpreted as obvious signals of an intent to fake a journey to the North Pole. Instead of travelling directly north through the familiar channels beyond Smith Sound, on the favoured 'American' route towards the Pole, he travelled northwest to the northernmost point of Axel Heiberg Island in the Canadian Arctic. This was a crazy route that left him, after a long and arduous journey, still over 500 nautical miles from the Pole. In retrospect, it can only be explained by the fact that it would leave no evidence, neither proof nor disproof, of what he had done; nobody else would dream of following such a route. Other evidence which, in retrospect, can also be considered damning, is that Cook chose to leave behind on Axel Heiberg Island most of his Eskimo companions and his only European companion, Rudolph Francke. He set out north over the sea ice with only two Eskimo companions, E-tuk-i-shuk and Ah-weh-lah. This gives rise to enormous suspicions. Where Peary, Cagni and others had failed to get near to the Pole with intricately prepared plans, using large backup sledge-teams carrying supplies, and even cutting a trail and building igloos, Cook apparently breezed to the Pole with just two Eskimos and no backup at all. His journey is hardly worth reporting because it is almost certainly not true, but this is how he recorded his supposed arrival at the North Pole. His prose, alone, is a clue. It is vague but colourful fiction – and it reads like fiction.

With the Pole only twenty-nine miles distant, more sleep was quite impossible. We brewed an extra pot of tea, prepared a favorite broth of pemmican, dug up a surprise of fancy biscuits and filled up on good things to the limit of the allowance for our final feast days. The dogs, which had joined the chorus of gladness, were given an extra lump of pemmican. A few hours more were agreeably spent in the tent. Then we started out with new spirit for the uttermost goal of our world.

Bounding joyously forward, with a stimulated mind, I reviewed the journey. Obstacle after obstacle had been overcome. Each battle won gave a spiritual thrill, and courage to scale the next barrier. Thus had been ever, and was still, in the unequal struggles between human and inanimate nature, an incentive to go onward, ever onward, up the stepping-stones to ultimate success. And now, after a life-denying struggle in a world where every element of Nature is against the life and progress of man, triumph came with steadily measured reaches of fifteen miles a day!

We were excited to fever heat. Our feet were light on the run. Even the dogs caught the infectious enthusiasm. They rushed along at a pace which made it difficult for me to keep a sufficient advance to set a good course. The horizon was still eagerly searched for something to mark the approaching boreal centre. But nothing unusual was seen. The same expanse of moving seas of ice, on which we had gazed for five hundred miles, swam about us as we drove onward.

Looking through gladdened eyes, the scene assumed a new glory. Dull blue and purple expanses were transfigured into plains of gold, in which were lakes of sapphire and rivulets of ruby fire. Engirdling this world were purple mountains with gilded crests. It was one of the few days on the stormy pack when all Nature smiled with cheering lights.

As the day advanced beyond midnight and the splendour of the summer night ran into a clearer continued day, the beams of gold on the surface snows assumed a more burning intensity. Shadows of hummocks and ice ridges became dyed with a deeper purple, and in the burning orange world loomed before us Titan shapes, regal and regally robed.

From my position, a few hundred yards ahead of the sleds, with compass and axe in hand, as usual, I could not resist the temptation to turn frequently to see the movement of the dog train with its new fire. In this backward direction the colour scheme was reversed. About the horizon the icy walls gleamed like beaten gold set with gem-spots of burning colours; the plains represented every shade of purple and blue, and over them, like vast angel wings outspread, shifted golden pinions. Through the sea of palpitating colour, the dogs came, with spirited tread, noses down, tails erect and shoulders braced to the straps, like chariot horses. In the magnifying light they seemed many times their normal size. The young Eskimos, chanting songs of love, followed with easy, swinging steps. The long whip was swung with a brisk crack. Over all arose a cloud of frosted breath, which, like incense smoke, became silvered in the light, a certain signal of efficient motive power.

With our destination reachable over smooth ice, in these brighter days of easier travel our long chilled blood was stirred to double action, our eyes opened to beauty and colour, and a normal appreciation of the wonders of this new strange and wonderful world.

As we lifted the midnight's sun to the plane of the midday sun, the shifting Polar desert became floored with a sparkling sheen of millions of diamonds, through which we fought a way to ulterior and greater glory.

Our leg cramps eased and our languid feet lifted buoyantly from the steady drag as the soul arose to effervescence. Fields of rich purple, lined with running liquid gold, burning with flashes of iridescent colours, gave a sense of gladness long absent from our weary life. The ice was much better. We still forced a way over large fields, small pressure areas and narrow leads. But, when success is in sight, most troubles seem lighter. We were thin, with faces burned, withered, frozen and torn in fissures, with clothes ugly from overwear. Yet men never felt more proud than we did, as we militantly strode off the last steps to the world's very top!

Camp was pitched early in the morning of April 20. The sun was northeast, the pack glowed in tones of lilac, the normal westerly air brushed our frosty faces. Our surprising burst on enthusiasm had been nursed to its limits. Under it a long march had been made over average ice, with the usual result of overpowering fatigue. Too tired and sleepy to wait for a cup of tea, we poured melted snow into our stomach and pounded the pemmican with an axe to ease the task of the jaws. Our eyes closed before the meal was finished, and the world was lost to us for eight hours. Waking, I took observations which gave latitude 89°46'.

Late at night, after another long rest, we hitched the dogs and loaded the sleds. When action began, the feeling came that no time must be lost. Feverish impatience seized me.

Cracking our whips, we bounded ahead. The boys sang. The dogs howled. Midnight of April 21 had just passed.

Over the sparkling snows the post-midnight sun glowed like at noon. I seemed to be walking in some splendid golden realms of dreamland. As we bounded onward the ice swam about me in circling rivers of gold.

E-tuk-i-shook and Ah-we-lah, though thin and ragged, had the dignity of the heroes of a battle which had been fought through to success.

We all were lifted to the paradise of winners as we stepped over the snows of a destiny for which we had risked life and willingly suffered the tortures of an icy hell. The ice under us, the goal for centuries of brave, heroic men, to reach which many had suffered terribly and terribly died, seemed almost sacred. Constantly and carefully I watched my instruments in recording this final reach. Nearer and nearer they recorded our approach. Step by step, my heart filled with a strange rapture of conquest.

At last we step over coloured fields of sparkle, climbing walls of purple and gold – finally, under skies of crystal blue, with flaming clouds of glory, we touch the mark! The soul awakens to a definite triumph; there is sunrise within us, and all the world of night-darkened trouble fades. We are at the top of the world! The flag is flung to the frigid breezes of the North Pole!

Looking about me, after the first satisfactory observation, I viewed the vacant expanse. The first realization of actual victory, of reaching my lifetime's goal, set my heart throbbing violently and my brain aglow. I felt the glory which the prophet feels in his vision, with which the poet thrills in his dream. About the frozen plains my imagination evoked aspects of grandeur. I saw silver and crystal palaces, such as were never built by man, with turrets flaunting 'pinions glorious, golden'. The shifting mirages seemed like the ghosts of dead armies, magnified and transfigured, huge and spectral, moving along the horizon and bearing the wind-tossed phantoms of golden blood-stained banners.

The low beating of the wind assumed the throb of martial music. Bewildered, I realized all that I had suffered, all the pain of fasting, all the anguish of long weariness, and I felt that this was my reward. I had scaled the world, and I stood at the Pole!

By a long and consecutive series of observations and mental tabulations of various sorts on our journey northward, continuing here, I knew, beyond peradventure of doubt, that I was at a spot which was as near as possible, by usual methods of determination, five hundred and twenty miles from Svartevoeg, a spot toward which men had striven for more than three centuries – a spot known as the North Pole, and where I stood first of white men. In my own achievement I felt, that dizzy moment, that all the heroic souls who had braved the rigours of the Arctic region found their own hopes' fulfilment. I had realized their dream. I had culminated with success the efforts of all the brave men who had failed before me. I had finally justified their sacrifices, their very death; I had proven to humanity humanity's supreme triumph over a hostile, death-dealing Nature. It seemed that the souls of these dead exulted with me, and that in some sub-strata of the air, in notes more subtle than the softest notes of music, they sang a paean in the spirit with me.

We had reached our destination. My relief was indescribable. The prize of an international marathon was ours. Pinning the Stars and Stripes to a tent-pole, I asserted the achievement in the name of the ninety millions of countrymen who swear fealty to that flag. And I felt a pride as I gazed at the white-and-crimson barred pinion, a pride which the claim of no second victor has ever taken from me.

On his arrival back in the Canadian Arctic from his supposed Pole journey, Cook spent a winter in a remote spot on the north coast of the uninhabited Devon Island. Then, in spring 1909, he returned to northwest Greenland. Later, he joined the Danish supply ship *Hans Egede* on a voyage to Copenhagen, and on the way, at the telegraph office at Lerwick in the Shetland Islands, burst his bombshell.

At first, everything seemed to go perfectly for Cook. Peary was just a little too slow in announcing his own claim to the Pole. Cook's heroic conquest was fêted both in Europe and America, aided of course by the sensation-seeking popular press.

Soon, however, official and public opinion began slowly to drift away from him. The *New York Herald*, naturally enough, backed his story to the hilt, but some major American polar explorers voiced doubts from the start. On the day after Cook announced his claim from the Shetlands, George Melville, veteran of the *Jeannette* expedition, recorded in the *New York Times* that 'After reading the dispatches today, I am more convinced than ever that the reported discovery of the North Pole is a fake.' Soon after, the damaging story of the Mount McKinley fraud came to light. Then, in December, an even more serious blow fell when in Copenhagen, where originally Cook had been received with great enthusiasm, a committee appointed to investigate his claim came out against him. Cook had handed over his documentation of the journey for inspection, and the committee concluded that 'the documents submitted to us are of such an unsatisfactory character that it is not possible to declare with certainty that the astronomical observations referred to were actually made ... The Commission is therefore of the opinion that the material transmitted for examination contains no proof whatever that Dr Cook reached the North Pole.' Knud Rasmussen, who had been born in Greenland, a skilled polar traveller who later rose to become Denmark's most famous polar explorer, was even more damning: 'No schoolboy could make such calculations. It is a most childish attempt at cheating. Cook has killed himself by his own foolish acts.' Other evidence against Cook emerged later. It was pointed out that, if he had followed the route that he claimed, he should have come in sight of a previously undiscovered island, Meighen Island, but did not report it. One of Peary's supporters, D.B. MacMillan, interviewed the two Eskimos who had accompanied Cook, who reported that they had never been more than two days from land. Most recently, the experienced British polar explorer Wally Herbert found corroboration of their story in a photograph that purported to show new land sighted in the distance at about 85°N, far into the Arctic Ocean, which he named 'Bradley Land'. When, many years later, it was demonstrated that there is no land within 180 miles of that location, his supporters maintained that it must instead have been an ice island (that is, a very large floe originating from an ice shelf). Herbert has a ready answer to that theory: 'Anyone who has seen the north-west coast of Axel Heiberg Island, and has also seen ice islands from the surrounding sea ice will know that the picture in Cook's book is not an ice island, but a picture of land, and since there is no land where Cook claims to have taken this picture, we may take it that what Cook's companions told MacMillan was true.' This evidence that the picture was faked is indisputable. Herbert also observed that Cook was quite skilled at faking photographic evidence, and used some simple visual tricks to ensure that the real location of the shot would never be known. He would wait until low cloud obscured distinguishing features of the landscape before taking his picture and also, sometimes, printed the photograph the wrong way round to disguise the subject still more.

Not all the arguments against Cook are so carefully considered; some books and articles about him seem to be written in pure hatred. There have also been truly offensive dirty tricks. After Cook was convicted in the 1920s for yet another fraud – dealing in land that he falsely claimed to be oil-bearing – one of Peary's supporters wrote to the court to insist that he serve his full 14-year sentence. Later, the judgement proved to be wrong; much of the land was rich in oil. Nevertheless Cook served seven years' imprisonment. In the year of his death, 1940, he received a full pardon from President Roosevelt.

The debate about Cook's Pole journey continues, but for the most part it is now much more moderate, mature and reflective than it used to be. Wally Herbert's authoritative book concludes that by faking the journey, he 'took the easier route to fame', which is almost certainly true. But he still has a large group of supporters. One of the most recent contributions to the debate (R.J. Osczevski in *Polar Record*, July 1990) presents cogent reasons why he failed to spot Meighen Island. The argument is huge and complex, and we shall never know the truth about why Cook might have chosen to fake the attainment of the Pole. Probably, the best guess was made by Cook's adversary, Peary, when he wrote angrily of 'Dr Cook's action in going north . . . for the admitted purpose of forestalling me.' This could certainly have been Cook's sole purpose. Cook had seen how Peary abused his fellow men for his own selfish ends. White and black Americans and Eskimos alike were used as expendable appendages to his ambition. He had seen how Peary had gradually come to believe that north Greenland, the people who lived there, and ultimately the Pole itself, were his own possessions on which nobody should trespass. As a man with compassion for those whom Peary abused, Cook may well have chosen deliberately, in retribution, to spoil his long-awaited hour of glory. In that, he succeeded. Peary lived for 11 years after his polar triumph, but was never fully able to bask in his glory; he died a saddened, broken man. Cook survived him by 20 years; and even after the death of his adversary, consistently refused to relinquish his claim to the Pole. Only he knew the truth, and when he died in 1940 he took that secret with him.

2. Peary's Story: 1908–9

After his failure of 1906 Peary was, nonetheless, welcomed home with honours. He had achieved a new record, and he was confident that just one more attempt would be enough to claim the Pole. By now, though, the pressures against him were beginning to accumulate. His Arctic Club stood by him, willing to sponsor another expedition. But his age and physical condition were against him: he was now entering his fifties, and his feet were mutilated. In addition, as one recent study by A.C. Bonga has suggested, he was vulnerable to 'peripheral vascular disease, hypothyroidism, sympathetic dystrophy and dietary deficiencies'. This was no ideal state in which to undertake such a punishing, challenging journey of more than 800 miles to the North Pole and back, and he was thoroughly aware that there was time for only one more attempt. Worse, his ship *Roosevelt* needed a refit. The contractors were unable to complete the job in time for setting out for the north in 1907, so he lost another year. The main thing remaining in his favour now was his own irresistibly driving ambition. He had a sense of destiny, and when he heard of the year's delay he wrote 'I gathered myself together and faced the situation squarely. I realized that the project was something too big to die; that it never, in the great scheme of things, would be allowed to fall through.' Further fuel to his ambition was added by the news that Frederick Cook had announced, in a letter to the Peary Arctic Club in August 1907, an intention to attempt a journey to the Pole. Peary was outraged that anyone should trespass on his own preserve, his own Eskimos and dogs, his own North Pole. The only redeeming feature about Cook's expedition was that he did not trespass on Peary's route. Their relationship now turned to open hostility. When Peary returned to the Arctic in 1908, he would not permit anyone, or anything associated with Cook on board his ship.

Peary's final attempt on the North Pole began on 6 July

1908, when *Roosevelt* and the support ship *Erik* departed from New York. Early in August, the expedition stopped at the Cape York settlement in northwest Greenland to pick up a party of 39 Eskimo men and women and over 200 dogs. In September, *Roosevelt* reached Cape Sheridan at the northeast point of Ellesmere Island, where the expedition wintered. During the autumn and winter, expedition staff transferred supplies west to Cape Columbia, the northernmost point of Ellesmere Island, in readiness for the Pole journey, and the Eskimos were sent inland to Lake Hazen to hunt and fish, providing further provisions for Peary's party.

The Pole journey began in February 1909, when, as before, supporting parties, headed by the ship's captain Robert Abram Bartlett, set out to place provisions along the route, blaze a trail, and build igloos. Peary's party was the last to leave the ship, and after reaching Cape Columbia, set out over the ice on 1 March.

An hour after I left camp my division had crossed the glacial fringe, and the last man, sledge, and dog of the Northern party — comprising altogether twenty-four men, nineteen sledges, and one hundred and thirty-three dogs — was at last on the ice of the Arctic Ocean, about latitude 83°.

Our start from the land this last time was eight days earlier than the start three years before, six days of calendar time and two days of distance, our present latitude being about two marches farther north than Cape Hecla, our former point of departure.

When we were far enough out on the ice to be away from the shelter of the land, we got the full force of the violent wind. But it was not in our faces, and as we had a trail which could be followed, even if with heads down and eyes half closed, the wind did not impede us or cause us serious discomfort. Nevertheless, I did not like to dwell upon the inevitable effect which it would have upon the ice farther out — the opening of leads across our route.

When we dropped off the edge of the glacial fringe onto the pressure ridges of the tidal crack already described, in spite of the free use of our pickaxes and the pickaxes of the pioneer division, which had gone before, the trail was a most trying one for men, dogs, and sledges, especially the old Eskimo type of sledge. The new 'Peary' sledges, by reason of their length and shape, rode much more easily and with less strain than the others. Everyone was glad to reach the surface of the old floes beyond this crazy zone of ice which was several miles in width. As soon as we struck the old floes the going was much better. There appeared to be no great depth of snow, only a few inches, and this had been hammered fairly hard by the winter winds. Still the surface over which we traveled was very uneven, and in many places was distinctly trying to the sledges, the wood of which was made brittle by the low temperature, now in the minus fifties. On the whole, however, I felt that if we encountered nothing worse than this in the first hundred miles from the land we should have no serious cause for complaint.

Very soon, Peary encountered a familiar problem.

The first serious obstacle of the sledge journey was encountered the second day out from land. The day was cloudy, the wind continuing to blow from the east with unabated violence. Again I intentionally brought up the rear of my division, in order to see that everything was going right and that everyone was accounted for. The going was much the same as on the previous day, rough and trying to the endurance of men, dogs and sledges.

When we had made about three-quarters of a march we saw ahead of us a dark ominous cloud upon the northern horizon, which always means open water. There is always fog in the neighborhood of the leads. The open water supplies the evaporation, the cold air acts as a condenser, and when the wind is blowing just right this forms a fog so dense that at times it looks as black as the smoke of a prairie fire.

Sure enough, just ahead of us were black spots against the snow which I knew to be my various divisions held up by a lead. When we came up with them I saw a lane of open water, about a quarter of a mile wide, which had formed since the captain had passed the day before. The wind had been getting in its work!

I gave the word to camp (there was nothing else to do), and while the igloos were being built, Marvin and MacMillan made a sounding from the edge of the lead, getting ninety-six fathoms.

This march to the edge of the lead put us beyond the British record of 83°20' made by Captain Markham, RN, north of Cape Joseph Henry, May 12, 1876.

Before daylight the next morning we heard the grinding of the ice, which told us that the lead was at last crushing together, and I gave the signal to the other three igloos, by pounding with a hatchet on the ice floor of my igloo, to fire up and get breakfast in a hurry. The morning was clear again, excepting for the wind haze, but the wind still continued to blow with unabated violence.

With the first of the daylight we were hurrying across the lead on the raftering young ice, which was moving, crushing, and piling up with the closing of the sides of the lead. If the reader will imagine crossing a river on a succession of gigantic shingles, one, two, or three deep and all afloat and moving, he will perhaps form an idea of the uncertain surface over which we crossed this lead. Such a passage is distinctly trying, as any moment may lose a sledge and its team, or plunge a member of the party into the icy water. On the other side there was no sign of Bartlett's trail. This meant that the lateral movement (that is, east and west) of the ice shores of the lead had carried the trail along with it.

After an hour or two of marching, we found ourselves in the fork of two other leads, and unable to move in any direction. The young ice (that is, the recently frozen ice) on the more westerly of these leads, though too thin to sustain the weight of the sledges, was yet strong enough to bear an Eskimo, and I sent Kyutah to the west to scout for the captain's trail, while the other Eskimos built out of snow blocks a shelter from the wind, and repaired some minor damage to our sledges.

In half an hour or so Kyutah returned from the west, signalling that he had found Bartlett's trail. Soon after he reached us a movement of the shores of the lead to the west crushed up the narrow ribbon of unsafe young ice over which he had passed, and we were able to hurry across with sledges and push west for the trail, which was about a mile and a half distant.

It was that area of open water that provided the expedition with its one great tragedy. After making rapid progress and reaching 86°38′N, Peary sent back a support party led by the assistant, Ross Marvin, and Marvin, crossing the lead, fell through the ice. It was only much later, when Peary returned to the ship, that Captain Bartlett broke the news.

'Have you heard about poor Marvin?' he asked.

'No,' I answered.

Then he told me that Marvin had been drowned at the 'Big Lead', coming back to Cape Columbia. The news staggered me, killing all the joy I had felt at the sight of the ship and her captain. It was indeed a bitter flavour in the cup of our success. It was hard to realize at first that the man who had worked at my side through so many weary months under conditions of peril and privation, to whose efforts and example so much of the success of the expedition had been due, would never stand beside me again. The manner of his death even will never be precisely known. No human eye was upon him when he broke through the treacherous young ice that had but recently closed over a streak of open water. He was the only white man in the supporting party of which he was in command and with which he was returning to the land at the time he met his death. As was customary, on breaking camp he had gone out ahead of the Eskimos, leaving the natives to break camp, harness the dogs, and follow. When he came to the 'Big Lead', the recent ice of which was safe and secure at the edges, it is probable that, hurrying on, he did not notice the gradual thinning of the ice toward the centre of the lead until it was too late and he was in the water. The Eskimos were too far in the rear to hear his calls for help, and in that ice-cold water the end must have come very quickly. He who had never shrunk from loneliness in the performance of his duty had at last met death alone.

During the journey, however, Peary had no knowledge of Marvin's death. In his book, *The North Pole*, he recorded retrospectively the moment when Marvin turned for home.

No shadow of apprehension for the future hung over that parting. It was a clear, crisp morning, the sunlight glittered on the ice and snow, the dogs were alert and active after their long sleep, the air blew cold and fresh from the polar void, and Marvin himself, though reluctant to turn back, was filled with exultation that he had carried the Cornell colors to a point beyond the farthest north of Nansen and Abruzzi, and that, with the exception of Bartlett and myself, he alone of all white men had entered that exclusive region which stretches beyond 86°34′ north latitude.

I shall always be glad that Marvin marched with me during those last few days. As we tramped along together we had discussed the plans for his trip to Cape Jesup, and his line of soundings from there northward; and as he turned back to the land his mind was glowing with hope for the future – the future which he was destined never to know. My last words to him were:

'Be careful of the leads, my boy!'

So we shook hands and parted in that desolate white waste, and Marvin set his face southward toward his death, and I turned again northward toward the Pole.

Peary continued to make good progress, and on 28 March he surpassed his own record northerly latitude of 87°06′N established in 1906. On 1 April, the last supporting party, led by Bartlett, turned for home at 87°47′N. Peary was accompanied now by only Matt Henson and the four Eskimos Ooqueah, Ootah, Egingwah and Seegloo. A few days later, Peary recorded the final few miles.

The last march northward ended at ten o'clock on the forenoon of April 6. I had now made the five marches planned from the point at which Bartlett turned back, and my reckoning showed that we were in the immediate neighbourhood of the goal of all our striving. After the usual arrangements for going into camp, at approximate local noon, of the Columbia meridian, I made the first observation at our polar camp. It indicated our position as 89°57′.

We were now at the end of the last long march of the upward journey. Yet with the Pole actually in sight I was too weary to take the last few steps. The accumulated weariness of all those days and nights of forced marches and insufficient sleep, constant peril and anxiety, seemed to roll across me all at once. I was actually too exhausted to realize at the moment that my life's purpose had been achieved. As soon as our igloos had been completed and we had eaten our dinner and double-rationed the dogs, I turned in for a few hours of absolutely necessary sleep, Henson and the Eskimos having unloaded the sledges and got them in readiness for such repairs as were necessary. But, weary though I was, I could not sleep long. It was, therefore, only a few hours later when I woke. The first thing I did after awaking was to write these words in my diary: 'The Pole at last. The prize of three centuries. My dream and goal for twenty years. Mine at last! I cannot bring myself to realize it. It seems all so simple and commonplace.'

Everything was in readiness for an observation at 6 p.m., Columbia meridian time, in case the sky should be clear, but at that hour it was, unfortunately, still overcast. But as there were indications that it would clear before long, two of the Eskimos and myself made ready a light sledge carrying only the instruments, a tin of pemmican, and one or two skins; and drawn by a double team of dogs, we pushed on an estimated distance of ten miles. While we travelled, the sky cleared, and at the end of the journey, I was able to get a satisfactory series of observations at Columbia meridian midnight. These observations indicated that our position was then beyond the Pole.

Nearly everything in the circumstances which then surrounded us seemed too strange to be thoroughly realized; but one of the strangest of those circumstances seemed to me to be the fact that, in a march of only a few hours, I had passed from the western to the eastern hemisphere and had verified my position at the summit of the world. It was hard to realize that, in the first miles of this brief march, we had been travelling due north, while, on the last few miles of the same march, we had been travelling south, although we had all the time been travelling precisely in the same direction. It would be difficult to imagine a better illustration of the fact that most things are relative. Again, please consider the uncommon circumstance that, in order to return to our camp, it now became necessary to turn and go north again for a few miles and then to go directly south, all the time travelling in the same direction.

As we passed back along that trail which none had ever seen before or would ever see again, certain reflections intruded themselves which, I think, may fairly be called unique. East, west, and north had disappeared for us. Only one direction remained and that was south. Every breeze which could possibly blow upon us, no matter from what point of the horizon, must be a south wind. Where we were, one day and one night constituted a year, a hundred such days and nights constituted a century. Had we stood in that spot during the six months of the arctic winter night, we should have seen every star of the northern hemisphere circling the sky at the same distance from the horizon, with Polaris (the North Star) practically in the zenith.

All during our march back to camp the sun was swinging around in its ever-moving circle. At six o'clock on the morning of April 7, having again arrived at Camp Jesup, I took another series of observations. These indicated our position as being four or five miles from the Pole, towards Bering Strait. Therefore, with a double team of dogs and a light sledge, I travelled directly towards the sun an estimated distance of eight miles. Again I returned to the camp in time for a final and completely satisfactory series of observations on April 7 at noon, Columbia meridian time. These observations gave results essentially the same as those made at the same spot twenty-four hours before.

I had now taken in all thirteen single, or six and one-half double, altitudes of the sun, at two different stations, in three different directions, at four different times. All were under satisfactory conditions, except for the first single altitude on the sixth. The temperature during these observations had been from minus 11° Fahrenheit to minus 30° Fahrenheit, with clear sky and calm weather (except as already noted for the single observation on the sixth).

In traversing the ice in these various directions as I had done, I had allowed approximately ten miles for possible errors in my observations, and at some moment during these marches and countermarches, I had passed over or very near the point where north and south and east and west blend into one.

Of course there were some more or less informal ceremonies connected with our arrival at our difficult destination, but they were not of a very elaborate character. We planted five flags at the top of the world. The first one was a silk American flag which Mrs Peary gave me fifteen years ago. That flag has done more travelling in high latitudes than any other ever made. I carried it wrapped about my body on every one of my expeditions northward after it came into my possession, and I left a fragment of it at each of my successive 'farthest norths': Cape Morris K. Jesup, the northernmost point of land in the known world; Cape Thomas Hubbard, the northernmost known point of Jesup Land, west of Grant Land; Cape Columbia, the northernmost point of North American lands; and my farthest north in 1906, latitude 87°6' in the ice of the polar sea. By the time it actually reached the Pole, therefore, it was somewhat worn and discoloured.

A broad diagonal section of this ensign would now mark the farthest goal of earth – the place where I and my dusky companions stood.

After a few more ceremonials, on the afternoon of 7 April, he turned his back on the Pole and headed for home.

Though intensely conscious of what I was leaving, I did not wait for any lingering farewell of my life's goal. The event of human beings standing at the hitherto inaccessible summit of the earth was accomplished, and my work now lay to the south, where four hundred and thirteen nautical miles of ice-floes and possibly open leads still lay between us and the north coast of Grant Land. One backward glance I gave – then turned my face toward the south and toward the future.

The return was swift, indeed suspiciously swift, and with few incidents. The only obstacle anticipated by Peary was his one last crossing of 'The Big Lead', but that presented a problem different from the one he had expected. It was frozen over and easily crossed, but he found that Bartlett, ahead of him, had lost the well-worn main trail at that point, and had needed to blaze a new, less satisfactory trail. This was a minor hindrance, however, and on 25 April he completed the journey. 'My heart thrilled as, rounding the point of the cape, I saw the little black ship lying there in its icy berth with sturdy nose pointing straight to the Pole.' All that remained now was the impatient wait for the ice to break up around the ship in July, and the voyage home to the anticipated triumphant welcome. But before he was even halfway home, the prospect of a triumphant welcome was already tarnished. At the Eskimo settlement of Etah in north-west Greenland, where *Roosevelt* arrived on 17 August, he first learned the devastating news that Cook was making a rival claim to an earlier attainment of the Pole. In his biography of Peary, Wally Herbert describes eloquently how that revelation must have hit him then, and later changed his life, creating 'a bitterness and sense of hurt which because he was unable to express it may already, up at Etah, have started turning in on Peary to become that cancer in his soul which by slow degrees destroyed him.'

Peary managed, somehow, to disguise his distress, and at Indian Harbour, Labrador, on 6 September, he went ahead with his intended telegraphic announcement to the world: 'Have nailed the Stars and Stripes to the Pole.' From that moment, the world looked on in astonishment as the feud between Cook and Peary simmered to boiling point.

In the end, Peary's better and more detailed calculations, his more plausible account of his journey, the support of powerful sponsors including the National Geographic Society, and the destructive evidence against Cook, won the argument. Nonetheless, Peary's own story is by no means watertight, and there have been frequent suggestions in the last 80 years that neither man reached the Pole. Two of the arguments most commonly raised against Peary concern his mileages after Bartlett turned back at 87°47'N, and that rapid return journey. In one eight-day period he claimed an average of over 38 miles per day; in a period of 21 days he claimed over 30 miles per day. That is quite exceptional by any standard of travelling by dog-sledge over sea ice. Most travellers on comparable journeys could at best claim daily averages of well under 20 miles. The implication is that as soon as Peary had sent back Bartlett, the last remaining person capable of calculating his position, he began to falsify the calculations and fake the mileages to cover up the fact that he turned back while still short of the Pole. Wally Herbert, who crossed the Arctic Ocean with dogs in 1968–9, and is one of the greatest living experts on the subject, expresses very serious doubts about Peary's ability to sustain such mileages, deeming them 'truly incredible!' Herbert also raises a new argument against Peary's claim. He argues that Peary took insufficient account of the westerly drift of the ice. That, plus other navigational errors, would have placed his final position not at the Pole, but about 50 nautical miles to the west of it, a little to the north of 89°N. Herbert's theory, published in 1989, was strongly challenged in the *National Geographic Magazine* in the following year.

We shall never know the truth with any certainty. The main outstanding question is whether it matters. An error of 50 miles is not a great distance for a man who over the years had struggled for thousands of miles in horrific conditions, to achieve the one great goal of his life. It is close enough to the Pole for all reasonable purposes. Peary was not a particularly agreeable man, but he was a man of truly heroic stature. Wally Herbert concludes, surely rightly, that Peary should now be allowed to rest in peace. There is no further point in quibbling; Peary should be allowed to have his North Pole. But, just as the feud between Peary and Cook continues to simmer, the likelihood is that the debate about Peary's last Pole journey will never end.

Peary's feat, real or imagined, effectively put an end to exploration towards the Pole before the First World War. The Norwegian
explorer Roald Amundsen, who had planned his own attempt
on the North Pole, swiftly changed his plans, and in 1910 headed
for the South Pole instead.

There was just one more attempt on the North Pole before the
war began. Georgiy Yakovlevich Sedov, veteran of four previous
Arctic expeditions and an experienced and distinguished polar
navigator, wanted to be the first Russian to get there. This,
however, was a rather sad affair. Sedov organized his expedition
with funding from scientific institutions and the public, and set
out from Archangel on his ship *Foka* in August 1912. His aim
was to use Franz Josef Land as his base, but in his first season
the weather and ice were against him. He spent the winter
of 1912–13 in northern Novaya Zemlya, and filled his time
there carrying out a range of scientific projects, exploring and
surveying. In summer 1913 he was able to transfer his base to
Hooker Island (Ostrov Gukera) in the south of the Franz Josef
archipelago, where he spent his second winter.

On 2 February 1914, accompanied by two seamen, and using
dogs and sledges, he set out on his journey to the Pole. He first
headed through the archipelago towards Rudolf Island, where
he hoped to find supplies left by Abruzzi and Fiala, but in the
very early stages of the journey his health began to fail rapidly,
and just as he was approaching Rudolf Island, on 5 March, he
died. The two seamen buried him on the island and returned to
the ship. The expedition remained on Hooker Island to complete
its summer scientific programme, then headed south to Cape
Flora, Jackson's old wintering site, to salvage some fuel and
supplies. It was then that there occurred another of those
remarkable instances of survival and rescue for which Cape
Flora has justly become famous. In the same year, the ship
belonging to another Russian expedition was stuck fast in the
ice to the north of Franz Josef Land. Some of the crew tried to
escape to the south with sledges and kayaks, but most died on
the route. Only two, Valerian Al'banov and a seaman, managed
to struggle to Cape Flora, and they were preparing to winter
there when, by pure chance, Sedov's ship *Foka* turned up.

The war brought most Arctic exploration to a standstill. When
exploration resumed with the coming of peace, the North Pole

was still a popular goal, but by then both the circumstances and the motives had changed entirely.

– 13 –

The Coming of Aviation

1. Roald Amundsen: 1925

The First World War interrupted exploration towards the North Pole, but neither that, nor the widespread belief that the Pole was already conquered by Peary, inhibited explorers from continuing to try to reach it. On the contrary, the war period, and the years immediately following it, brought major technological advances which completely changed the face of Arctic exploration, and stimulated a whole new era of attempts to attain the Pole. The object now was not to be the first to get there, but to be the first to get there by other means. From the 1920s onwards, polar explorers had at their disposal a new generation of aircraft, airships, icebreakers, submarines and motorized land transport, all of which were rapidly becoming more reliable, more powerful, and safe enough to be deemed suitable for use in remote Arctic areas. In addition, the coming of wireless communications gave explorers the added confidence that even if an accident befell them, they were still not entirely lost.

The first person to attempt to reach the Pole by air was the Norwegian explorer Roald Amundsen (1872–1928). In common with Peary, Amundsen was one of the few men of his day who could hope to make a lifelong career out of polar exploration. His poor business sense ensured that it was sometimes a very precarious career, but for over 30 years, from 1897 until his tragic death in an aircraft accident in 1928, his life was entirely devoted to exploiting the prevailing public enthusiasm for polar exploration with a long series of spectacular accomplishments. Strictly speaking, also like Peary, he was more adventurer than explorer; he did sometimes explore entirely new ground, and his expeditions usually had a scientific element, though it was often insignificant. What he did best was to achieve a wide variety of polar 'firsts' for public entertainment. After beginning his career as a member of the first expedition to winter in the Antarctic, he was the first to make a complete navigation of the Northwest Passage (1903–6), and the first to attain the South Pole (1910–12). Later, after disruption by the First World War, then after attempting his one major scientific expedition, an ice-drift on the Arctic Ocean on the ship *Maud* (1918–21), his mind turned to aerial exploration. He attempted the first flight by aircraft to the North Pole (1925); and accomplished the first airship flight to the North Pole, and, on the same expedition, the first crossing of the Arctic Ocean (1926). In 1928, he disappeared during an aerial search for his airship colleague Umberto Nobile, who had crashed in the Arctic Ocean.

Amundsen's interest in aerial exploration dated back to as early as 1909, and he had bought his first aircraft in 1914. In 1921 he left the *Maud* expedition in the hands of its scientists (who continued the expedition until 1925) and began seeking the means to attain the Pole by air. He first prepared a flight to the Pole in 1923, but on that occasion he lost confidence in his aircraft at a late stage, and abandoned the flight.

In 1925, he tried again. On this occasion he collaborated with the American Lincoln Ellsworth, whose millionaire father financed the purchase of two Dornier-Wal flying boats (code-named N24 and N25). They set up their base at Kongsfjorden, northwest Svalbard, and waited several weeks for suitable ice and weather conditions, making trial runs across the ice of the fjord. By 21 May they were ready, and they prepared to take off with Amundsen, Hjalmar Riiser-Larsen (pilot) and Feucht (mechanic) in N25, and Ellsworth, Leif Dietrichson and Oskar Omdal (mechanic) in N24. Their take-off was hair-raising; Amundsen describes it in his account of the flight.

It was now ten minutes past five. The motors were quite warm and Green nodded approvingly. His smile expressed complete satisfaction. A last handshake from Director Knutsen and then good-bye. The motor was running at top speed as N25 trembled and shook. The plan was that our machine should make the first start. First to try if possible to start out over the fjord with the wind in order to glide and swing at a low altitude between the fjord boundaries.

If this were not successful we were to set our course direct against the wind, towards King's Bay. It was also agreed that the machines should try to keep together during the entire flight. What the one did the other should do afterwards. One last pull and then N25 was free and glided gracefully down the slide on to the frozen fjord. The trip was started. 'Welcome back tomorrow,' was the last I heard as with tremendous speed — 1,800 revolutions a minute — it set off towards the starting-place in the middle of the fjord. There we noticed all at once that the ice was bending right over and the water surging up. In a second the machine was across the fjord, heading straight for the glacier and making 2,000 revolutions. This was one of the most anxious moments. Could the machine bear the tremendous excess weight or must we stop and lighten it? The pilot sat at the wheel. Had he been seated at the breakfast-table he could scarcely have looked less concerned. As the speed still continued, and we were nearing the glacier at a mighty rate, the pilot's coolness seemed greater than ever. His mouth was the only indication of his resolution and determination. We went over the ice like a hurricane. The speed continued and continued; then, suddenly the miracle happened. With a mighty pull the machine raised itself from the earth. We were in the air. The master-stroke was accomplished. It seemed to me after the breathless anxiety that I at last heard a light 'Ah!' which grew into a ringing shout of joy.

After this calmness again took possession of the man who had performed this master-stroke, and it left him no more during the whole trip. Feucht was always going up and down between the tank compartment and the motor; his duty was to keep the pilot advised of everything: how the engine worked: how much petrol had been used, etc. All seemed in the finest order and Feucht announced 'All clear.' Before we rose I had tried to get my things in order as the space was limited and my belongings numerous.

Over Cape Mitra we had already risen to 400m. and everything beneath us seemed exceedingly small. Time after time I turned round and looked for the other machine, but never managed to discern it. Therefore we turned our plane completely round, flying back to look for N24. One never knew what might have happened. It was possible that something had struck it as it tried to rise. The ice might have broken, or its load might have been too heavy for it. Suddenly something blazed in the sun; it glittered like gold. It was the sun playing on N24's wings. There it came in full flight to meet us. Everything seemed to be in order . . . Then the machine turned its nose again towards the north, and the two enormous birds started their flight together towards the 'Unknown' . . .

We passed quickly over the north-west coast of Spitzbergen, where the sea below us was entirely free from ice. Then we reached Magdalena Bay, the South Gate with the Moss Islands, and then came the Danske Öen. I knew them all again from my trip with Gjoa in 1901. After an hour's flight we were level with the Amsterdam Islands. Here we met most unpleasant weather. Fog as thick as porridge. First it came densely, thickeningly from the north-east – then thicker – thicker. The pilot rose higher and we were flying above the woollen blanket. The other machine accompanied us at a somewhat lower altitude. Here I saw the strangest optical illusion I have ever seen, and nothing seems to me to have ever equalled it in beauty. Directly pictured in the fog I could see a complete reflection of our own machine surrounded by a halo of all the spectrum's colours. The sight was miraculously beautiful and original.

We took our bearings from the Amsterdam Islands and steered north for Taakeheimen. Here the fog came down quite unexpectedly. We had not looked for it so quickly, nor such a big stretch of it; it was certainly not local, but a field of colossal dimensions lay before us. For two complete hours we flew over it; a stretch of fully 200 kilometres. Occasionally we passed over a little break or hole in it, but never big enough to give me an opportunity to take my bearings. These holes were of great interest. Through them I got an idea of the territory below. The sea here was filled with small ice with water amongst it. These conditions continued to 82°n.br., and I am certain that a vessel with any power at all could have navigated it. A little after eight o'clock it began suddenly to clear, and in a second the fog disappeared as though charmed. And there below us and in front of us lay the great shining plain of the notorious pack-ice. 'How many misfortunes have you been responsible for during the passage of years, you vast Whiteness? What have you not seen in the way of need and misery? And you have also met those who set their foot upon your neck and brought you to your knees. Can you remember Nansen and Johansen? Can you remember the Duke of the Abruzzi? Can you remember Peary? Can you remember how they crossed over you and how you put obstacles in their way? But they brought you to your knees. You must respect these heroes. But what have you done with the numbers who sought to free themselves from your embrace in vain? What have you done with the many proud ships which were steered direct towards your heart never to be seen again? What have you done with them, I ask? No clue, no sign – only the vast white waste.'

Quite naturally an airman's thoughts turn towards a landing-place. Should his motor fail and he has no place to land, he is indeed in a bad way. But no matter where we looked there was not the sign of a landing-place. So far as we could see the ice looked like a number of furrows, stretched out without rhyme or reason, and between the furrows rose a high stone fence. Conditions, however, were unusual, the fence took up more room than the ploughed field. Had the field been even and flat it would not have appeared so strange, but a flat part simply did not exist. The plough seemed to have been everywhere between stones and stubble. A little brook was also there, but so small that one could have jumped over it anywhere. A more monotonous territory it had never been my lot to see. Not the slightest change. Had I not been engaged in making many kinds of observations and notes it is certain that the uniformity of the outlook and the monotony of the engine's hum would have sent me to sleep, but fortunately my task kept me awake. Riiser-Larsen confessed to me later that he had had a little snooze. I can understand that, as he had monotonous work to do.

The mean temperature during the flight had been −13°C. N24 kept beside us with no thought of separating. I tried continually to take the sun, but unsuccessfully. The sun was alright, but the horizon was useless. Our plane level was fastened to the sextant (a bulb sextant, of American make). We had used it several times at a trial in King's Bay, but the results were most unsatisfactory, so much so that we had stopped using it. Therefore I was left to use whatever Nature placed at my disposal. But Nature was not obliging. There was no horizon. Sky and ice blended into one.

Two hours after I had taken soundings at the Amsterdam Islands I got an opportunity to calculate our speed and the deviation. What had happened in two hours? It was exceedingly difficult to say. If one does not get an opportunity to calculate the speed and the deviation it is naturally difficult to know the direction of the wind when one comes flying at a speed of 150 kilometres. The sky was quite clear as we came out of the fog with a few high cirri in the east. About ten o'clock a fine mist crept up from the north, but too high and fine to annoy one. The sun was not quite visible, but from the sun's position and the compass's variations it was quite clear that we were well over to the west. There was, therefore, nothing else to do but to steer eastwards. I have never seen anything more deserted and forlorn; at least I thought we might see a bear or something to break the monotony a little, but no – absolutely nothing living. Had I been sure of this condition before I would have taken a flea with me in order to have life near.

At five o'clock in the morning of the 22nd we came to the first waterway. It was not a small brook, but a big dam with arms stretching in different directions. It offered our first possibility of finding a landing-place. According to our bearings we should now be in 88°N Lat., but with regard to longitude we were quite confused. That we were westerly was certain, but where? Feucht announced here that half the petrol was used, so it became necessary to look for a landing-place. Our intention was, therefore, to descend, take the necessary observations, and act in the best way according to the conditions. The question now was where should we land? Naturally a landing on the water would have been safest, so far as the landing was concerned, but there was always the fear that the ice might close in and crush us before we were able to rise again. We decided unanimously that if it were possible we should land on the ice. In order to observe the territory as conveniently as possible we descended in big spirals. During these manoeuvres the aft motor began to misfire and changed the whole situation. Instead of choosing a place now we would have to take what offered. The machine was much too heavy to remain in the air with one motor. A forced landing became necessary. At this low altitude we could not reach the main dam, but had to be satisfied with the nearest arm. It was not particularly inviting – full of slush and small ice. But we had no choice. Under such conditions it was worth much to have a cool, unruffled pilot who never lost his self-possession, but even in flight was able to make a clear decision and act accordingly. The slightest wobbling and the game would have been lost. The arm was just wide enough for the machine, so it was not so dangerous. Every clump of ice could have torn it through; the danger lay in the high icebanks which lay at each side. It took a master to guide the machine in between these and save the wings. We landed squat in the slush, and here arose the most difficult problem any airman could have to solve. It was a piece of luck for us that we landed in the slush, for that slowed down our speed somewhat. But on the other hand it reduced the boat's manoeuvring powers. We were passing a small iceberg on the right. The machine turned to the left, with the result that the wings stroked the top of the iceberg and loose snow was whirled in the air. Here we zig-zagged along in a manner which was most impressive and alarming. Could we clear it? The anxiety was great for those who were only spectators; it seemed not to have the slightest effect on the pilot; he was quite cool and calm. When I say we cleared the iceberg by two millimetres it is no exaggeration. I expected every moment to see the left wing destroyed. The speed now slackened in the thick slush, and we stopped at the end of the arm – nose up against the iceberg. It was again a question of millimetres. A little more speed and the nose would have been stove in.

They now faced a series of problems: they had a faulty engine; they had no idea where N24 was; and the slushy lead in which they had landed was freezing over, so they soon had no runway for taking off again. Eventually, though, they saw that N24 had landed far in the distance to render assistance, and the crew were walking towards them. But as they came close, there was a heart-stopping incident as they disappeared from sight behind a pressure ridge.

I stood on the old ice and waited, when I was alarmed by a ringing shriek – a shriek which went to my marrow and made my hair stand up on end. It was followed by a number of cries, each one more alarming and terrifying than the last. I had not the slightest doubt but that a drama of the most horrible kind was being played on the other side of the iceberg. A man was in danger of drowning. There I must stand and listen to it without being able to raise a finger to help him. The situation seemed hopeless. The dying cries got less, and I thought to myself: 'Yes, now all is over. How many of them and who?' Just then came a head from the back of the iceberg. 'Fortunately all three are not drowned.' One appeared and then another one joined him; then all three were there. To say I was glad is a mild expression. The two first shook themselves like dogs, but the third conducted himself normally. Riiser-Larsen carried them quickly over the fissure. Dietrichson and Omdal were wet to the skin, but Ellsworth was dry. We got them quickly on board the boat and their wet clothes were changed for dry ones.

After they had dried out, they explained the incident to Amundsen.

When they found that the old ice was difficult to negotiate on account of small open cracks, they decided it would be better to link hands and cross the new ice. The result was better than one might have expected, and they got safely near to the old ice. But that lay on *our* side, and in such a condition that they preferred to continue on the new ice. Omdal went first, then Dietrichson and last Ellsworth. The first to break through was Dietrichson, in fact one could hardly use the word 'break', as 'sink' suits the situation

better. The slush is very treacherous; it disappears underneath without a sound. When Dietrichson fell through he
quite reasonably gave a loud cry, and Omdal turned round
to see what was wrong. In the same moment he himself
fell through, and both lay there. Without a thought, and
with brilliant presence of mind, Ellsworth rushed to them,
pulled Dietrichson out and together they ran to Omdal. It
was in the last moment that they reached him, loosened
his rucksack, and hauled him out. He had stuck his nails
into the ice and held on with the greatest desperation,
but it did not help him much as the current carried his
legs under the ice and threatened to draw him under if
help had not come to him in the last moment. Lincoln
Ellsworth was later decorated with the medal for bravery
by HM the King of Norway, and no one who wears it has
earned it more bravely. There is no doubt that by his action
he saved the whole expedition, as later experience showed
us, for without the power of six men the N25 could never
have got home.

The three men brought with them more bad news. N24 had
been damaged on take-off and further damaged on landing; N25
was the only serviceable aircraft. Its engine was soon enough
mended, and the aircraft was just barely powerful enough to fly
with all six men aboard; but they still had no runway, and spent
much of the next three weeks preparing an area of packed snow
long enough to attempt a take-off. By 15 June it was ready, and
they clambered aboard.

At 10.30 everything was in order. In the pilot's seat sat
Riiser-Larsen, behind him Dietrichson and I, in the petrol tank Omdal and Feucht, and Ellsworth in the mess.
Dietrichson was to navigate us homewards and should
really have taken his place in the observer's seat in front
of the pilot. But as that was too exposed in view of the
nature of the task we were undertaking, his place was
allotted further back at the start. This was undeniably a
most anxious moment. As soon as the machine began to
glide one could notice a great difference from the day
before. The hasty forward glide was not to be mistaken.

One hundred metres off, we started at top-speed, 2,000 revolutions a minute. It trembled and shook, shivered and piped. It was as though N25 understood the situation. It was as though the whole of its energy had been gathered for one last and decisive spring from the floe's southern edge. Now – or never.

We rushed over the three-metre wide crack, dashed down from the 40-metre broad floe, and then? Was it possible? Yes, indeed! The scraping noise stopped, only the humming of the motor could be heard. At last we were in flight. A smile and a nod and Dietrichson disappeared into the observation compartment.

And now started the flight which will take its place amongst the most supreme in flying's history. An 850-kilometre flight with death as the nearest neighbour. One must remember that we had thrown practically everything away from us. Even though we had managed by a miracle to get away with our lives, after a forced landing, still our days would be numbered.

The sky was low and for two hours we were compelled to fly at a height of 50 metres. It was interesting to observe the ice conditions, so we eased down. We believed that in different places we observed from the sky that we could distinguish open water all around us. But it was not the case. Not a drop was to be seen anywhere. Ice in a chaotic jumble all around. It was interesting also to see that the floe, which from first to last had given us freedom, was the only floe within a radius of many miles which could have been of any use to us. N24 got a farewell wave and was thus lost to sight for ever. Everything worked excellently, the engines went like sewing-machines and gave us unqualified confidence. Both solar-compasses ticked and worked, and we knew that if only the sun would appear, they would be of invaluable assistance to us. The speedometers were placed. By the wheel sat the pilot, cool and confident as always. In the navigating compartment was a man I trusted absolutely, and by the engines two men who knew their work perfectly. Ellsworth spent his time making geographical observations and photographs. I myself managed to get what was impossible on the journey north, a splendid opportunity to study the whole flight. The course was set towards Spitzbergen's north coast land, around Nord Kap. In the two first hours we steered by the magnetic compass. This had been considered an impossibility, hitherto, so far north, but the result was excellent.

When the sun broke through after two hours and shone direct on the solar compass, it showed us how exactly we had steered. For three hours the atmosphere had been clear, but now it turned to thick fog. We rose to a height of 200 metres, flying over it in brilliant sunshine. Here we derived much benefit from the solar compasses and were able to compare their readings with the magnetic compass. We had fog for an hour and then it cleared again. The condition of the ice was as on the northern trip, small floes, with icebergs on all sides. There was apparently no system in its formation; everything was a jumble. There was more open water than on the northern tour, but no waterways, only basins.

In 82°N Lat. the fog descended again. The pilot tried for some time to fly under it, and this was a flight which would have delighted people who seek for nerve-splitting thrills. The fog got lower and lower, till at last it stretched right over the icebergs. With a speed of about 120 miles, one gets a different impression of flying. With a rush we passed over the top of the icebergs, one after the other. At a great height one does not notice the terrific speed. One is, on the contrary, astonished how slowly one appears to be travelling. Several times icebergs peeped up directly under us, so close, in fact, that I thought 'We shall never clear that one!' But the next moment we were across it. There could not have been more than a hair's breadth to spare. At last the conditions became impossible; fog and ice blended into one. It was impossible to see. There was another point as well which was of special weight, namely, the nearness of Spitzbergen. Should we fly into the high cliff walls with a speed of 120 kilometres there would not be much left of us. There was only one thing to do – to fly over the fog, and that was exactly what the pilot decided to do.

Up 100 metres high – and we were above the fog in brilliant sunshine. It was observable soon that the fog was thinning, began to lift more and more in big masses, and soon we could see territory under it. It was not inviting; nothing but small ice with a little water amongst it. When I speak of the impossible landing conditions it is only to show that to land here would have meant certain death. Such a landing would have crushed the machine and sent it to the bottom. The fog lifted steadily and soon disappeared entirely. It was a fresh southerly breeze which brought about this welcome change. The fog had lain thickest in the south, but now that began to move away as well. Large sections of it tore themselves away from the great mass and disappeared in small driving clouds. Where was Spitzbergen? Had we steered so mistakenly that we had flown to the side of it? It was quite possible. One had no experience in the navigation of the air in these regions. Over and over again the general opinion of the magnetic compass's uselessness in this district came back to my mind as I sat there. The solar compass had – as soon as we got the sun – shown a reading in agreement with the magnetic compass, but it was set at –? At what? If only I knew! There was probably no ground for anxiety, yet I felt dubious. We ought to see land by now. We had not enough petrol to last long – and still no land. Then suddenly a big heavy fog-cloud tore itself away and rose slowly, disclosing a high glittering hill-top. There was scarcely any doubt – it must be Spitzbergen. To the north lay some islands. They coincided with Syv Öene [Seven Islands] and the land stretched out in a westerly direction. But even if it were not Spitzbergen, it was still land – good, solid land. From the islands there stretched a dark strip northwards. It was water – the great open sea. Oh! what a delightful feeling – sea and land and no more ice. Our course lay southwards, but to get more quickly away from the ugly conditions beneath us, the course was set westwards and downwards to the open sea. It was more than a clever move on the part of the pilot – it was refreshing to see how instinct came to his aid – because the controls were showing signs of wear. It is enough to say before we had got right across the sea the controls jammed and an immediate landing was necessary. It blew with a cold blast from what we later learned was Hinlopen Strait and the sea was high and rough. The forced landing was accomplished with all the assurance and experience which always distinguished our pilot. We left our places and all went aft in order to allow the nose to lift as high as possible. The pilot was the only one left fore. He flew most carefully, guiding the boat and manoeuvring it against the highest waves, which were of tremendous dimensions. We who were aft kept warm and dry, but it was a different matter for the man at the wheel. Time after time the waves lashed over him, wetting him to the skin in a few minutes. It was not 'spray' which we shipped when the waves broke over us. Unused as I was to manoeuvres of this kind, I expected every moment to see the bottom stove in. It was seven in the evening when the forced landing was accomplished, and it was not until eight that we reached land. It was a fairly shoaly bay we entered into, and the landing-places it offered us were not of the best. We found a sloping side of the coast ice where we could climb ashore. The wind now laid and the sun shone against the heavy stones which lay on the beach. Here and there a little fresh rill ran between them, singing as it descended from the hillsides. The sweet voices of birds fitted in with our gentle mood of eventide, and inspired in us a feeling of solemnity. There was no need to look for a church wherein to praise God the Almighty and offer up to Him our burning thanks.

Later that day, their astonishing battle for survival was over. A ship appeared in the bay:

What should we do? What should we do to communicate with it? 'Nothing easier,' said the flying-men. 'Just sit tight and you shall see.' In a second everything was brought on board the plane, the motor started and we rushed over the sea, stopping exactly beside the cutter. It was the cutter *Sjöliv* of Balsfjord – Captain Nils Wollan. A jolly-boat was lowered and with two men rowed across to us. They seemed in doubt as to who we could be, dirty and bearded as we were. But when I turned slightly round I exposed my profile – and they knew us at once. Would they tow us down to King's Bay as our petrol was almost done? They would be delighted to do this, in fact Wollan would have certainly towed us to China if we had asked him, so glad was he to see us, so beaming with kindness and goodwill.

Such an ordeal would be expected to discourage any ordinary person for life. But not Amundsen and Ellsworth. One year later they were back, still battling to be the first to fly to the Pole.

2. Richard Evelyn Byrd: 1926

In 1926, two quite separate expeditions attempted to reach the Pole by air, and a situation developed which the world's press, in spite of objections from both sides, was delighted to seize upon as a close-fought race. Amundsen and Ellsworth were trying again in a very different sort of flying machine; pitted against them was an aviator who later rose to become, alongside Peary, one of America's most famous polar explorers, Richard Evelyn Byrd (1888–1957).

Byrd, already a seasoned pioneer of aviation, had been to the Arctic once before, in 1925, and had immediately realized the potential of aircraft in polar exploration. His stated reasons for his attempt to reach the Pole were entirely practical and unsentimental. 'There were two fairly good reasons for our wanting to fly to the North Pole: first, by travelling at high altitude over unexplored regions we might discover some new land or unexpected scientific phenomena; second, a successful flight would, like the first crossing of the Atlantic, be sure to accelerate public interest in aviation.'

Byrd had financial backing from Edsel Ford, John D. Rockefeller, Vincent Astor and others, and he also had the support of the US Navy (in which he was a Commander). His aircraft was a three-engined Fokker monoplane fitted with ski runners, and was named *Josephine Ford* after Edsel Ford's daughter. The pilot was Floyd Bennett, who had been in the Arctic with Byrd in 1925. The expedition's chosen point of departure was Kings Bay (Kongsfjorden) in northwest Spitsbergen, which coincidentally was also the place selected by Amundsen and Ellsworth. After their arrival there on 29 April 1926, they prepared a snow take-off ramp and runway, made a short trial flight, then after overcoming several difficulties, including the excessive weight of their fuel and equipment, they prepared to start for the Pole just after 12.30 a.m. on 9 May. Byrd narrates the story of the flight.

With a total load of nearly 10,000 pounds we raced down the runway. The rough snow ahead loomed dangerously near but we never reached it. We were off for our great adventure!

Beneath us were our shipmates – every one anxious to go along, but unselfishly wild with delight that we were at last off – running in our wake, waving their arms, and throwing their hats in the air. As long as I live I can never forget that sight, or those splendid fellows. They had given us our great chance.

For months previous to this hour, utmost attention had been paid to every detail that would assure our margin of safety in case of accident, and to the perfection of our scientific results in the case of success.

We had a short-wave radio set operated by a hand dynamo, should we be forced down on the ice. A hand-made sledge presented to us by Amundsen was stowed in the fuselage, on which to carry our food and clothing should we be compelled to walk to Greenland. We had food for ten weeks. Our main staple, pemmican, consisting of chopped-up dried meat, fat, sugar and raisins, was supplemented by chocolate, pilot-bread, tea, malted milk, powdered chocolate, butter, sugar and cream cheese, all of which form a highly concentrated diet.

Other articles of equipment were a rubber boat for crossing open leads if forced down, reindeer-skin, polar-bear and seal fur clothes, boots and gloves, primus stove, rifle, pistol, shotgun and ammunition; tent, knives, axe, medical kit and smoke bombs – all as compact as humanly possible.

If we should come down on the ice the reason it would take us so long to get back, if we got back at all, was that we could not return Spitzbergen way on account of the strong tides. We would have to march Etah way and would have to kill enough seal, polar-bear and musk-ox to last through the Arctic nights.

The first stage of our navigation was the simple one of dead reckoning, or following the well-known landmarks in the vicinity of Kings Bay, which we had just left. We climbed to 2,000 feet to get a good view of the coast and the magnificent snow-covered mountains inland. Within an hour of taking [to] the air we passed the rugged and glacier-laden land and crossed the edge of the polar ice pack. It was much nearer to the land than we had expected. Over to the east was a point where the ice field was very near the land.

We looked ahead at the sea ice gleaming in the rays of the midnight sun – a fascinating scene whose lure had drawn famous men into its clutches, never to return. It was with a feeling of exhilaration that we felt that for the first time in history two mites of men could gaze upon its charms, and discover its secrets, out of reach of those sharp claws.

Perhaps! There was still that 'perhaps', for if we should have a forced landing disaster might easily follow.

It was only natural for Bennett and me to wonder whether or not we would ever get back to this small island we were leaving, for all the airmen explorers who had preceded us in attempts to reach the Pole by aviation had met with disaster or near disaster . . .

As we sped along over the white field below I spent the busiest and most concentrated moments of my life. Though we had confidence in our instruments and methods, we were trying them for the first time over the Polar Sea. First, we obtained north and south bearings on a mountain range on Spitzbergen which we could see for a long distance out over the ice. These checked fairly well with the sun-compass. But I had absolute confidence in the sun-compass.

We could see mountains astern gleaming in the sun at least a hundred miles behind us. That was our last link with civilization. The unknown lay ahead.

Bennett and I took turns piloting. At first Bennett was steering, and for some unaccountable reason the plane veered from the course time and time again, to the right. He could glance back where I was working, through a door leading to the two pilot's seats. Every minute or two he would look at me, to be checked if necessary, on the course by the sun-compass. If he happened to be off the course I would wave him to the right or left until he got on it again. Once every three minutes while I was navigating I checked the wind drift and ground speed, so that in case of a change in wind I could detect it immediately and allow for it.

We had three sets of gloves which I constantly changed to fit the job in hand, and sometimes removed entirely for short periods to write or figure on the chart. I froze my face and one of my hands in taking sights with the instruments from the trapdoors. But I noticed these frostbites at once and was more careful thereafter. Ordinarily a frostbite need not be dangerous if detected in time and if the blood is rubbed back immediately into the affected parts. We also carried leather helmets that would cover the whole face when necessary to use them.

We carried two sun-compasses. One was fixed to a trapdoor in the top of the navigator's cabin; the other was movable, so that when the great wing obscured the sun from the compass on the trapdoor, the second could be used inside the cabin, through the open windows.

Every now and then I took sextant sights of the sun to see where the lines of position would cross our line of flight. I was very thankful at those moments that the Navy requires such thorough navigation training, and that I had made air navigation my hobby.

Finally, when I felt certain we were on our course, I turned my attention to the great ice pack, which I had wondered about ever since I was a youngster at school. We were flying at about 2,000 feet, and I could see at least 50 miles in every direction. There was no sign of land. If there had been any within 100 miles' radius we would have seen its mountain peaks, so good was the visibility.

The ice pack beneath was criss-crossed with pressure ridges, but here and there were stretches that appeared long and smooth enough to land on. However, from 2,000 feet pack ice is extraordinarily deceptive.

The pressure ridges that looked so insignificant from the plane varied from a few feet to 50 or 60 feet in height, while the average thickness of the ice was about 40 feet. A flash of sympathy came over me for the brave men who had in years past struggled northward over that cruel mass.

We passed leads of water recently opened by the movement of the ice, and so dangerous to the foot traveler, who never knows when the ice will open up beneath and swallow him into the black depths of the Polar Sea.

I now turned my mind to wind conditions, for I knew they were a matter of interest to all those contemplating the feasibility of a polar airway. We found them good. There were no bumps in the air. This was as we had anticipated, for the flatness of the ice and the Arctic temperature was not conducive to air currents, such as are sometimes found over land. Had we struck an Arctic gale, I cannot say what the result would have been as far as air roughness is concerned. Of course we still had the advantage of spring and 24-hour daylight.

It was time now to relieve Bennett again at the wheel, not only that he might stretch his legs, but so that he could pour gasoline into the tanks from the five-gallon tins stowed all over the cabin. Empty cans were thrown overboard to get rid of the weight, small though it was.

Frequently I was able to check myself on the course by holding the sun-compass in one hand and steering with the other.

I had time now leisurely to examine the ice pack and eagerly sought signs of life, a polar-bear, a seal, or birds flying, but could see none.

On one occasion, as I turned to look over the side, my arm struck some object in my left breast pocket. It was filled with good-luck pieces!

I am not superstitious, I believe. No explorer, however, can go off without such articles. Among my trinkets was a religious medal put there by a friend. It belonged to his fiancée and he firmly believed it would get me through. There was also a tiny horseshoe made by a famous blacksmith. Attached to the pocket was a little coin taken by Peary, pinned to his shirt, on his trip to the North Pole.

When Bennett had finished pouring and figuring the gasoline consumption, he took the wheel again. I went back to the incessant navigating. So much did I sight down on the dazzling snow that I had a slight attack of snow blindness. But I need not have suffered, as I had brought along the proper kind of amber goggles.

Twice during the next two hours I relieved Bennett at the wheel. When I took it the fourth time, he smiled as he went aft. 'I would rather have Floyd with me', I thought, 'than any other man in the world.'

We were now getting into areas never before viewed by mortal eye. The feelings of an explorer superseded the aviator's. I became conscious of that extraordinary exhilaration which comes from looking into virgin territory. At that moment I felt repaid for all our toil.

At the end of this unknown area lay our goal, somewhere beyond the shimmering horizon. We were opening unexplored regions at the rate of nearly 10,000 square miles an hour, and were experiencing the incomparable satisfaction of searching for new land. Once, for a moment, I mistook a distant, vague, low-lying cloud formation for the white peaks of a far-away land.

I had a momentary sensation of great triumph. If I could explain the feeling I had at this time, the much-asked question would be answered: 'What is this Arctic craze so many men get?'

The sun was still shining brightly. Surely fate was good to us, for without the sun our quest of the Pole would have been hopeless.

To the right, somewhere, the rays of the midnight sun shone down on the scenes of Nansen's heroic struggles to reach the goal that we were approaching with the ease of an eagle at the rate of nearly 100 miles an hour. To our left, lay Peary's oft-traveled trail.

When I went back to my navigating, I compared the magnetic compass with the sun-compass and found that the westerly error in the former had nearly doubled since reaching the edge of the ice pack, where it had been eleven degrees westerly.

When our calculations showed us to be about an hour from the Pole, I noticed through the cabin window a bad leak in the oil tank of the starboard motor. Bennett confirmed my fears. He wrote: 'That motor will stop.'

Bennett then suggested that we try a landing to fix the leak. But I had seen too many expeditions fail by landing. We decided to keep on for the Pole. We would be in no worse fix should we come down near the Pole than we would be if we had a forced landing where we were.

When I took to the wheel again I kept my eyes glued on that oil leak and the oil-pressure indicator. Should the pressure drop, we would lose the motor immediately. It fascinated me. There was no doubt in my mind that the oil pressure would drop any moment. But the prize was actually in sight. We could not turn back.

At 9.02 a.m., May 9, 1926, Greenwich civil time, our calculations showed us to be at the Pole! The dream of a lifetime had at last been realized.

We headed to the right to take two confirming sights of the sun, then turned and took two more.

After that we made some moving and still pictures, then went on for several miles in the direction we had come, and made another larger circle to be sure to take in the Pole. We thus made a non-stop flight around the world in a very few minutes. In doing that we lost a whole day in time and of course when we completed the circle we gained that day back again.

Time and direction became topsy-turvy at the Pole. When crossing it on the same straight line we were going north one instant and south the next! No matter how the wind strikes you at the North Pole it must be travelling north and however you turn your head you must be looking south and our job was to get back to the small island of Spitzbergen which lay somewhere south of us!

There were two great questions that confronted us now. Were we exactly where we thought we were? If not – and could we be absolutely certain? – we would miss Spitzbergen. And even if we were on a straight course, would that engine stop? It seemed certain that it would.

As we flew there at the top of the world, we saluted the gallant, indomitable spirit of Peary and verified his report in every detail.

Below us was a great eternally frozen, snow-covered ocean, broken into ice fields or cakes of various sizes and shapes, the boundaries of which were the ridges formed by the great pressure of one cake upon another. This showed

a constant ice movement and indicated the non-proximity
of land. Here and there, instead of a pressing together of
the ice fields, there was a separation, leaving a water-lead
which had been recently frozen over and showing green
and greenish-blue against the white of the snow. On some
of the cakes were ice hummocks and rough masses of
jumbled snow and ice.

At 9.15 a.m. we headed for Spitzbergen, having abandoned the plan to return via Cape Morris Jesup on account
of the oil leak.

But, to our astonishment, a miracle was happening. That
motor was still running. It is a hundred to one shot that a
leaky engine such as ours means a motor stoppage. It is
generally an oil lead that breaks. We afterward found out
the leak was caused by a rivet jarring out of its hole, and
when the oil got down to the level of the hole it stopped
leaking. Flight Engineer Noville had put an extra amount
of oil in an extra tank.

The reaction of having accomplished our mission, together
with the narcotic effect of the motors, made us drowsy
when we were steering. I dozed off once at the wheel
and had to relieve Bennett several times because of his
sleepiness.

I quote from my impressions cabled to the United States
on our return to Kings Bay:

The wind began to freshen and change direction soon after
we left the Pole, and soon we were making over 100 miles
an hour.

The elements were surely smiling that day on us, two
insignificant specks of mortality flying there over that great,
vast, white area in a small plane with only one companion, speechless and deaf from the motors, just a dot
in the centre of 10,000 square miles of visible desola-
tion.

We felt no larger than a pinpoint and as lonely as the
tomb; as remote and detached as a star.

Here, in another world, far from the herds of people, the
smallnesses of life fell from our shoulders. What wonder
that we felt no great emotion of achievement or fear of

death that lay stretched beneath us, but instead, impersonal, disembodied. On, on we went. It seemed forever onward.

Our great speed had the effect of quickening our mental processes, so that a minute appeared as many minutes, and I realized fully then that time is only a relative thing. An instant can be an age, an age an instant.

We were aiming for Grey Point, Spitzbergen, and finally when we saw it dead ahead, we knew that we had been able to keep on our course! That we were exactly where we had thought we were!

It was a wonderful relief not to have to navigate any more. We came into Kings Bay flying at about 4,000 feet. The tiny village was a welcome sight, but not so much so as the good old *Chantier* that looked so small beneath. I could see the steam from her welcoming and, I knew, joyous whistle.

It seemed but a few moments until we were in the arms of our comrades, who carried us with wild joy down the snow runway they had worked so hard to make.

Among the first to meet us had been Captain Amundsen and Lincoln Ellsworth, two good sports.

On his return home, Byrd's records of the flight were scrutinized by the National Geographic Society, which pronounced itself satisfied that he had, indeed, reached the North Pole. Byrd rapidly gained acclaim as one of the great heroes of aviation and polar exploration, and for many years he and Bennett were almost universally recognized as the first men to reach the Pole by air. In 1960, however, doubts began to arise. The meteorologist G.H. Liljequist published an analysis of the prevailing meteorological conditions and of *Josephine Ford*'s technical records, and concluded that the aircraft could not have maintained the cruising speed (87 knots) required to fly to the Pole and back in 15½ hours, and that at a more probable speed of 75 knots it would have reached only 88°17.5'N. Other subsequent investigations produced evidence supporting Liljequist's findings, leaving Byrd's claim to priority in some doubt. Unlike Cook and Peary, however, he was never publicly pilloried;

history has treated him more kindly, especially since in later life he made some magnificent contributions to the exploration of the Antarctic. Even if he did not, technically, attain the North Pole, his claim to have done so is generously treated as a mistake rather than a deception; his flight unquestionably helped to shape the course of polar exploration, and is still regarded as one of the great moments in the history of aviation.

From Nansen in 1895 to Peary in 1909, the sheer glory of being first was the main driving force in expeditions towards the Pole. The 1920s showed the beginning of a return to practicalities; to Byrd, and to some extent to Amundsen and others also, a flight to the Pole was a proving ground for new technologies; a dramatic and very public way of showing that new-fangled creations worked, even in the most extreme conditions. It was Byrd and his contemporaries who proved that trans-Atlantic flights, trans-polar flights to the Far East, were all coming within the scope of human capability; and such things changed the world forever.

3. *Amundsen, Ellsworth and Nobile: 1926*

While Byrd was making his historic polar flight, Amundsen's expedition was still making its final preparations for take-off. This, too, was an attempt to use the North Pole as a means of drawing attention to a new technology – in this case, airships.

Wellman's series of failures around the turn of the century had done the airship lobby no favours, but there had been great advances since then, especially in Germany and Italy, and in the 1920s a growing body of opinion thought that airships had an important role to play in Arctic exploration and research. Amundsen and Ellsworth shared that belief, and in 1926 they teamed up with the Italian airship engineer Colonel Umberto Nobile to attempt the first crossing of the Arctic Ocean, by way of the North Pole. The first ideas for such an expedition arose during the Amundsen/Ellsworth expedition of 1925, when several men fell into casual conversation about it, and concluded that the Italian airship N1 was the best fitted for the enterprise. Immediately after the expedition of 1925, its designer Nobile was summoned to Oslo, and the new expedition came to life. Ellsworth once again provided much of the funding, the Italian government agreed to the use of N1, and a Norwegian aviation club undertook the formal management of the expedition.

This was one of the most international of all polar expeditions to that date, with participants from Norway, the United States, Italy and Sweden, and it displayed some of the advantages, as well as some of the drawbacks, of international cooperation. The obvious advantages were that only Italy had the airship, only Ellsworth the money, and only Amundsen the charismatic leadership to make a success of it. On the other hand, there was always a little tension among the leading participants over whose expedition it really was. Amundsen won the upper hand: the organizing body was Norwegian, the airship, once handed over, was renamed *Norge* (*Norway*); and he and Ellsworth later wrote the main published narrative which they dedicated, rather provocatively, to 'The Norwegian Flag'. On the other hand, Nobile had every right to feel a little miffed at being publicly overshadowed by his Norwegian and American colleagues. After all, it was he who designed and built the airship, served as its captain and chief pilot, and provided some of the most essential staff, the mechanics. He was understandably hurt when Amundsen grabbed most of the credit, but in later life he was gracious enough about it.

On 7 May, *Norge* arrived in northwest Spitsbergen, where Amundsen's advance party was already waiting. On 11 May, with 16 men on board, the airship departed on the trans-Arctic flight. Amundsen relates the story of the flight; rather too noticeably, his account makes virtually no reference to the Italian crew; only the Scandinavians and Ellsworth. The Norwegians heroically man the rudders, write telegrams, plot the course; Ellsworth heroically holds the chronometer; the Italians invisibly keep the thing in the air.

At 9.55 a.m. the order 'Let go' was given, and lightly and without effort the *Norge* rose gracefully up into the fresh clear air. It was about −4.5° centigrade, and almost perfectly still. Our friends below became smaller and smaller, and at last unrecognizable.

Now that our connection with *terra firma* was broken we were a little world to ourselves, swaying lightly and freely in space. The motors were started, and the *Norge* began the last part of its voyage. It had been declared by some that the most difficult part of the journey was over, but I wonder if these gentlemen were not a trifle uncertain on this point. Who could tell what was before us? Who dared prophesy?

Soon, however, we discovered we were not quite alone, for Byrd's machine suddenly whizzed past us. It was quite a comforting sight: there were still other human beings in this world! The Fokker accompanied us for an hour and then turned back.

As has previously been mentioned, the gondola was very small. In order to save weight the original gondola had been cut down, and this had been done so thoroughly that it was now extremely difficult to find room for the ten men who were to be accommodated in it. When the foreign Press sought to give sensational particulars of the *Norge*'s flight, and stated that discord and wrangling prevailed, that relations were even more like two armed camps, then there is only this to be said – that there was simply no room for quarrelling. A certain amount of elbow-room is required for exhibitions of temper, but here there was none at all. Only under the most cordial conditions could this flight be accomplished, and we assure these imaginative gentlemen of the foreign Press that a more peaceful and tranquil spot than the *Norge* during the flight has never existed. Let it be said at once with emphasis that we never heard an angry word nor saw an unpleasant expression during the whole flight. And, indeed, how could anybody find time? That question seems enough to knock all ill-disposed fabrications to pieces. Let us take a glance inside and see how the situation shaped itself the whole time.

In the front of the gondola Horgen has settled down on his Bovril case. He is busy controlling the *Norge*'s course, and has his time fully occupied. He dare not let go of the helm for a second. Well, then, Horgen is quite harmless. The next man we set eyes on is Wisting, at the main rudder. He is in the same class as Horgen, and entirely absorbed in a peaceful avocation. Amundsen is sitting on one of the two aluminium water-tanks, placed in the commander's cabin. He is for the most part occupied in the peaceful occupation of looking out through the window and studying the ice-conditions that are constantly changing. His gaze is often far away and dreamy: 'I wonder what I shall see next.' Everything around is unknown, and the most surprising object may show itself at any moment. 'Land ahead' perhaps. How he can possibly get into a bloodthirsty frame of mind is difficult to imagine. Nobile is the fourth person in the commander's cabin. He moves about smiling and composed. His movements consist in marking time, for no other space for exercise is available. Peace, then, prevails in this part of the ship.

In the chart-room there prevails indescribable industry. The second-in-command is taking astronomical observations, observations of drift and speed, which are constantly altering the position on the chart. This goes on incessantly and leaves no time for sleeping or eating or drinking, much less for quarrelling. Ellsworth keeps calm and quiet, always ready to read off on the chronometer each time Riiser-Larsen takes an observation of latitude. Malmgren with great difficulty moves about in a circle amongst the various meteorological instruments. Here also Ellsworth is ready to help. It is not easy to manage without assistance. Ramm is scribbling and sending off telegrams without cessation. Heaven knows what he writes about, but certainly not of the alarms of war! Captain Gottwaldt and Storm-Johnsen are busy in the little radio cabinet. Perhaps they are tearing each other's hair out? If so, they are doing it in solemn silence for we hear nothing. The motors are roaring and throbbing, so it is very unlikely that the mechanics are looking after their work and at fisticuffs at the same time. No, my dear scribblers, your 'armed camp' was absurd and your stories untrue from beginning to end.

The feeling of safety on board the *Norge* was very much in evidence. Possibly this feeling was strong when we recalled last year's flight. In case any mishap befell the motors we could now merely stop and make repairs whilst we quietly floated on. It was very different last year. An accident to a motor was then synonymous with landing, and landing on this territory was in nine cases out of ten synonymous with a catastrophe. The ice-conditions seemed exactly the same now as in 1925. We did not see a single landing-place on the long way from Svalbard to Alaska. Not one. But it requires experience to be able to decide this. I remember that several times some of our companions on board the *Norge* cried out excitedly: 'See what a splendid landing-place.' The four of us who had seen and experienced these 'splendid landing-places' looked at each other and smiled – a smile that expressed our meaning better than any words. In spite of Byrd's fine flight our advice is: 'Do not fly over these ice-fields before aeroplanes have become so perfect that one can be quite sure of not having to make a forced landing.'

Flying northwards all went splendidly. If we did not look out and assure ourselves that we were in the air, we should not have realized it. The ice lay considerably farther towards the south than last year; it lay practically right down to Amsterdam Island. Whilst last year we saw broken ice right up to 82°N latitude, this year we came in entirely over unbroken polar ice. But the humps were the same – always the same.

It is only under conditions like this one rightly comes to see what a remarkable age we live in. It is even strange when we for instance are sitting in the smoking-saloon of one of the large Transatlantic liners and are enjoying our coffee with two or three friends, to get a little scrap of paper containing a greeting from dear ones, many hundred miles away. Still there are amongst us a few that are not so blasé that they do not on such an occasion exclaim: 'It is very wonderful after all, this wireless.' We elders, who have known nothing other than cables will certainly never overcome this feeling. But I really first felt the complete effect when in 81°30′N latitude. I received a telegram from a friend in Melbourne with his good wishes for our voyage. At 7 p.m. I stood with the headphones and listened to the time-signal from Stavanger wireless-station. It was just as if I stood in my room at home and heard the clock ticking. It made a great impression on me. Here we were flying north-ward – always farther northward – into the great infinite ice desert, whilst at the same time we heard those at home sending us messages and trying to help us on our way. It is then that one can best realize what a wonderful age we live in. In 87°30′N latitude Captain Gottwaldt was decorated with the King's gold service medal for his eminent work in connection with the radio. I have always admired His Majesty's great talent for doing everything at the right moment and in the right place, but this time I could not find expression for what I felt. With ringing cheers from us all, so that the *Norge* shook again, Captain Gottwaldt received the announcement of this high honour. That was the only time I heard shouting on the *Norge*!

It was easy to describe the feeling with which we now, light and safely, passed over our highest latitude of last year, 87°43′. We do not know whether we shook our fists or not. Possibly we made a grimace and said: 'Not this time, dear friend, not this time.' It is most probable we

took off our hats to our worthy opponent. Certain it is
that we looked out on the humpy ice-field with endless
relief knowing that we were over it and not on it.

As we neared the Pole the work of the navigator became
more and more intense. He must endeavour to find the
point as accurately as possible. We first had, however,
another event to attend to – namely to celebrate Ellsworth's
birthday. At 12 midnight all work ceased for a moment
and all congratulated the esteemed leader who under such
unique circumstances entered his forty-sixth year. This
short ceremony, besides being a rare one, was also quite
surprisingly pleasant, and Nobile conjured forth a flask of
egg-punch. With handshakes and with egg-punch therefore
we conducted the birthday hero into a new year. It will be
long before he forgets it.

'Ready with the flags.'

Riiser-Larsen knelt and through the open window followed the sun with his sextant.

'Now we are there.'

Out flew the beautiful double-sewn silk Norwegian flag.
It was on a cross-bar fastened to a long aluminium staff
exactly like a standard, which resulted in its making a
splendid descent. It landed correctly, fixed itself in the
ice, and the light breeze unfolded the Norwegian colours.
Amundsen at the same moment turned round and grasped
Wisting's hand. No word was uttered; it was unnecessary,
for these two men's hands planted the Norwegian flag at
the South Pole on the 14th of December, 1911.

Then the Stars and Stripes flew out. It was with an
extraordinary, quite indescribable feeling that Ellsworth
undertook this task. When again will a man plant the flag of
his country at the Pole on his birthday? Not for many a year
perhaps. Lastly Nobile threw down the Italian flag. Thus all
three flags stand a few yards apart as near the Geographical
North Pole as any human beings can determine with instruments. It was then 1.25 Greenwich time on the twelfth of
May 1926. Ellsworth received two congratulatory telegrams
here from relations and friends. The ice was much broken
up at the Pole and a mass of small ice-floes were observable.
It was quite different from the other ice we had passed over.

We were uncommonly fortunate with the weather, having, as a matter of fact, been in fog just before reaching the Pole. This disappeared, however, and permitted our navigator to take his observations.

As the technical sections of the book will probably contain a mass of figures, such as the time of day, temperature, distances, speed and so on, we shall endeavour as far as possible to avoid them in this our part.

The ice continued in a very broken-up condition, except with a few closer-packed stretches right down to 86°N latitude. There it assumed quite the same character as the ice between Svalbard and the Pole, and at the Ice-pole itself there was not a particle of open water to be seen. The Ice-pole – or, as it up to this time was called, the Inaccessible Pole – is the centre of the great ice-covered region and as such, of course, is the most difficult place to reach.

Of animal life we had seen extremely little. North of Svalbard we saw a good many bear tracks and indeed two bears. They were so alarmed when they saw and heard us that they threw themselves headfirst into the nearest opening in the ice. We saw no more bear tracks until we came to the Ice-pole. There were no signs of bird life, nor of seal nor walrus. This was only a confirmation of the previous year's observations.

At 8.30 a.m. we came into a thick fog and this kept on with occasional breaks until 6 p.m. It was thus a tremendous sea of fog we passed over and in some places of extraordinary density. It is clear that this, in a high degree, prevented our taking observations. We may well therefore have passed over islands at low altitude. There can be no question that land exists, even flat land, to any great extent on the course we took, as we time and again observed the ice under us. The greatest danger we encountered on our journey was met here. The damp fog settled in the form of ice on the various external metal parts. This ice became loosened from time to time, was sucked into the propellers and was then slung against the outer part of the balloon-envelope, with the result that it was much battered and had constantly to be repaired.

At 6.45 a.m. (Greenwich) on the 13th we sighted land on

the port bow. It was a great moment. The flight had been accomplished and the goal reached! It is difficult to obtain land-bearings in these parts of the world and especially from the air. The flat land seemed all alike – a heap of gravel here and there. Wherever we were on the Alaska coast we had to alter our course westward along the shore so as to come out in Bering Strait. We supposed, however, according to the last observation, that we had struck the coast some miles west of Point Barrow, but we did not see it. That our supposition was correct was proved a little later, as we then passed over Wainwright, Amundsen's and Omdal's place of sojourn from 1922 to 1923. We were now no longer in doubt. We knew every single house. The inhabitants had heard the sound of the motors, and all of them had collected outside on the slope. What in the world were their thoughts? They expected indeed that we should come, but it is scarcely reasonable to suppose that they had formed any conception of the real appearance of an airship in mid-air. Indeed, to us an airship seems an imposing sight. What then must these people think when such a monster suddenly shoots out of the clouds? Some years ago they would certainly have shot at us. Not so now; they knew that Amundsen and Omdal, their good friends, were on board. All waved and shouted and took their hats off. But it lasted only a moment before Wainwright was lost to sight. Shortly after we passed over our own familiar Maudheim, the house we ourselves had built and had lived in for a whole year. The people who now lived there all gathered on the roof and clearly showed their excitement. Memories came and went. On the 20th of November 1922, Amundsen left this house with one Esquimaux, one sledge, and fifteen dogs in order to go southward to more civilized regions, whilst Omdal remained behind to look after the house and the aeroplane. They accomplished the journey to Kotzebue Sound in ten days – a distance of 500 miles. It was a fine achievement for a man who had passed his fiftieth birthday – fifty miles a day for ten days. There was no question of sitting on the heavily laden sledge; not the slightest. They walked the whole way, holding on to the sledge for support. It was a record trip of high rank. But now we could record something considerably greater.

Soon the house had disappeared and the journey began along the low coast covered with lagoons. It is difficult enough to proceed with sledges and dogs in this kind of region, as the land often entirely disappears. But from the air it is still worse. At Cape Lisburne we came into a fog, so we rose and sailed above it. We were obliged to be at a considerable height so as to be sure of clearing the mountains. Our journey from now onwards – after the real voyage was ended – became the most adventurous. A furious gale blew up from the north, and partly in and partly out of the fog we drove quite out of our course. Probably we were, according to observations, at about 6 p.m. (Greenwich) on the 13th of May, not far from Cape Serdze Kamen on the Siberian coast. We then set our course due east so as to reach the coast of Alaska again. At 11 p.m. (Greenwich) we at last reached the coast. An observation showed us to be in the vicinity of Kevalina on the north side of Kotzebue Sound. Here we had quite a pleasant experience: we saw a hut with an Esquimaux and his dogs outside it. We passed in over the land at quite a low height above him. He danced and gesticulated. What his thoughts were I leave the reader to imagine.

Ice conditions in the Polar Sea, north of Bering Strait, were peculiar. Here – where we year after year had tried to force our way northwards, drifting with the *Maud*, but had met with quite impenetrable ice only – it was now quite open. Indeed it was so open that we thought that we had been driven out into Bering Strait before we got our bearings. From Kevalina it then bore southward along the land. We also got our bearings from the Serpentine River, which from the air is impossible to mistake, with its distinct snake-like twists. Here we had another experience, as, at quite low altitude, we passed two Esquimaux with their dog-teams. We were then so low that we could very easily have recognized them had we known them before. The dogs were, as can reasonably be imagined, startled, and we can well suppose that their owners were also, for they had difficulty in managing them. The journey

from here along the coast was not altogether pleasant;
the northerly gale had increased to a storm and the drifting
of the immense balloon became enormous. At times it
appeared as if it would be difficult to prevent it from
drifting in over the high mountains on Seward Peninsula.
All went well, however, and we passed Cape Prince of
Wales at 3.30 a.m. (Greenwich) on the 14th of May. Bering
Strait was quite free of ice, and the strong wind over the
open sea was very troublesome. We could now really feel
the difference between a flight over ice and one over sea.
We had during the long voyage over ice been accustomed
to absolutely calm conditions. It was now quite different:
like a ball were we tossed up and down by the strong wind
and not infrequently the *Norge* drove sideways through
Bering Strait.

In order to have all in readiness for landing, which should
now, according to our plan, soon take place, Riiser-Larsen
wrote a note to the acting Norwegian consul, Mr Ralph
Lomen, with detailed instructions as to what was to be
done from the slope during landing. The coast, however,
had entirely disappeared in the fog. The wind howled
worse than ever and the apprehension of drifting out of
our course and out into Bering Strait was not groundless.
In order not to be exposed to this the airship was steered
towards land. We were now in 'waters' with which both
Amundsen and Wisting were familiar, after their various
trips in the course of years. As Wisting was fully occupied
at the main rudder, it fell to Amundsen to act as guide.
There is an enormous difference between acting in this
capacity on sea and in the air. One is accustomed to the
former; but the latter one is totally unfamiliar with. When
you add storm and fog to this, the 'guide's' position is
not an enviable one. As we steered towards the coast
we saw faint outlines of an island on the starboard side.
In the haste and tumult that now arose in making all
ready for landing, Amundsen took this to be Sledge Island
and we hugged the coast expecting that before very long
we should be at our destination. Under more tranquil
circumstances one would scarcely have committed such
an error as this, but conditions were far from tranquil.

As mentioned before, there prevailed chaotic disturbance – everything having been brought down into the lowest gondola in readiness for anchoring. If it had been crowded before, one was now entirely prevented from making the slightest movement. That part of the coast we now came to appeared quite strange, a fact (as was later proved) that was not so very remarkable, as we had never been there before. At 7 a.m. (Greenwich) on the 14th of May, we reached a spot where there were a few houses. What could this be? Not the originally intended landing-place, for the houses were too few, and moreover were lacking that best of identification-marks, the high telegraph-mast. We now all agreed that a landing ought to be attempted, especially as the ice was even and unbroken outside the little village. We would not, however, give up finding the landing-place originally fixed upon without first examining the coast a little. This was then done, but without result. The 'guides' had to acknowledge that they had never been here before.

Now came the question, should we leave the place where conditions seemed better – though this is not saying very much – than any other place? Besides, we got the announcement that we had petrol for only seven more hours' flight. We believe, we venture to say with conviction, that all on board desired to land even if it were risky. It must be remembered that we had been in the air for about seventy hours, and most of us entirely without sleep. The result was that we were dead tired and unfit for work. Indeed, some even began to see visions. During our flight to and fro we again came to the little village, which now with its small, even surface of ice gave greater possibilities for a safe landing than any we had hitherto seen. The wind here was also strong and came in dangerous squalls, but there was some protection. 'All right, then let us try.'

The landing was one of the achievements one will always remember. It was splendidly done and we take off our hats to the skipper of the vessel for the quiet, neat manner in which he accomplished it. But if conditions had remained the same on landing as when we started, the result might well have been doubtful, even if the skipper had been ever

so skilful. But the remarkable thing happened – it can well
be called the miracle – something that causes us to sometimes stop and think. There must indeed be an over-ruling
Providence. Whilst we were descending there were still
strong, quick gusts of wind from the land. Suddenly, and
without any warning whatsoever, it became quite calm and
remained so during the time we were landing. As we began
to approach the ice, people came running out to meet us.
An attempt to anchor the airship failed. The ice was too
poor and the anchor that was cast out could not grip. Nor
was it really necessary. Gently and quietly we approached
the ice – nearer and nearer until we at last touched. The
gondola was supplied with an enormous air-fender on the
bottom, so this overcame the shock. But for the bump
against the air-fender causing us to spring some metres
into the air, we should scarcely have noticed the landing,
so finely and skilfully was it done. The ice we landed upon
lay just outside the village. The whole population had now
come to the spot and most of them helped to hold the
anchor-rope. The door of the gondola was now opened,
and one by one we jumped down upon the ice. They were
a peculiar people that we found here: they did not show
the slightest perturbation or excitement; quietly and calmly
they gave us a warm welcome. One would almost think
that they were accustomed to receive airships every day.
At last we got our curiosity satisfied: 'Where in the world
are we?' 'In Teller,' was the reply. We had therefore flown
ninety kilometres away from our original landing-place.

    The first flight from continent to continent via the North
Pole had been accomplished without any injury whatsoever
to anyone.

– 14 –

The *Italia* Disaster

1928

In spite of his unhappy relationship with Amundsen, by the end of the flight of the *Norge*, Umberto Nobile had already convinced himself that his airships had an important role to play in Arctic exploration. Within days of landing at Teller, he was discussing plans for another expedition and saying, 'After all, our journey has been practical proof that the airship is the best means of exploring unknown country from above. There is still so much to be done.' In addition, he already had a newer, better airship under construction in Italy, and an airship hangar in Spitsbergen. There were still 1,500,000 square miles of Arctic Ocean to be explored for new land, including areas north of Greenland, Siberia and Canada that had always been inaccessible to ships. There were also scientific questions that could best be investigated from an airship. By the end of 1927 he had persuaded the Italian Royal Geographical Society, the City of Milan, and finally, by authority of Benito Mussolini, the Italian government, to support an expedition to explore, geographically and scientifically, those unknown areas.

Nobile's new airship *Italia* reached the hangar in Kongsfjorden, northwest Spitsbergen, on 6 May 1928. The first flights, intended to explore Russian Arctic waters, were only partly successful, being hampered by bad weather. On the third flight, Nobile planned to explore to the north of Greenland, then head along an unexplored route to the North Pole. *Italia* took off for this flight in the early morning of 23 May. One of his companions on the flight, mentioned frequently in Nobile's narrative, was the Swedish meteorologist Finn Malmgren (1895–1928), who was charged with the crucial task of determining the airship's best course in the prevailing weather conditions. Later, after

establishing their position over Cape Bridgman in northeast
Greenland, the North Pole flight began.

Having recognized Cape Bridgmann, we turned back and
steered for the Pole, along the 27th meridian W of
Greenwich.

At six o'clock, a few miles from Cape Bridgmann, the sky
– until then covered with clouds – cleared up.

With the blue sky above, the radiant sun lighting the
inside of the cabin, and the wind astern increasing our
speed, the journey to the Pole proceeded in joyous excitement. All on board were happy, and contentment shone
from every face.

One of the Naval officers stood at the steering-wheel,
whilst the other two divided their time untiringly between
solar observations and measurements of drift and speed.
Trojani and Cecioni, as usual, manned the elevator-wheel.

Malmgren was standing up, with his spectacles on, to
mark on a chart fixed to the wall of the wireless cabin the
meteorological data which Biagi, as he intercepted them,
came to communicate to us. Pontremoli and Behounek
attended imperturbably to their instruments, without troub-
ling in the least about what was going on around them.
One would have thought they were working in the quiet
of their laboratories.

The three mechanics were at their posts, vigilant and
attentive as ever: Pomella in the stern engine-boat, Caratti
on the left, and Ciocca on the right. But only the stern
engine and one of the side ones were in motion.

Arduino was walking backwards and forwards along
the gangway, to supervise the mechanics and check and
regulate the consumption of petrol.

Alessandrini, after visiting all the accessible parts of the
ship during the first hours of flight to make sure that
nothing was wrong, and pulling up the handling-ropes that
dangled outside – to prevent their offering an unnecessary
resistance to the air and getting coated with ice – had come
down into the cabin, some time before, to help Trojani and
Cecioni and take a spell at the steering-wheel.

With such a strong wind astern we advanced rapidly

towards our desired goal. At 6 p.m. we had reached the 84th parallel; by 10.30 p.m., 88°10′.

The region over which we were flying was unknown to man. It lay between the route of the *Norge*, to the right of us, and that of Peary, to the left. Not a trace of land in sight, although the visibility was exceptional, as we could see clearly up to 60 miles all round.

The height at which we were sailing gradually increased: at 6 p.m. it was 750 ft; at 8 p.m., 1,500; at 10 p.m., 1,650; at 10.30 p.m., 1,800.

I was delighted at such splendid visibility occurring unexpectedly after the 8 hours' fog which had made the first part of our voyage so trying. But the strong wind, although it helped us on our way to the Pole, made me regretfully consider that I should have to give up the descent we had planned.

Meanwhile I watched Malmgren at work. He was now tracing the curves of two cyclonic areas which apparently existed, one above the Arctic Ocean towards the Siberian coast, the other above the Barents Sea.

Which was the best route to follow, after leaving the Pole? This was the problem which had been preoccupying me for some time.

The notion of sailing against a wind as strong as the one at present behind us did not at all appeal to me, especially as I feared it might be accompanied by fog. So I thought that, having reached the Pole, it would be better to fly before the wind to the Siberian coast, or steer for the coast of Canada, where the meteorological bulletins forecast fog, it is true, but with atmospheric calm.

I discussed it with Malmgren, who dissuaded me.

'It would be better to return to King's Bay,' he said. 'Then we shall be able to complete our programme of scientific research.'

I remained undecided. I knew from long experience what a hard – and often intolerable – strain it was to fight for hours against a strong wind, and so instinctively I shrank from it. But Malmgren reassured me.

'No!' he said. 'This wind will not last long. When we are

on our way back it will drop, after a few hours, and be succeeded by north-west winds.'

Eventually I was won over and followed his advice.

The conversation on this subject was resumed, in dramatic circumstances, four days later. On May 27th, on the pack after the catastrophe, Malmgren asked me if I thought that all would have been well had we followed out my idea of reaching the mouth of the Mackenzie. Probably it would, because the airship would have been spared the torment of a prolonged struggle against the wind – but who can tell whether, on this route too, some other peril would not have been lying in wait for us?

At the Pole

Whilst I was talking to Malmgren, we continued to draw rapidly nearer to the Pole.

Towards ten o'clock there was an unexpected change in the sky, which until then had been blue all over. In front of us, an hour or two away, a barrier of cloud over 3,000 ft high rose from the horizon, standing out against the azure of the sky above. With its weird outlines it looked like the walls of some gigantic fortress.

That band of cloud, dark and compact, had a menacing aspect which struck my imagination. 'There's no getting through that!' I thought. 'We shall be bound to turn back.'

At 10.30 we encountered a bank of thick cloud. And as at that moment it did not suit us to lose sight of the sun – height measurements being more than ever necessary – we rose above the fog, to about 2,400 ft.

We were then at 88°10'. Another 54 miles and we should be at the Pole.

Meanwhile the Naval officers were making their solar observations. We were getting nearer and nearer to the goal, and the excitement on board was growing.

Twenty minutes after midnight, early on May 24th, the officers who were observing the sun with a sextant cried: 'We are there!'

The *Italia* was at the Pole.

We had covered 425 miles from Cape Bridgmann at an average speed of 62 m.p.h.

I had the engines slowed down and ordered the helmsman to steer in a circle.

It was impossible, alas! to descend on the pack, but we had a promise to keep: to deposit on the ice of the Pole the Cross entrusted to us by Pius XI, and by its side the Italian flag. We prepared ourselves in religious silence to carry out this gesture — so simple and yet so solemn. I ordered Alessandrini to get ready.

Then I had the engines accelerated once more, to pass under the fog. It was 12.40. Twenty minutes later we were in sight of the pack. We went on circling round at a reduced speed until the preparations were completed. I had had a large tricolour cloth fastened to the Cross, to catch the wind and guide it down.

At 1.20 a.m. I leaned out of the cabin and let fall the Italian flag. Then followed the *gonfalone* of the City of Milan, and a little medal of the Virgin of the Fire, given me by the inhabitants of Forli. For the second time our tricolour spread itself over the ice of the Pole. Beside the flag we dropped the Cross. It was 1.30, and we were about 450 ft up.

At the moment when these rites were completed, I felt a thrill of pride. Two years after the *Norge* flight we had come back to the Pole, and this time the bad weather, from Italy onwards, had made it much more difficult.

Inside the cabin, now that the engines were almost still, a little gramophone was playing an old folk-song: 'The Bells of San Giusto', bringing back memories, taking us all of a sudden to Italy, to our homes. We were all moved: more than one had tears in his eyes. Zappi cried: 'Long live Nobile!' I was grateful to him, as I was to Malmgren, when he came and said, clasping my hand: 'Few men can say, as we can, that we have been twice to the Pole.'

Few men indeed: six Italians and one Swede.

After that ceremony, matters became much more serious. The flight back to Spitsbergen was severely hampered by strong headwinds and fog. Eventually, it became extremely difficult to determine where they were, and how fast they were moving, and Nobile decided that 'It was essential to find the pack again, so that we could go on checking our drift and speed. We plunged back into the fog and slowly descended until the frozen sea appeared clearly in sight. We were about 900 ft up.' Soon after, he and his crew lost control of their airship.

We were flying between 600 and 900 ft up. The dirigible was still light, so to keep it at the proper height we had to hold the nose down.

At 10.30 I again ordered a speed measurement. When this had been taken I walked to the front of the cabin and looked out of the right-hand porthole, between the steering-wheel and the elevator. To test the height, I dropped a glass ball full of red liquid, and stood there, timing its fall with a stop-watch.

While I was attending to this, I heard Cecioni say excitedly: 'We are heavy!'

I turned with a start to look at the instruments.

The ship was right down by the stern, at an angle of 8 degrees to the horizon; nevertheless, we were rapidly falling.

The peril was grave and imminent. A short distance below us stretched the pack. I at once gave the orders which had to be given, the only ones that could save the ship in this emergency – if that was possible: to accelerate the two engines, start the third, and at the same time lift the nose of the dirigible still higher. I hoped by these means to overcome the unexpected heaviness.

Simultaneously, I shouted to Alessandrini to run out on the top of the ship and inspect the stern valves, as I thought gas might be escaping – the only explanation that occurred to me at the moment of this serious and rapid increase in weight.

Meanwhile, the mechanics had carried out my orders. Pomella and Caratti had speeded their engines up to 1,400 revolutions and Ciocca, with surprising promptness, had started his own. The ship began to move faster, and tilted at an angle of 15 or 20 degrees.

The dynamic lift obtained in this way must certainly have represented several hundredweight.

But unfortunately we went on falling. The variometer – on which my eyes were fixed – confirmed it; in fact, we seemed to be dropping even faster.

I realized that there was nothing more to be done. The attempt to combat the increased weight by propulsion had failed . . . A crash was now inevitable; the most we could do was to mitigate its consequences.

I gave the necessary orders: to stop the engines at once, so as to avoid fire breaking out as we crashed; and to drop the ballast-chain. Sending Cecioni to do this, I put Zappi in his place.

It was all that could have been ordered; it was ordered promptly and with absolute calm. The perfect discipline on board was unbroken, so that each man carried out my orders as best he could, in the vertiginous rapidity of the event.

In the meantime the pack was approaching at a fearful speed. I saw that Cecioni was finding it difficult to untie the rope which held the chain. 'Hurry up! Hurry up!' I shouted to him. Then noticing that the engine on the left, run by Caratti, was still working, I leaned out of a porthole on that side, and at the top of my voice – echoed, I think, by one of the officers – repeated the order: 'Stop the engine!' At that moment I saw the stern-boat was only a few tens of yards from the pack. I drew back into the cabin.

The recollection of those last terrible instants is very vivid in my memory. I had scarcely had time to reach the spot near the two rudders, between Malmgren and Zappi, when I saw Malmgren fling up the wheel, turning his startled eyes on me. Instinctively I grasped the helm, wondering if it were possible to guide the ship on to a snow-field and so lessen the shock . . . Too late! . . . There was the pack, a few yards below, terribly uneven. The masses of ice grew larger, came nearer and nearer . . . A moment later we crashed.

There was a fearful impact. Something hit me on the head, then I was caught and crushed. Clearly, without any pain, I felt some of my limbs snap. Some object falling from a height knocked me down head foremost.

Instinctively I shut my eyes, and with perfect lucidity and coolness formulated the thought: 'It's all over!' I almost pronounced the words in my mind.

It was 10.33 on May 25th.

The fearful event had lasted only 2 or 3 minutes!

When I opened my eyes I found myself lying on the ice, in the midst of an appalling pack. I realized at once that others had fallen with me.

I looked up to the sky. Towards my left the dirigible, nose in air, was drifting away before the wind. It was terribly lacerated around the pilot-cabin. Out of it trailed torn strips of fabric, ropes, fragments of metal-work. The left wall of the cabin had remained attached. I noticed a few creases in the envelope.

Upon the side of the crippled, mutilated ship stood out the black letters *Italia*. My eyes remained fixed on them, as if fascinated, until the dirigible merged in the fog and was lost to sight.

It was only then that I felt my injuries. My right leg and arm were broken and throbbing; I had hurt my face and the top of my head, and my chest seemed all upside down with the violence of the shock. I thought my end was near.

Suddenly I heard a voice – Mariano's – asking: 'Where is the General?' And I looked around me.

I had never seen such a terrible pack: a formless, contorted jumble of pointed ice-crags, stretching to the horizon.

Two yards away on my right, Malmgren was sitting, and a little farther off lay Cecioni, moaning aloud. Next him was Zappi. The others – Mariano, Behounek, Trojani, Viglieri, and Biagi – were standing up. They appeared unhurt, except for Trojani, whose face was stained by a few patches of blood.

Here and there one could see wreckage – a dreary note of grey against the whiteness of the snow. In front of me a strip of bright red, like blood which had flowed from some enormous wound, showed the spot where we had fallen. It was the liquid from the glass balls.

I was calm. My mind was perfectly clear. But now I was feeling the seriousness of my injuries – worst of all, a terrible convulsion in my chest. Breathing was a great effort. I thought I had probably sustained some grave internal injury. It seemed that death was very near – that maybe I had only 2 or 3 hours to live.

I was glad of this. It meant that I should not have to watch the despair and slow death-agony of my comrades. What hope was there for them? With no provisions, no tent, no wireless, no sledges – nothing but useless wreckage – they were lost, irremediably lost, in this terrible wilderness of ice.

I turned towards them, looking at them with an infinite sadness at heart. Then I spoke: 'Steady, my lads! Keep your spirits up! Don't be cast down by this misfortune.' And I added: 'Lift your thoughts to God!'

No other words, no other ideas, came to me in those first unforgettable moments when death seemed imminent. But suddenly I was seized by strong emotion. Something rose up from my soul – from the depths of my being: something stronger than the pain of my tortured limbs, stronger than the thought of approaching death. And from my straining breast broke out, loud and impetuous, the cry: '*Viva l'Italia!*'

My comrades cheered.

Beside me on the right Malmgren was still sitting silent in the same place, stroking his right arm. On his face, frowning and ashen pale, a little swollen from his fall, was a look of blank despair. His blue eyes stared fixedly in front of him, as if into the void. Lost in thought, he seemed not even to notice the other men around him.

I had been very fond of this young scientist, ever since we had shared in the *Norge* expedition. And lately my affection for him had grown. He had become my most valued collaborator – the only one to whom I confided my plans, my ideas, my thoughts. I attached a good deal of weight to his judgment and advice. Some days previously we had decided the general lines of our future flight – the bold scheme which, if carried out, would have utilized to the utmost the possibilities afforded by our ship and crew . . . But now all our plans had come to naught.

Wishing to speak to him, I said softly: 'Nothing to be done, my dear Malmgren!'

Nothing to be done! . . . A painful confession for men of action!

He looked at me and answered: 'Nothing, but die. My arm is broken.'

Suddenly he got up. He could not stand erect, for his injured shoulder made him stoop. Once more he turned to me and said in English: *'General, I thank you for the trip . . . I go under the water!'*

So saying, he turned away.

I stopped him: 'No, Malmgren! You have no right to do this. We will die when God has decided. We must wait. Please stop here.'

I shall never forget the look he turned on me at that moment. He seemed surprised. Perhaps he was struck by the gentle and affectionate seriousness of my tone. For a moment he stood still, as if undecided. Then he sat down again.

Malmgren was feeling remorse for having wrongly predicted a change in the wind; he thought the crash was largely his fault. He made another attempt to kill himself later, but Nobile again dissuaded him.

Nobile's own condition was scarcely much better. He felt himself dying, and after calling to his tiny pet dog Titina to come to him, he settled down to await death; but death never came. Titina, quite unconcerned, continued to scamper about on the ice.

Others had been far less fortunate: one man died in the crash. Six others were carried away when the airship, lightened by the crash, rose up again and drifted away to the east, never to be seen again.

Meanwhile, the nine survivors pitched the one four-man tent that, to their great good fortune, had fallen out in the crash, and dyed it red to make it conspicuous. The two most seriously injured, Nobile and the engine mechanic Natale Cecione, were placed inside it; the others searched around for any provisions that might have fallen out. Luckily, they found enough for over a month. Just as luckily, their radio had also fallen out, and they began to transmit and listen for messages. Then they just settled down despondently to await help. Their despair deepened as, day after day, their radio messages appeared to fall on deaf ears. They could, however, hear the expedition's ship, *Città di Milano*, based in Svalbard, repeating that help was being organized. The problem was that those on the ship could have no way of telling where they were; they were clearly failing to pick up Nobile's messages.

Help was certainly being organized. A huge international relief effort was already under way, with participants from Norway, Sweden, Finland, Russia, and the USA as well as Italy. In fact, Mussolini's fascist Italian government was one of the most reluctant to help, yet at first opposed the international rescue on the grounds that Italy did not need help from outsiders.

One of the first to volunteer was Nobile's old adversary Roald Amundsen. Incensed by the official Italian attitude, he organized a rescue flight. It was his last. After taking off from Tromsø in northern Norway on 18 June, he disappeared. A great explorer died in action seeking to rescue a former colleague for whom he had little regard. Polar exploration produces many strange circumstances.

Before that, out on the ice towards the end of May, the nine survivors had been comforted by the knowledge that rescue was being organized, but alarmed that the rapid drift of the ice was taking them away from the zone where the rescuers were planning to look for them. When they drifted into sight of land, the tiny Karl-XII (Karl XII-øya) island in the far northeast of Svalbard, they began to quarrel among themselves about whether or not to head for it. Nobile and Cecioni were still far too badly injured to contemplate such a march. Nobile records that the first arguments occurred on 28 May.

After our meal that day, I heard this suggestion discussed for the first time. Mariano was talking about it to Malmgren. He proposed that we should set out on a march. Malmgren, indicating Cecioni and me, asked: 'With them?' And when Mariano nodded, he replied: 'No! That's impossible!'

Later on Zappi and Mariano came to speak to me . . . They judged the situation desperate. The drift would carry us farther and farther from the zone where the *Città di Milano* was organizing rescue work. We could not depend on the wireless any longer.

I objected that the technicians who had chosen this set had surely tested it before handing it over to us.

'Yes!' replied Zappi. 'They did test it, but under very much more favourable conditions. They even got in touch with Rhodes once, but that was at night.'

I did not share Zappi's pessimism, nor was I convinced that the drift must inevitably carry us eastwards. At bottom, the matter depended on the winds. These might change, and one fine day we should find ourselves drifting before an easterly wind towards the region they were searching, instead of away from it.

In any case, Zappi and Mariano's proposal was clear enough; a group composed of the Naval officers and Malmgren should make for the coast and send help.

I replied that we would all gather in the tent, to discuss the proposal thoroughly and come to a decision.

Meanwhile, when the two had gone out, I had to start calming down Cecioni, who at the bare idea of our staying there alone became overwrought and began to cry like a child.

The argument continued throughout that day and the next, and even the shooting of a bear, which greatly extended their stock of provisions, could not dissuade three of the party from heading for land. One of these was Finn Malmgren, and Nobile asked him what he thought would become of them.

He paused a moment; then, lowering his voice as if to be heard by me alone: 'Both parties will die!' he concluded.

He said these words as tranquilly as I listened to them. It was as if we were discussing matters in which we had no personal interest.

Malmgren's fate provides one of the most distressing episodes in the history of expeditions to the North Pole. He was a young Swedish meteorologist with a fine career ahead of him; he had been torn over whether or not to leave Nobile, and one of his motives for leaving was that he, alone of the men who wanted to leave, was experienced in Arctic conditions. But the march was too much for him. His colleague Filippo Zappi gave the following account to Nobile.

Having left us on May 30th, Malmgren, Mariano and Zappi made for Broch Island, which Malmgren expected to reach in a day or two. But the state of the pack made the march very difficult. Their progress was not much over half a mile a day, instead of the six they had foreseen. To make things much worse, the drift carried them in the opposite direction, so that after fourteen exhausting days on the march they were even farther from the island than when they started. This tragic situation must have weighed heavily on Malmgren's spirits, since when he left me he had declared that he expected to reach Cape North in a fortnight.

In these circumstances it is not surprising that Malmgren, by this time convinced of the futility of their attempt, should have confessed himself beaten. On the fourteenth day of the march, according to Zappi, at the end of his strength, he let himself drop in the snow, declaring that he could go no farther, and asking the others to go on alone to try and reach land. 'Leave me to die here in peace,' he had said, insisting that Mariano and Zappi should take his share of provisions. He made them dig him a shallow trench in the ice, and lay down in it, after having given Zappi a little magnetic compass with the request that it should be sent to his mother.

The two Italians, after walking about a hundred yards, sat down to rest, hoping that Malmgren would change his mind and come to join them. They waited there about 24 hours, and then Malmgren, raising his head from the trench, called to them: 'Why don't you go? Go on quickly: don't waste time!' This was the last time that Mariano and Zappi saw their companion. It was June 16th. They set off again on their march.

Nearly three weeks later, Malmgren's two companions, Zappi and Adalberto Mariano, also decided to settle themselves down on the ice and await death. They had not yet reached land, and their supply of food was exhausted. Then, on the evening of 10 July, they were spotted from the air by the Russian pilot Boris Chuknovskiy, who directed the Russian icebreaker *Krasin* towards them. On 12 July, they were saved.

Back in the red tent, Nobile and his five remaining colleagues continued their monotonous vigil. Their original deep depression had lifted, and their state of mind began to be controlled in a curious way by a tiny island in northeast Svalbard, Foyn Island, that had drifted into sight.

> 'The Island' regulated our moods, which changed with its distance from us. When its silhouette stood out clearly on the white horizon-line, we were happy; it saddened us to see it fading into the distance. And when it disappeared altogether pessimism overcame us, and dreary days began; we felt lonelier, more abandoned than ever in the white desert around us.

There were also some amusing incidents.

> Suddenly we heard our little dog barking furiously. When the men ran out to see what on earth was happening, they watched the curious spectacle of Titina chasing a poor bear who had come over to investigate our camp. She only gave up when the bear saved itself by diving into a lead and swimming away.

The sight of a 12-pound dog, 10 inches high, chasing off one of the world's largest and most fearsome predators, entertained them greatly.

On 6 June occurred what Nobile described as 'the miracle of the radio'. They had continued to transmit messages giving their location, and continued to realize, dishearteningly, that no one was hearing them; but Nobile was sure that, one day, somebody would. The radio operator Giuseppe Biagi was listening for messages that evening, when he suddenly shouted out: 'They've heard us!' Nobile wrote: 'I could hardly contain my joy. At last my prophecy had come true! Someone had heard us, if only by chance!' A young Russian radio enthusiast in Archangel had heard one of their signals, and passed it on to the Russian authorities. Soon, they began to receive more and more messages; then one day they heard that the *Città di Milano* could now hear them. Their mood changed from buoyant to ecstatic. 'We all looked radiant: the lines graven by the previous days had been blotted out. How splendid it was to see my men laughing again – dirty, grimy, and ragged as they were! The laughter lit up the bearded faces, clouded with all the dirt of a fortnight. Mutually, we lifted a grateful thought to Providence for this hour of indescribable joy.' As the days went by and news of the various rescue missions continued to reach them, they waited anxiously to see some sign of these rescuers. On 17 June there was temporary excitement when two Norwegian planes appeared nearby, but they turned away without noticing the red tent. Similar incidents happened several times. Finally, on 20 June, they were able to guide towards them, by radio, an Italian flying boat laden with supplies.

At 7.35 we got into touch with the plane by wireless. At 8.15 we heard the first throb of its engines. We waited anxiously.

At last the aircraft appeared and the signals began. It seemed at first not to hear us, then all at once it began to obey our orders: 'Turn so many degrees to the right,' 'Reverse your direction,' 'Turn so many degrees to the left.'

In a few minutes we managed to bring the flying-boat towards us: 'The tent is on your course, less than 2 miles in front. Go ahead!' And the plane obediently went straight on. A moment later it caught sight of us. We saw it swoop down to about a hundred yards ... 'VVV ... You are on top of us!' We were feverish with excitement. Here it was! The throb of its engines grew louder, and now we could clearly see the colours painted on its wings. It was very close ... was passing overhead ... One or two men leaned

out of the cabin and wildly waved their arms in greeting.
My throat was constricted with excitement. I wanted to
shout, but I only waved an answering greeting with my
hand. The others were shouting and laughing. Even Titina
rushed madly about the ice, barking.

The flying-boat overshot us and went on, the sonorous
hum of its engines growing fainter. We expected it would
turn back at once to throw down provisions and other
things. Following it anxiously, we saw it wheel round, but
in the wrong direction. It passed some distance from us and
then changed its course again, as if searching round; but it
was a long way off. It had lost sight of us!

We persevered with our signals. Biagi kept running to
and fro, between the transmitter outside the tent and the
receiver inside, sending his message and then rushing to
put on the ear-phones; to find out if it had been heard. At
last, after half an hour, the aircraft picked us up. We drew a
breath of relief as it began to obey our orders with docility.
We guided it back in our direction till it sighted the tent. It
came straight for us and in a few seconds was overhead.

'KKK,' I ordered Biagi the moment the plane was above
us. This was the code-signal for 'Drop the provisions!' and
I hastened to give the order for fear they should lose us
again. We saw someone leaning out of the back of the
cockpit to drop parcels. The first packets fell and we greeted
them joyously. Then the flying-boat turned and started to
throw out afresh. It was not losing us now.

We followed the parcels with our eyes to see exactly
where they fell. Then the cascade ceased and the aircraft
swiftly turned homewards.

An even more cheering event happened on 23 June.

It was now evening. The sky was still blue and a light NW
breeze was blowing. The hour fixed for communicating
with the *Città di Milano* (five minutes to nine) had passed
without our receiving any news. From time to time the
silence was broken by someone asking me the state of the
barometer, which had been slowly falling for some days.

We sat down to supper. My companions were all

rather depressed, and everyone was silent. More than ever annoyed at the silence of the radio and the lack of news, I began to turn over in my mind an old idea: to have our boats ready loaded with provisions and materials, and a few weeks later, when the pack had broken up, to embark all together in the biggest boat and steer through the ice to the nearest shore. Once we had touched land, wherever it might be, I considered we were safe. I was not even alarmed at the idea of wintering there.

I was thinking over these things and waiting till the end of supper to speak to my comrades, when a slight humming came to our ears. We all started.

It was a moment of great excitement. We guessed that it was the Swedes, who had come to fetch us.

Viglieri and Biagi dashed out of the tent and stood listening. The throbbing grew louder, and now it came more distinctly – a slight rhythm familiar to our ears: 'The aeroplanes are coming!'

Dragging myself along the ice, I also left the tent, followed by Cecioni. Now the rhythm of the engines came clearly, rejoicing us like the sweetest music. I looked round for the planes, but the masses of ice round our encampment hid them. Viglieri, Biagi, and Behounek, standing up, were scanning the horizon.

'There they are!'

Two aeroplanes were coming towards us. The rhythm grew steadily more sonorous. I gave the order: 'Make a smoke-signal!'

The smoke rose, dense and black, and the aeroplanes wheeled. They had seen us.

'Viglieri and Biagi! Go straight to the field, both of you, and lay down the landing-signal. Hurry up! Run!'

Run! It was all very well to say this! As the crow flies, the field was about 150 yards from our camp, but to cover this short distance one needed rare acrobatic skill. Here and there were crevasses, sometimes hidden by snow, hummocks to climb, channels or little pools to cross, using a piece of ice as a raft, which often threatened to overturn under a man's weight. Although they had already made the journey several times, Viglieri and

Biagi would do well to reach the field in a quarter of an hour.

I watched them go. Meanwhile the aircraft began to circle overhead. Then I turned to Cecioni, who was beside me at one corner of the tent, and ordered: 'Get the sledge ready at once!'

The sledge was all in a muddle. A number of loose parts had to be tied together.

'Trojani! Look in the box for the wire! Quickly!'

Trojani, who had a temperature, was lying in his sleeping-bag inside the tent. He found the wire and brought it out.

Whilst Cecioni was busy tying up the disconnected parts, I watched the flight of the planes. One of them – the sea-plane – stayed high in the air and circled widely round our encampment. The other gradually came lower, continuing to manoeuvre round the landing-field.

I followed it anxiously with my eyes, giving news to my companions . . . Now it was flying over the field – coming lower – skimming the ground – disappearing behind the masses of ice. All at once it rose again. Perhaps it had difficulty in landing? Then I guessed that the pilot was trying to get some idea of the state of the field. There he was, flying round once more, and yet again. The aeroplane swooped down afresh and seemed to touch the ice.

I followed the manoeuvre, holding my breath. Yes! Now it had touched and not risen again. It skimmed along the ground . . . It had landed – and landed safely!

I drew a long breath of relief, and irrepressible joy filled my heart. The long, unutterable torment was at an end – the alternatives of hope and despair, the wearing suspense, the anxiety about the radio . . . At last we were in contact with humanity. Very soon we should greet the lucky man who, alone of all those who had been trying during a whole month to reach us, had succeeded in his purpose.

The pilot was the Swede Einar Lundborg. He had come with instructions to collect Nobile first, so that he could direct the whole search operation, including the search for those carried away with the airship, from the *Città di Milano*. At first, Nobile protested.

Eagerly awaiting his arrival, I spurred Cecioni up to finish his preparations. At last the men appeared. The stranger, dressed in flying-kit, had a pleasant expression – a frank, rather rugged face and blue eyes. Viglieri introduced him to me: 'Here is the General!' The stranger saluted respectfully. I answered by thanking him in the name of us all; then, feeling that words were inadequate to express our gratitude, I asked Viglieri and Behounek to lift me, so that I might embrace him. Then they laid me down again.

Lundborg began to speak: 'General, I have come to fetch you all. The field is excellent. I shall be able to take away the lot of you during the night. You must come first.'

'But that's impossible!' I replied, and pointed out Cecioni: 'Take him first. That is what I have decided.'

Lundborg answered firmly: 'No! I have orders to bring you first, because we need your instructions to start looking for the others.'

Then I remembered that, only two or three days before, the *Città di Milano* had asked me to give 'data and instructions to search for the airship', which I had not been able to send, owing to the bad wireless communication. Instinctively I considered Lundborg's words in relation to this request. So the seaplanes were ready to start their search? We had to take advantage of the weather, which was still fine: a clear sky, perfect visibility, calm. Perhaps it was a case of snatching a few hours, for such favourable conditions could not last long: the barometer had been going down for some days.

Still, though the vision leaped to my mind of those seaplanes ready to start and impatiently awaiting my arrival, I was reluctant. I did not like the idea of coming back to *terra firma* before my companions, even when I thought it simply meant anticipating them by an hour or two. For sentimental reasons I would rather have followed and not preceded them. So I insisted firmly: 'Please take him first. That is my decision.'

'No, General, don't insist!' replied Lundborg. 'We will take you to our base not far from here; then I can come back quickly for the others.'

As I showed signs of protesting again he interrupted me

curtly, as if to cut short any further discussion: 'No! I can't take him now' (indicating Cecioni); 'he is too heavy. It is impossible, without leaving my companion behind, and I cannot do that. Later on I will come back alone to fetch him. Besides, it would take too long to carry him to the plane, and we have no time to lose. In a few hours I will bring you all away. Please come quickly.' And he pointed to the machine, of which we could see the propeller still revolving: 'Do please hurry up!'

Nobile was persuaded by his colleagues to go. He was crippled and so a burden to them, and was needed at the centre of the rescue effort. He went.

When he reached the ship, he was immediately attacked for obeying the orders Lundborg had brought him; required to explain why he, the leader, had allowed himself to be rescued first. The Italian fascists had turned against him, and his 'indescribable bitterness' was clear.

The disappearance of the *Italia*, the mystery which wrapped our fate, had moved the whole civilized world. Sweden, Norway, Russia, Finland – all the countries bordering on the frozen Arctic Ocean – in a generous impulse of solidarity had immediately decided to organize rescue expeditions. But in Italy the Fascist Government had made no move. On the day when the newspapers published the story of our disappearance, Balbo landed at Alcazar aerodrome near Madrid. He was met on the field by a professor of Aeronautical Law at the University of Rome, who gave him the sad news. Balbo, in a tone of absolute indifference, remarked: 'Serve him right!' and gave orders that the Press should devote as little space as possible to the expedition, but publicize his own flight of sixty aeroplanes across the Mediterranean. A still more serious episode was reported to Viglieri after our return to Rome: at a banquet given during that mass cruise, Balbo had toasted the disappearance of the *Italia*!

This hostility explains why Italy was so tardy in organizing an aerial rescue expedition. The attitude of the Fascist Government had been severely criticized not only in Italy but also abroad. The King of Norway, when on a visit to Helsingfors [Helsinki] he received the Italian Ambassador, could not help pointing out the inertia of our Government in face of the catastrophe. Still more explicit had been the Soviet Vice-Commissar for War, Kamenev, who in an interview published on June 12th in the newspaper *Izvestia* regretted that in Italy 'the practical measures taken to help the castaways were so few that they virtually amounted to nothing.'

But already public opinion in Italy had begun to make itself felt, urging that something should be done. Its mouthpiece was Arturo Mercanti, of Milan, who asked permission to go to our help with two flying-boats. Thanks to this initiative, it was finally decided to send to King's Bay Maddalena and Penzo, the brave officers who brought us supplies with their flying-boats. But in his letter to Mercanti, Balbo gave vent to a number of insulting remarks about me, explicitly affirming that ours was no Fascist enterprise, and that therefore there was no obligation to go to our help.

Lundborg's mishap had given Balbo the opportunity to launch a direct attack on me. In Rome, during a meeting of Ministers, he impugned me in the most violent manner. At the same time, the foreign Press was incited against me. In Paris, *Le Matin* published the cheapest slanders, excusing themselves on the ground that they were only repeating what had been said by 'a high Fascist personage'. Instructions were sent from Rome to the Italian Legations in various countries to prevent demonstrations of sympathy for me. The peak of insolence was reached by Balbo's paper, the *Corriere Padano*, which asserted that I had broken my leg when running to meet the Swedish aeroplane that had descended on the pack. This grave insinuation was made at a time when other Italian newspapers had already stated several weeks previously that my injuries had been caused when the airship crashed.

In the meantime, other things were going wrong with the search. Lundborg, paying a return visit to the red tent, crash-landed, and became one of the party awaiting rescue. Italian, Swedish and Finnish aircraft were delayed from starting out by

bad weather. Nobile, trying to co-ordinate the search, experienced a 'month of hell' on the *Città di Milano*. But the Russian
icebreaker *Krasin* was still in the region and trying to get
through to the red tent. The expedition leader on *Krasin*,
Rudol'f Lazarevich Samoylovich, was one of the Soviet Union's
most experienced and most respected Arctic scientists; he had no
intention of returning without success. His first achievement was
to rescue Zappi and Mariano. In his book *My Polar Flights*, Nobile
quotes from Samoylovich's account of this encounter.

> I turned to look at him. Mariano's eyes were shining with
> joy. A radiant, childlike smile lit his tortured face, like that
> of a man unexpectedly called back to life, whose sufferings
> were finished and who was now recovering consciousness
> in the midst of his friends and rescuers.
>   I stroked his hand, and if I had not been embarrassed in
> front of so many people, I would have stooped down and
> kissed this happy man. A lump rose in my throat: I was
> so moved that I could not say a single word . . . One of
> our stokers came up to me, sweating, with blackened face,
> just as he had come from the engine room: 'So, in spite of
> everything, they've been saved!' he said, smiling. I was not
> at all surprised to see the white streaks that tears of joy had
> drawn through the coal-dust on his face.

Krasin then continued her voyage towards the red tent, and on
the same day accomplished its mission. Nobile was not present,
but he records what happened.

> At 8 p.m. on board the *Krasin* a great column of smoke
> was seen rising from a wide field of ice. The sailors cheered
> exultantly. It was the field where Lundborg had landed
> twice, and to which the tent had been shifted on the day
> after his aeroplane capsized. Both the tent and the machine
> could be clearly seen through a telescope.
>   Half an hour later the *Krasin*, having approached the
> icefield, moored about a hundred yards from the tent.
> Several men disembarked. It was a large field, almost
> rectangular in shape and about 350 × 120 yards. Here

and there multicoloured flags had been spread out as a
signal to airmen. The field was covered with snow – soft
snow on the point of melting; footprints in it made large
holes, quickly filled with water. There were tracks in all
directions around the camp. Quite near the tent there was
a large rubber dinghy: about 40 yards farther away was the
Swedish aeroplane – or what was left of it after the men had
used its plywood wings to make a raised platform on which
to pitch the tent. The skeleton of the aeroplane lay tilted at
an angle, with its tail and skis in the air. On the fuselage
one could see three crowns painted inside a circle, and the
number 31. Between the aeroplane and the tent, anchored
by wire guy-ropes, was the wireless mast.

At 8.45 Viglieri, Behounek, Trojani, Cecioni and Biagi
were on board the *Krasin*: our anxiety for them was at
an end.

They told me afterwards that, almost as soon as he set
foot on the ice-breaker, Behounek had asked Samoilovitch:
'May I go on with my scientific work on board the *Krasin*?'
'Of course!' Samoilovitch had replied, smiling. 'We too are
making scientific observations, and we shall be glad to
help you.'

The last to come had been Biagi. He had stopped to send
a wireless message written by Viglieri. It got lost on the air,
conveying among other things: 'Greetings and good wishes
to our beloved General Nobile.'

This, of course, pleased me very much, as I was pleased
when Behounek, saying goodbye to me some days afterwards, added that he was proud to have shared in my
expedition.

But I was still more deeply moved, on our return to
Italy, when, at the moment of parting in the train, Viglieri,
Trojani and Biagi embraced me with emotion and said:
'Thank you for taking us with you.' Without realizing
it, they were repeating the very words that Wisting had
used two years earlier, upon the arrival of the *Norge*
– and that Malmgren had stoically pronounced in that
terrible moment just after the crash: '*Thank you for the
trip.*'

Simple words – but expressive of deep feeling.

The search for the men carried away in the airship continued, but they were never found.

Travelling home, Nobile was given the worldwide newspaper reports of his venture, and discovered that many were hostile to him. The bitterness that then arose in him remained with him for the rest of his life.

In the train at Narvik, as if to round off the fearful ordeal, they brought me a bundle of newspapers. There I read everything that had been printed in the European Press during the last month against the *Italia* expedition. The full, brutal, unexpected revelation showed me, as if in a mirror, the spectacle of a world which, after having sympathized with our disaster and vied in efforts to save us, had then tried almost as eagerly to demolish with the vilest calumnies a daring scientific enterprise, which was fine and noble even if unfortunate. The most ignominious things had been written about me and my companions. They had even gone so far as to represent as an act of petty cowardice what had been obedience to an order, the fulfilment of a high and definite duty. Everything had served as material for calumny, insinuations, insults. I felt crushed under the avalanche of abuse hurled at me by mean spirits throughout the world, whilst I had been unable to defend myself during that terrible month on the *Città di Milano*, fighting with all my might for the rescue of the castaways. A great sadness took possession of me, a profound disgust with life and humanity.

Then at Vindeln, the first Swedish station where the train stopped, a little fair-haired, blue-eyed girl came towards me, smiling sweetly, to offer me a bunch of flowers. Choked with emotion I thanked her, stammering.

After all, there were still pure and gentle spirits among mankind. Not all were beasts of prey.

Ebba Håggström . . . I memorized her name and impressed it on my heart, never to forget it again.

Throughout the rest of his journey home he encountered many similar incidents. In Italy, despite official opposition, enthusiastic crowds swarmed around him. In the end, from the people, he won the glory he deserved. The courageous perseverance of Nobile and his companions was summed up with eloquent simplicity by Pope Pius XI: 'one of those feats which attain the highest beauty and sublimity that can be encountered in this life'.

– 15 –

From New Technology to New Adventure

1931–85

Once the Pole had been attained, or generally thought to have been attained, on foot, by aircraft, and by airship, there began a quest to find new ways of achieving 'first' conquests by all manner of different means. Some have been ingenious, many have been entertaining but otherwise quite pointless except in the minds of the participants. The earliest of them, though, had serious scientific or practical aims. In 1931, the Australian explorer Sir Hubert Wilkins made the first attempt to attain the Pole by submarine. Wilkins, who had already distinguished himself in a series of aerial exploring expeditions to the Antarctic and the Arctic Ocean, wished to carry out a wide range of scientific investigations under the ice. These included oceanography, depth sounding, and studies of the sea ice. The expedition was not a great success, chiefly because its vessel was a decrepit American submarine, built in 1916–18 and chartered by the expedition for the nominal sum of one dollar. Wilkins gave it the name *Nautilus*. Even before it reached the Arctic, *Nautilus* suffered a series of mechanical failures requiring repair, and it became increasingly apparent that the vessel was not fit for a long voyage beneath the ice. Nonetheless, Wilkins remained determined at least to make a few short dives under the ice, and to carry out part of his scientific programme. On 10 August, after long delays, the submarine left Norway for Svalbard waters, where the under-ice voyage was to start. On arrival, further repairs were needed. In addition, there were suspicions of sabotage; somebody on board, Wilkins mused later, did not want to go under the ice. They could hardly be blamed. When, on 31 August, Wilkins managed to force the submarine under a large floe, the noise of the ice scraping along the superstructure, which at first seemed to be destroying the vessel, and other noises caused by the propeller colliding with ice, terrified them all. But when, after a short time, *Nautilus* resurfaced, there was found to be no damage.

Wilkins made some more short dives and ultimately he was happy with the scientific results obtained, but as an attempted voyage under the ice to the Pole, it was a complete failure. The age of the submarine had not yet arrived in the Arctic Ocean. It was not until the coming of nuclear vessels in the 1950s that their full potential in the Arctic could be realized.

Later in the 1930s Russian explorers resumed an interest in the North Pole for the first time since Sedov's expedition in 1912–14. By this time, the Soviet Union had a rapidly increasing vested interest in the seas of the Arctic. With improving technology, the Northeast Passage, or, as it is now usually called, the Northern Sea Route, was becoming an ever more important artery of trade. Thus, the Soviet government was eager to understand the oceanography and meteorology of the Arctic Ocean in general. At the same time, it had basic practical and political reasons for wishing to know more about conditions over the ocean and around the Pole. In 1937, for two different reasons, they launched four separate expeditions involving the North Pole.

The first of these began a novel and remarkable series of scientific experiments which the Soviets later pursued for many years. This was to establish drifting scientific stations on ice islands (that is, very large, old and stable ice floes) in the Arctic Ocean. In some ways this was an extension of Nansen's *Fram* drift: part of the experiment to determine the circulation of Arctic Ocean currents. Another aim was to determine the meteorological conditions of the North Polar region for the benefit of aviators. With the coming of increasingly reliable passenger aircraft capable of flying ever greater distances, the Soviets were beginning to contemplate polar air routes from Moscow to the United States, with missions that some called 'Wings of Friendship'. Friendship between the two nations was not then as imperilled as it later became.

The ice-drift station was to be commanded by Ivan Papanin. It would be established as near as possible to the North Pole, and be manned for at least one year. The materials for building the station, supplies and scientific instruments were to be transported to the Pole by four large Tupolev aircraft, each with four engines and with a flying weight of 24 tons. On 21 May, the first of these transport aircraft, piloted by one of the Soviet Union's most famous air pioneers, Mikhail Vodopyanov, took off from Moscow with Papanin on board. Soviet reports of arrivals at the North Pole are more laconic than those of some of their more excitable predecessors:

At 10.30 a.m. Professor Schmidt reported that the plane had reached Lat. 88°35′N, and that since they had passed the 88th degree visibility had improved considerably. Huge ice-fields below were cut up by long leads. The temperature was 23°C below zero ... Lat. 89°N, Long 58°E was reached at 10.34 a.m., and Vodopyanov followed this meridian in a northerly direction, and reached the North Pole at 11.10 a.m. The party flew a little farther and then descended from 1750 to 200m, breaking through heavy clouds, and began to look for a suitable landing place. At 11.35 a.m. Vodopyanov made a perfect landing on an ice-floe about 20 km the other side of the Pole ... The floe, which will drift in the polar basin, is described as being entirely suitable for a scientific station, and the party set about preparing for the reception of other planes.

Vodopyanov's account of the landing is even briefer, but marginally more emotional:

On May 21, 1937, the first of four heavy Soviet air machines accomplished a landing on the perennial ice of the North Pole. A few days later the remaining three aircraft joined the first.

Thus a long cherished hope of mankind was realized by Soviet fliers and arcticians.

When the Polar observatory was set up, our aerial expedition retraced its course to the mainland. Papanin, Krenkel,

Fyodorov and Shirshov, the four dauntless Polar explorers, were now alone on the ice floe in the middle of the Polar basin.

In fact, Papanin never claimed to have been exactly at the Pole or even within 35 kilometres of it, but it hardly matters. This was the first of many Soviet ice stations in the Arctic Ocean. The experiments had to be discontinued during the Second World War, but were resumed afterwards, and the Soviets occupied over 30 ice stations before the fall of the Soviet government and the subsequent Russian economic crisis forced a suspension of the experiments.

The three other Soviet aerial expeditions to the North Pole in 1937, although independent of one another, all had the same object of trying out a commercial air route from the USSR to the USA. There was also a large measure of Stalinist propaganda in them; not only to demonstrate that the Soviet Union could achieve feats that were beyond the capability of other nations, but also that Stalin himself was a man of impeccable character. In the English-language accounts of the flights, published in Moscow, Stalin is repeatedly represented as a charming, cheery and caring gentleman, which is now known to be distant from the truth. The first of the three flyers was Valeriy Pavlovich Chkalov, another veteran of pioneering flights, and when he and his co-pilot and navigator were invited to discuss their plan at the Kremlin, much was made of Stalin's concern.

Stalin was in a humorous mood.

'Feeling cramped again? Getting ready to start off on another flight?'

'Yes, Comrade Stalin,' answered Chkalov. 'The time is propitious. We are here to ask permission of the government to fly over the North Pole.'

In recalling this conference, Chkalov wrote:

. . . Questioned by Stalin, we went into the details of the work we had done. We felt that Stalin was fully posted on the subject and understood us thoroughly, even if we only hinted at things.

'So you think, Comrade Chkalov, that this machine is the right choice?' he asked.

Then he added:

'Still, there's only one engine . . . We mustn't forget that.'

I replied:

But a first-class engine, Comrade Stalin. That has been proved and there's nothing to worry about. Furthermore, I jested, with one engine, the risk is one hundred per cent, with four, it's four hundred per cent.

Then came the decisive moment. Comrade Stalin asked a few more questions, became thoughtful for a bit, then said:

'I'm for it, but propose to obligate Comrade Chkalov, who is in charge of the flight, to make a landing in Canada, if there should be the slightest danger.'

Stalin repeated the same injunction . . .

'Stop the flight as soon as there is any sign of danger.'

The fliers left the Kremlin as if treading on air. Everything now depended on them themselves.

The report of the attainment of the Pole by Chkalov and his two companions was rather less detailed, but they do give some details of the flight. They took off from Moscow early in the morning of 18 June 1937. Their route took them to a familiar starting point for journeys over the Arctic Ocean, Rudolf Island, in Franz Josef Land. As they approached that island, Chkalov encountered growing difficulties. Their story is told by Vodopyanov (though he was not with them).

The plane had to forge its way through a solid mass of suspended mist. Although the thermometer registered 24° below zero and the ice formation on the aircraft was not to be expected at such a low temperature for lack of moisture, yet this is precisely what happened.

But this time the layer was thicker than before, the wings, the stabilizer, the rear trusses, the aerial and the frame of the radio compass were instantly covered with a layer of ice. The plane again swerved upward and had difficulty in reaching sunlight. It took more than an hour for the ice crust to thaw. Although the plane was now flying at a height of more than 13,100 feet and breathing became difficult in the rarefied atmosphere, the fliers did not resort to the respirators. They decided to use their oxygen sparingly, since a difficult stretch lay ahead and no one knew what still might be in store for them.

On June 18, at 8.20 p.m. Greenwich time, the plane was over Franz Josef Land. From there it headed North. The crew approached the Pole with palpitating hearts, for somewhere hereabouts the heroic Papanin four were drifting on their ice floe.

On June 19, at 4.15 a.m., the Pole was crossed. To the great regret of the fliers, a thick sheet of clouds hid the drifting Polar station from their view.

On the part of the Papanin group, the disappointment was equally great. They knew the time when the plane was supposed to pass above them and awaited it full of impatience. They were all set to give the 'Go' signal to the first aerial craft to pass their station, but the clouds were so heavy that they could discern nothing but the distant din of the passing plane.

The problem with the accumulation of ice became so acute that on one occasion, when they could no longer see through the windscreen, a novel solution was needed:

> The front pane was so covered with ice that nothing could be seen through it. Baidukov stuck his hand through the side window of the cabin and began to scrape off the ice with a bowie knife. It appeared that some water from the motor had been spurted on the cabin window and changed instantly to an icy crust.

After battling for 63 hours against ice, cloud, storms and all manner of lesser problems, the three men landed safely on an airfield in the state of Washington on 20 June. They had covered a distance of 5,670 miles.

The symbolic 'Wings of Friendship' aspect of the flight was taken very seriously by both sides. Before returning home, the three flyers were taken to the White House for a reception hosted by President Roosevelt; and Vodopyanov wrote of the flight:

> The heroic crew of the NO25 had established the shortest airway between Moscow, the heart of the USSR, and the

United States of America, by this historic flight via the North Pole, and had thus strengthened the bonds uniting these two great peoples.

The second of the trans-polar flights was piloted by Mikhail Mikhaylovich Gromov, and took off from Moscow on 12 June. Because Chkalov had already pioneered the route, Gromov's aim was slightly different: in addition to crossing the Arctic Ocean, he intended also to attempt a new world record for long-distance flying. Otherwise, his flight followed much the same pattern as Chkalov's, except that he met better weather. He reported his passage over the Pole just as unemotionally as Vodopyanov had reported Chkalov's: '. . . at 3.14 a.m., we passed over the North Pole. We were then at an altitude of 8,850 ft and were making a speed of 100 m.p.h. The temperature of the air was −8°C. The crew were in excellent spirits.' After flying for a little over 62 hours, they landed at San Jacinto, California; they had flown 6,302 miles and beaten the world distance record.

The third flight, piloted by Sigismund Aleksandrovich Levanevskiy, with four companions, was dogged by misfortune and ended in tragedy. Levanevskiy took off from Moscow on 12 August. As he passed over the Pole on the following day, he reported by radio a catalogue of problems: strong headwinds, dense cloud, and icing; he was already three hours behind schedule. An hour later, he reported the failure of one of his four engines. Further incomplete messages reached Moscow in the next few hours, but then he fell silent. Several expeditions searched for the five missing men, including two headed by Sir Hubert Wilkins, but they were never found.

The achievements of Chkalov and Gromov initially did nothing to advance commercial aviation. There were not then aircraft of sufficient power, capacity and reliability to provide an air service across the Arctic Ocean. But they had laid the foundations of an achievement for which Barentsz and Hudson had struggled over 300 years previously: the successful exploration of the most direct route from Europe to the Pacific Ocean. After the Second World War, a new generation of passenger jet aircraft was able to use this short 'great circle' route from one side of the world to the other. Today, every day, many aircraft criss-cross the Arctic Ocean on flights between Europe, Asia and America, though not necessarily by way of the Pole. The objective of those early explorers has been achieved. Their route is now a northern passage of great value to the world, though not in a way that they could ever have envisaged. For that achievement, the pioneers Vodopyanov, Papanin, Chkalov, Gromov, Levanevskiy and their companions all fully deserve their share of the credit.

After the Second World War, attempts to attain the North Pole became ever more diverse and imaginative. Science and international politics played a part. Feats of courage abounded, but so, too, did attempted feats of madness. The history of the North Pole entered a new age of adventure, when many persons tried to get there by many different means, and for many different purposes: as a personal challenge, for money, for publicity, pleasure, or all of those things. It is impossible, and hardly worthwhile, to present details of all of them. But the most significant and interesting, the most worthwhile 'firsts' should at least be summarized.

In 1948, another Soviet pilot, P.A. Gordiyenko, landed at the Pole on 23 April. It has sometimes been claimed that, since all previous attainments of the Pole had either been disputed or acknowledged to be only approximate, or accomplished in the air without landing, Gordiyenko was the first man indisputably to stand at the Pole.

Next came submarines. The Second World War had proved the value of submarines in warfare. It had also accelerated the emergence of nuclear power. The Cold War that followed turned the Arctic Ocean into a region of great strategic importance; it was the shortest route by which nuclear missiles could be directed between the world's two great powers, the USA and the USSR. It also provided a means by which nuclear-powered submarines carrying nuclear weapons, and capable of staying submerged for very long periods, could make a close approach into the adversary's territory, unobserved under the ice. The activity of submarines under the Arctic ice is, in all the countries involved, classified information and there is much that we do not know. Some feats, though, as a matter of demonstrating prowess, were deliberately made public. Two such were widely publicized in 1958, and involved the arrival of two of the United States Navy's nuclear-powered submarines at the North Pole.

The first of these was named *Nautilus*, and the fact that it shared the same name as Sir Hubert Wilkins's submarine in 1931 is no coincidence. The United States Navy made a careful study of Wilkins's scientific observations in 1931, and one naval officer described the data collected by Wilkins as 'invaluable' in the preparation for the under-ice voyage of the second *Nautilus*. The first attempt to reach the Pole on the new *Nautilus* took place in August 1957, but an instrument failure forced the expedition to turn back from 87°N. The commander of *Nautilus*, W.R. Anderson, tried again in 1958. The submarine, with 116 men aboard, submerged off Point Barrow, Alaska, on 1 August. Cruising at a depth of about 400 feet, the vessel reached the North Pole on 4 August, and emerged on the opposite side of the Arctic Ocean on the following day.

Another US Navy submarine, USS *Skate*, commanded by James Calvert, followed closely behind *Nautilus*, and surfaced near the North Pole on 12 August 1958.

On 17 March 1959, *Skate* and Calvert returned to the Pole. The submarine carried the ashes of Sir Hubert Wilkins, who had died on 1 December 1958, and the ashes were scattered at the Pole.

The next significant expedition was in 1968, when a joint Canadian/United States expedition led by Ralph Plaisted reached the Pole by snowmobile (motorized sledges). Plaisted had tried to attain the Pole by this means in 1967, but had been forced back by the break-up of the ice. On the second attempt, using four Skidoo snowmobiles, his party of six men set out on 7 March from Ward Hunt Island, off the north coast of Ellesmere Island. Four of the men reached the Pole on 19 April, and were then evacuated by their Otter support aircraft.

In the same year as Plaisted's successful expedition, Wally Herbert and three companions set out on the British Trans-Arctic Expedition, an attempt to make the first surface crossing of the Arctic Ocean by way of the North Pole. The party, using four dog-sledges, set out from Point Barrow, Alaska, on 24 February 1968. They were supported by air-drops by aircraft of the Royal Canadian Air Force. The journey was fraught with difficulties and dangers; they encountered broken ice, frequent leads, and rough ice surfaces. By 14 July, when they set up their summer camp to await easier travelling conditions in the autumn, they were still only at 82°27'N, about 450 miles from the Pole. By the time they started out again on 4 September, the ice had done some of their work for them by drifting to about 84°N, but even greater difficulties lay ahead of them. Almost immediately after setting off again, one of the party put his foot through a hole in the ice and damaged his back. They had to return to their summer camp, and summon help, but the weather and ice conditions were too bad for a rescue aircraft to land and evacuate him. The party remained in the same place for the winter, using a hut provided by the last RCAF air-drop of the year. Even then, there was more danger to come. In October their ice floe began to break up, and they had to spend ten days shifting their camp and all their supplies to another floe – all this in the dark.

They started out again on 24 February 1969, and despite continuing rough ice surfaces, reached the Pole on 5 April. As they pressed on towards Svalbard, they suffered another mishap when a tent and a sleeping bag caught fire, forcing all four men into uncomfortable, cramped conditions in a single tent until the next air-drop provided replacements. Finally, on 29 May they reached land: the tiny Table Island (Tavleøya) in the extreme north of Svalbard. In attempting to press on they were repeatedly plagued by open water, but on 11 June they were lifted out by helicopter to the research ship *Endurance*.

This was a fine, courageous adventure, shared throughout by readers of the two sponsoring newspapers to which Wally Herbert sent regular radio bulletins. It also had scientific merit, with observations on glaciology, meteorology, physiology and geophysics. But most of all, it was one of the last truly great adventures in the history of the North Pole.

A decade later, there was another remarkable adventure when Naomi Uemura, a Japanese, made a 55-day solo journey to the Pole and back. Using dogs, and travelling along Peary's route, he reached the Pole on 29 April 1978. Two others merit a mention: in 1985 Will Steger led an international expedition to the Pole along Peary's route, using dog-sledges. In the following year, the Frenchman Jean-Louis Etienne made the first successful solo man-hauling journey.

Doubtless, there are many more 'firsts' to come. Every day, there is somebody, somewhere, wondering how they, too, can claim a different sort of first conquest of the North Pole. One day, there will be the first hang-glider, the first solo woman, the first motor cycle, the first walking backwards, but most of the great, stirring firsts have been done.

Only one other remains to relate.

– 16 –

Full Circle

1977–93

Nearly 400 years ago, men tried to reach the North Pole by ship. In the nineteenth century, the hope of getting there by ship persisted for 80 years. So, it is ironic to reflect that after every conceivable method had been tried, the very last means of successfully reaching the Pole has been by ship. By the middle of the 1970s it had been attained by sledge, aeroplane, airship, submarine, snowmobile. But it was still, then, impossible to do it by ship. Now, that too is possible. The quest for the North Pole has most satisfyingly turned full circle.

Neither seventeenth-century sailing ships, nor nineteenth-century steamships, nor the icebreakers of the first three-quarters of the twentieth century, had any chance of getting even remotely close to the North Pole. The ice they needed to penetrate can be anything between 10 and 15 feet thick, and they had neither the strength of hull nor the power. But modern 75,000 horse-power Russian nuclear icebreakers can do it, and now do so quite regularly. What is more, they can do it for sound economic reasons, which Barentsz, Hudson and their successors had hoped to achieve, but which disappeared almost completely in the nineteenth century as the motives of science and adventure took over. Neither Barentsz nor Hudson, though, would have imagined the newest economic incentive.

The best and most powerful icebreakers in the world are Russian for one simple reason. They are essential to the Russian economy. Most of Russia's great rivers flow north into the Arctic seas surrounding the Arctic Ocean, and in such a huge country with inadequate road and rail networks, those rivers are needed for both international and domestic trade. But to export the rich mineral and agricultural wealth of Russia and Siberia, two more links in the chain are needed: sea-going ships that can receive cargoes from the river vessels, and icebreakers to clear a path through the ice for convoys of these cargo ships. It has been estimated that in 1992 the Russian north accounted for 60 per cent of all of Russia's foreign currency exchange, and much of that came from goods exported in this manner. It is little wonder, then, that since the beginning of the twentieth century Russia has led the world in icebreaker development.

There are four main principles on which most icebreakers operate. It is not merely a matter of strengthening the bow to cut through the ice. First, the bow is certainly strengthened, to a thickness of 50 centimetres (20 inches), and at the strongest point of the hull, about 20 metres (66 feet) behind the bow, there is an area of 2-metre (6½ feet) thick cast steel. But the most important part of the bow's design is that the underside is shaped to ride up on the surface of the ice, so that this reinforced area, above which much of the weight of the ship is concentrated, can, by sheer weight, carve a path downward and forward through the ice. The third essential is the forward velocity of the ship, and Russian icebreakers with their nuclear reactors driving sets of huge, six-ton propeller blades, predominate in this field. Finally, an air-bubble system, with powerful jets of air flowing along the side of the hull below the level of the ice, provides a kind of lubrication to assist the ship's passage. The most powerful Russian icebreakers are designed to break through a thickness of 2.3 metres (7½ feet) of ice, but they have proved capable, though with some difficulty, of breaking through ice twice as thick. To see them in action, to see the white-blue-green ice floes, solid to the horizon, thicker than the height of two full-grown men, fragmenting and folding away from the ship as it carves its way through them at a speed of anything up to 21 knots, is one of the most breathtakingly beautiful experiences in life.

The first ship to reach the North Pole was the Russian nuclear icebreaker *Arktika*, on an expedition led by T.B. Guzhenko, minister of the merchant fleet, with Captain O.G. Pashnin commanding the ship. *Arktika* left the Russian port of Murmansk on 9 August 1977, and attained the Pole on 17 August. The expedition was carried out without fuss; no major announcement was made; it was described by the Soviet government as merely a 'scientific-practical experimental voyage'. This was an expression used quite frequently by Russian polar scientists, and appears to mean a scientific investigation with practical ends in view. One of these would have been to test this new class of icebreaker to its limits, in ice conditions far worse than could normally be anticipated in Russian Arctic waters.

The other practical aim was still over a decade away, and would probably have caused great surprise to those who took part in that first pioneering voyage. It is tourism. After *Arktika*, ten years passed before another Russian icebreaker reached the Pole in 1987; three more years passed before another one did in 1990. Over the next three years there were a further eight voyages to the North Pole, mostly Russian, but also two on Swedish and German diesel-powered icebreakers.

Most have resulted from a collaboration between a Russian shipping company and foreign travel companies that, only a few years ago, might have seemed impossible. But with the fall of communism, Russia opened its doors to foreign innovations. Also, Russia's economic crisis, its desperate need for foreign currency, brought to life a success story that seems bound to continue. The Murmansk Shipping Company supplies the icebreakers and the foreign travel companies provide the passengers. Since 1991, the Russian nuclear icebreaker *Sovetskiy Soyuz*, commanded by Anatoly Gorshkovskiy, has visited the Pole three times; in 1993 alone, the icebreaker *Yamal*, commanded by Andrey Smirnov, reached the Pole three times, all for the purpose of tourism.

The compiler of this book had the privilege of taking part, as a lecturer, on the most recent of these voyages, on *Yamal*, travelling from the port of Provideniya in the Russian Far East to the North Pole, and then back to Murmansk in European Russia. On that voyage, I observed in myself and in the other passengers many of the emotions that have inspired mankind to seek the Pole over four centuries. But, it must be said quickly, the comparison ends there. The tale of the quest for the North Pole has many victims: many who died, many who never recovered physically or mentally from their experience. The tourist, by comparison, travels in pampered luxury. A Russian nuclear icebreaker is not quite in the class of a purpose-built luxury holiday-cruise vessel; it is, as the Chief Engineer says, a workhorse, not a thoroughbred; but the passenger has nothing to complain about. It is, in every respect, a beautiful, awe-inspiring ship. Cabins are spacious and comfortable, but overheated; paradoxically, the greatest problem is keeping the temperature down, not up. One of the most exhilarating experiences is to lean out of the cabin window, feeling the cool breeze and watching the ice tumble away from the bow as the ship powers its way irresistibly forward. The fact that we were all living, eating and sleeping almost directly above a Russian nuclear reactor, a thing of poor repute in recent years, appeared to trouble nobody except the ship's engineers, who took great trouble to demonstrate its safety. The only minor discomfort was the constant noise of thumping ice against the hull and the shuddering of the ship as it carved its path through the ice.

I could find nobody among the passengers who could describe, in any adequate terms, why they wanted to be at the Pole. I did not know my own reasons. Yet, as we entered the last few minutes of latitude and were summoned to the bridge to watch the Global Positioning Satellite monitor registering our approach to 90° North, the atmosphere seemed almost electrically charged. When we finally got there, there was a feeling of joyous relief.

But how different from the experiences of those who had gone before. Peary invested nearly ten years of his life and thousands of miles of agonizing struggle to get there. Charles Francis Hall, George Porter of the Nares expedition, De Long and 19 of his men, Andrée and his two companions, three of the Duke of Abruzzi's men, Ross Marvin of Peary's expedition, eight of Nobile's men, Roald Amundsen, Levanevskiy and his crew, all died while making or supporting attempts to reach the North Pole. In starkest contrast, on 30 August 1993, assembled in the warm comfort of *Yamal*'s bridge, we drank champagne. Then we went for a barbecue out on the ice. Some even took a dive into the icy-cold open water around the stern of the ship.

After the barbecue, I was asked to read to the multi-national company those celebrated words of Peary: 'The Pole at last. The prize of three centuries. My dream and goal for twenty years. Mine at last!' It was ironic to reflect that we were almost certainly nearer the Pole when hearing those words than Peary had been when he wrote them, but how very different the circumstances. He had toiled over 400 miles with his sledges, his mutilated feet, his endangered pride, after 20 years of bitter struggle. And having got somewhere near the Pole, he faced a 400-mile walk back again. We had arrived in the greatest of comfort, enjoyed a feast on the ice, shared the prospect of an even better feast in the evening, and could confidently leave the problem of getting home again to the captain and his crew.

Men and women will continue to visit the North Pole, in ever increasing numbers, either as tourists or adventurers; but new arrivals at the Pole, by whatever means, are now mere footnotes to history. The days of heroic conquest of the Pole are gone, and true explorers now look to the future and new achievements: who will be the first to stand at the North Pole of the Moon, or Mars?

Sources

AMUNDSEN, Roald (1925). *My polar flight*. London, Hutchinson.

AMUNDSEN, Roald and others (1927). *First crossing of the polar sea*. New York, George H. Doran.

ANDRÉE, Salomon August and others (1931). *The Andrée diries. Being the diaries of S.A. Andrée, Nils Strindberg and Knut Fraenkel written during their balloon expedition to the North Pole in 1897*. London, John Lane the Bodley Head.

ASHER, G.M. ed. (1860). *Henry Hudson the navigator. The original documents in which his career is recorded*. London, Hakluyt Society.

BARRINGTON, Daines (1818). *The possibility of approaching the North Pole asserted*. London, T. and J. Allman.

BARROW, John (1818). *A chronological history of voyages into the Arctic regions, undertaken chiefly for the purpose of discovering a North-east, North-west, or polar passage between the Atlantic and the Pacific*. London, John Murray (Reprinted by David and Charles Reprints, 1971).

BARROW, John (1846). *Voyages of discovery and research within the Arctic regions, from the year 1818 to the present time: under the command of the several naval officers employed by sea and land in search of a North-west Passage from the Atlantic to the Pacific; with two attempts to reach the North Pole*. London, John Murray.

BEECHEY, Frederick William (1843). *A voyage of discovery towards the North Pole, performed in His Majesty's Ships* Dorothea *and* Trent, *under the Command of Captain David Buchan, RN*. London, Henry Colburn and Richard Bentley.

BLAKE, E. Vale ed. (1874). *Arctic experiences: containing Capt. George E. Tyson's wonderful drift on the ice-floe, a history of the* Polaris *expedition . . . and rescue of the* Polaris *survivors*. New York, Harper and Brothers.

BRYCE, George (1910). *The siege and conquest of the North Pole*. London, Gibbings.

BYRD, Richard Evelyn (1928). *Skyward. Man's mastery of the air as shown by the brilliant flights of America's leading air explorer*. New York and London, G.P. Putnam's Sons.

COOK, Frederick Albert (1911). *My attainment of the Pole; being the record of the expedition that first reached the boreal center 1907–9 with the final summary of the polar controversy*. New York, Polar Publishing Co.; London, Arlen & Co.

DAVIS, C.H. ed. (1876). *Narrative of the North Polar expedition, US ship*

Polaris, *Captain Charles Francis Hall commanding*. Washington, DC, Government Printing Office.

DE LONG, George Washington (1884). *The voyage of the* Jeannette. *The ship and ice journals of George W. De Long . . . 1879–81*. Boston, Houghton Mifflin.

DE VEER, Gerrit (1853). *A true description of three voyages by the north-east towards Cathay and China, undertaken by the Dutch in the years 1594, 1595, and 1596*. London, Hakluyt Society.

GROMOV, Mikhail (1939). *Across the North Pole to America*. Moscow, Foreign Languages Publishing House.

HAKLUYT, Richard ed. (1965). *The principall navigations, voiages and discoveries of the English nation*. London, Hakluyt Society (Facsimile reprint of the original edition, London 1589).

HAYES, Isaac Israel (1867). *The open polar sea; a narrative of a voyage of discovery towards the North Pole, in the schooner* United States. London, Sampson Low, Sons & Marston.

HERBERT, Wally (1969). *Across the top of the world; the British Trans-Arctic Expedition*. London, Longmans.

HERBERT, Wally (1989). *The noose of laurels; the discovery of the North Pole*. London, Hodder and Stoughton.

HOLLAND, Clive (1994). *Arctic exploration and development, c. 500 BC to 1915: an encyclopedia*. New York and London, Garland Publishing.

JACKSON, Frederick George (1899). *A thousand days in the Arctic*. New York and London, Harper and Brothers.

JOHANSEN, Hjalmar (1899). *With Nansen in the north; a record of the* Fram *expedition in 1893–6*. London and New York, Ward, Lock and Co.

KANE, Elisha Kent (1856). *Arctic explorations; the second Grinnell expedition in search of Sir John Franklin, 1853, '54, '55*. Philadelphia, Childs and Peterson; London, Trübner.

LUIGI AMEDEO DI SAVOIA, duca degli Abruzzi (1903). *On the* Polar Star *in the Arctic sea*. London, Hutchinson.

NANSEN, Fridtjof (1897). *Farthest north; being the record of a voyage of exploration of the ship* Fram *1893–6*. London, Constable.

NARES, George Strong (1878). *Narrative of a voyage to the polar sea during 1875–6 in HM ships* Alert *and* Discovery. London, Sampson Low, Marston, Searle and Rivington.

NOBILE, Umberto (1961). *My polar flights; an account of the voyages of the airships* Italia *and* Norge. London, Frederick Muller.

PARRY, William Edward (1828). *Narrative of an attempt to reach the North Pole in boats fitted for the purpose, and attached to HM Ship* Hecla *in 1827*. London, John Murray.

PAYER, Julius von (1876). *New lands within the Arctic Circle. Narrative of the discoveries of the Austrian ship* Tegetthoff *in the years 1872–4*. London, Macmillan.

PEARY, Robert Edwin (1907). *Nearest the Pole; a narrative of the polar expedition of the Peary Arctic Club in the SS* Roosevelt *1905–6.* New York, Doubleday, Page & Co.

PEARY, Robert Edwin (1910). *The North Pole; its discovery in 1909 under the auspices of the Peary Arctic Club.* New York, Frederick A. Stokes.

PHIPPS, Constantine John (1774). *A voyage towards the North Pole undertaken by His Majesty's command.* London, J. Nourse.

RIFFENBURGH, Beau (1993). *The myth of the explorer. The Press, sensationalism, and geographical discovery.* London and New York, Belhaven Press and Scott Polar Research Institute.

VODOPYANOV, Mikhail (1939). *Moscow – North Pole – Vancouver, Washington.* Moscow, Foreign Languages Publishing House.

WELLMAN, Walter (1911). *The aerial age. A thousand miles by airship over the Atlantic Ocean. Airship voyages over the polar sea . . .* New York, A.R. Keller & Co.

WILKINS, Hubert (1931). *Under the North Pole; the Wilkins-Ellsworth submarine expedition.* New York, Brewer, Warren and Putnam.

Maps

The North Pole
Ellesmere Island Region
Franz-Josef Land
Svalbard

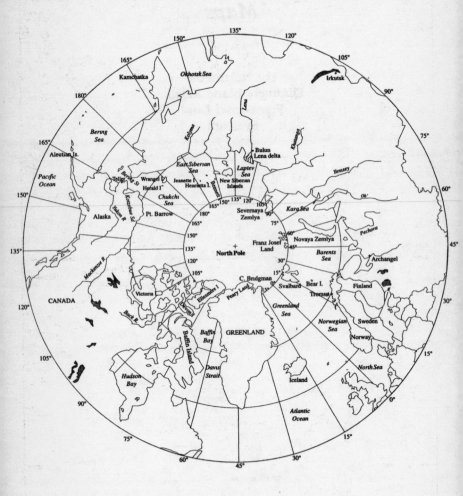

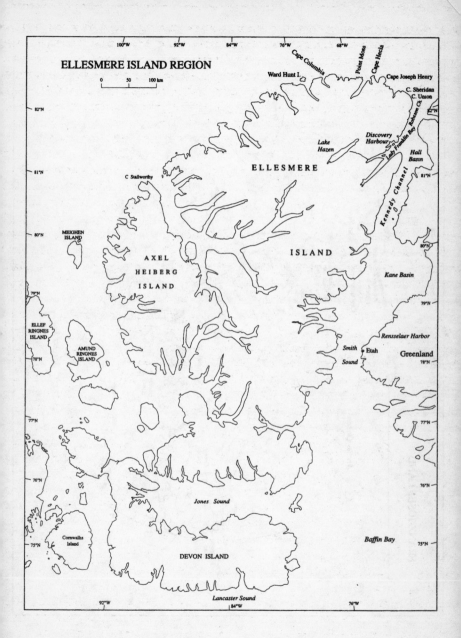

ELLESMERE ISLAND REGION

0   50   100 km

100°W   92°W   84°W   76°W   68°W

Cape Columbia
Point Moss
Cape Hecla
Cape Joseph Henry
Ward Hunt I.
C. Sheridan
C. Union
82°N
Discovery Harbour
Lake Hazen
Hall Basin
Robeson Ch.
Lady Franklin Bay
82°N
81°N
ELLESMERE
C Stallworthy
81°N
ISLAND
Kennedy Channel
80°N
MEIGHEN ISLAND
80°N
AXEL
Kane Basin
HEIBERG
ISLAND
79°N
79°N
ELLEF RINGNES ISLAND
Rensselaer Harbor
78°N
AMUND RINGNES ISLAND
Smith   Etah
Greenland
Sound
78°N
77°N
77°N
76°N
76°N
Jones Sound
75°N
Cornwallis Island
Baffin Bay
75°N
DEVON ISLAND
Lancaster Sound
92°W   84°W   76°W

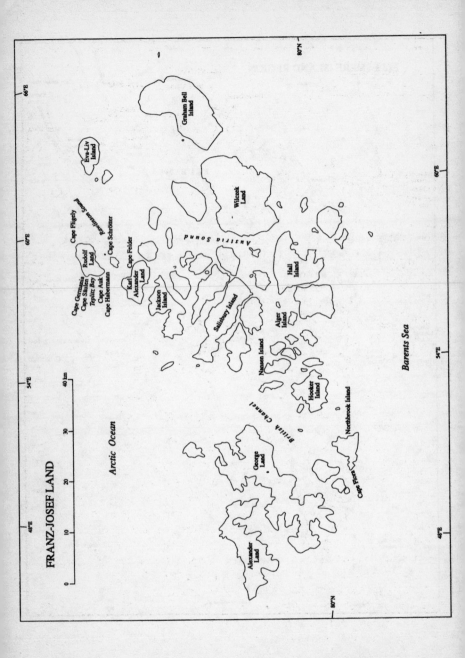

FRANZ-JOSEF LAND

Arctic Ocean

Barents Sea

Graham Bell Island

Eva-Liv Island

Cape Fligely
Rudolf Land
Cape Germania
Cape Säulen
Teplitz Bay
Cape Auk
Cape Habermann
Cape Schröter

Wilczek Land

Austria Sound

Karl Alexander Land
Cape Felder
Jackson Island

Salisbury Island

Hall Island

Alger Island

Nansen Island

Hooker Island

George Land

British Channel

Alexander Land

Cape Flora

Northbrook Island

0   5   10   20   30   40 km

48°E   54°E   60°E   66°E

80°N

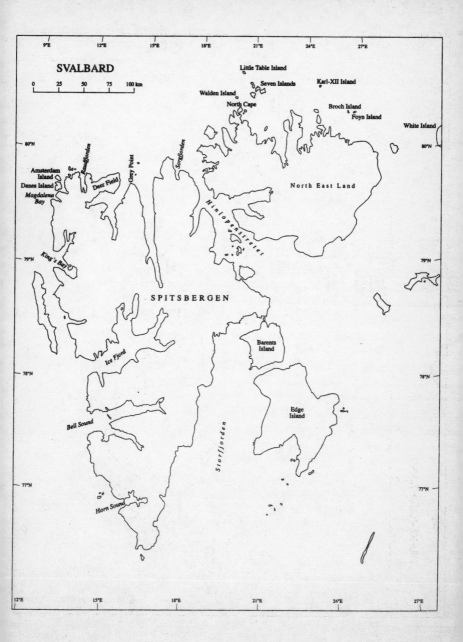